The Art of
Critical Decision Making
Part I

Professor Michael A. Roberto

THE TEACHING COMPANY ®

PUBLISHED BY:

THE TEACHING COMPANY
4840 Westfields Boulevard, Suite 500
Chantilly, Virginia 20151-2299
1-800-TEACH-12
Fax—703-378-3819
www.teach12.com

ISBN 1-59803-540-1

Michael A. Roberto, D.B.A.

Trustee Professor of Management, Bryant University

Michael A. Roberto is the Trustee Professor of Management at Bryant University in Smithfield, Rhode Island, where he teaches leadership, managerial decision making, and business strategy. He joined the tenured faculty at Bryant after serving for six years on the faculty at Harvard Business School. He also has been a Visiting Associate Professor at New York University's Stern School of Business.

Professor Roberto's new book, *Know What You Don't Know: How Great Leaders Prevent Problems before They Happen*, was published by Wharton School Publishing in 2009. It examines how leaders discover hidden problems and unearth bad news in their organizations before such problems escalate to become major failures. His 2005 book, *Why Great Leaders Don't Take Yes for an Answer*, was named one of the top-10 business books of that year by *The Globe and Mail*, Canada's largest daily newspaper. The book examines how leaders can cultivate constructive debate to make better decisions.

Professor Roberto's research focuses on strategic decision-making processes and senior management teams. He also has studied why catastrophic group or organizational failures happen, such as the *Columbia* space shuttle accident and the 1996 Mount Everest tragedy. He has published articles based on his research in *Harvard Business Review*, *California Management Review*, *MIT Sloan Management Review*, *The Leadership Quarterly*, and *Group and Organization Management*.

Professor Roberto's research and teaching have earned several major awards. His 2004 article, "Strategic Decision-Making Processes: Beyond the Efficiency-Consensus Tradeoff," was selected by Emerald Management Reviews as one of the top-50 management articles of 2004 from among 20,000 articles reviewed by that organization that year. His multimedia case study about the 2003 space shuttle accident, titled "Columbia's Final Mission," earned the software industry's prestigious Codie Award in 2006 for Best Postsecondary Education Instructional/Curriculum Solution. Finally, an article based on his research earned him the Robert Litschert Best Doctoral Student Paper Award in the year 2000 in the Academy of

Management's Business Policy Division. On the teaching front, Professor Roberto earned the Outstanding MBA Teaching Award at Bryant University in 2008. He also has won Harvard's Allyn A. Young Prize for Teaching in Economics on two occasions.

Professor Roberto has taught in the leadership-development programs of and consulted at a number of firms including Apple, Morgan Stanley, Coca-Cola, Target, Mars, Wal-Mart, Novartis, The Home Depot, Federal Express, Johnson & Johnson, Bank of New York Mellon, and Edwards Life Sciences. He also has presented at government organizations including the FBI, NASA, and the EPA. Over the past five years, Professor Roberto has served on the faculty at the Nomura School of Advanced Management in Tokyo, where he teaches in an executive education program each summer.

Professor Roberto received an A.B. with Honors from Harvard College in 1991. He earned an M.B.A. with High Distinction from Harvard Business School in 1995, graduating as a George F. Baker Scholar. He also received his D.B.A. from the Harvard Business School in 2000.

In the past, Professor Roberto worked as a financial analyst at General Dynamics, where he evaluated the firm's performance on nuclear submarine programs. He also worked as a project manager at Staples, where he played a role in the firm's acquisition integration efforts.

In his spare time, Professor Roberto enjoys gardening, running, hiking, and cooking. He lives in Holliston, Massachusetts, with his wife, Kristin, and his three children, Grace, Celia, and Luke.

Table of Contents
The Art of Critical Decision Making
Part I

The Art of Critical Decision Making

Scope:

Why did that leader make such a horrible decision? We have all asked that question when we have observed a poor decision, whether it be in politics, business, athletics, or the nonprofit sector. Too often, observers attribute such flawed choices to incompetence, inexperience, a lack of intelligence, or bad intentions. In most cases, though, the faulty decisions do not arise because of these factors.

In this course, we examine why leaders and organizations make poor choices, digging deep into cognitive psychology, group dynamics, and theories of organizational culture and systems to help us understand why well-intentioned, capable people blunder. Moreover, we examine the techniques and behaviors that leaders can employ to improve decision making in their organization. We focus on how leaders can design decision-making processes that marshal the collective intellect in their organizations, bringing together the diverse expertise, perspectives, and talents to determine the best course of action.

The course uses case studies to examine decision making at three levels: individual, group, and organizational. To begin, we examine how individuals make choices. We show that most individuals do not examine every possible alternative or collect mountains of information and data when making choices. Instead, most of us draw on our experience, apply rules of thumb, and use other heuristics when making decisions. Sometimes, that leads us into trouble. As it turns out, most individuals are susceptible to what psychologists call cognitive biases—decision traps that cause us to make certain systematic mistakes when making choices. From there, we examine the intuitive process in great depth, showing that intuition is more than a gut instinct. Intuition represents a powerful pattern-recognition capability that individuals have, drawing from their wealth of past experience. However, intuition can lead us astray, and this course explains how and why that can happen, particularly when we reason by analogy.

In the second major module of the course, we examine how teams make decisions, recognizing that most of us do not make all our choices on our own. Instead, we often work in groups to make complex choices. We begin by asking the question, are groups "smarter" than individuals? We see that they can be, but in many cases, teams do not actually employ the diverse talents and knowledge of the members effectively. Thus, teams may experience a lack of synergy among the members. We show the problems that typically arise, such as groupthink—that is, the tendency for groups to experience powerful pressures for conformity, which suppress dissenting views and lead to clouded judgments. In our section on group decision making, we also examine why teams often find themselves riddled with indecision. Most importantly, though, we examine how groups can stimulate constructive conflict, as well as achieve consensus and timely closure, so that they can overcome these problems and make better decisions.

Finally, we examine decision making at the organizational level of analysis. Here, we look at a number of large-scale failures such as the *Columbia* space shuttle accident and the Three Mile Island nuclear power plant incident. We show that one cannot attribute such failures to one faulty decision, nor to one poor leader. Instead, we must understand how the structure, systems, and culture of the organization shape the behavior of many individuals and teams. In these cases, we often see large-scale failures resulting from multiple small decision failures that form a chain of events leading to a catastrophe. We also look in this final module at how some organizations have discovered ways to encourage vigilant decision making in the face of high risks, such that they perform with remarkable reliability.

The course concludes with a lecture on how leaders must behave differently to improve decision making in their organizations. Specifically, leaders have to dispel the notion that they must come up with all the answers or solutions to tough problems. Instead, they must view their responsibility as designing the decision-making processes that help individuals come together to make better choices. Leaders have to create productive dialogues in their organizations, and to do so, they have to understand the pitfalls that are described in this course, as well as the techniques that can be used to enhance decision-making effectiveness.

Before applying these lessons, leaders must first learn to identify the true problems facing their organizations. By honing their skills as problem finders, leaders at all levels can preempt threats before they balloon into disasters.

Lecture One
Making High-Stakes Decisions

Scope:

Why did President John F. Kennedy choose to support an invasion of the Bay of Pigs by Cuban exiles in 1961? Why did NASA choose to launch the *Challenger* in 1986 despite engineers' concerns about O-ring failure? In each of these cases, leaders—and the organizations in which they worked—made flawed decisions that led to very poor outcomes. When we think about these types of blunders, we carry with us certain myths about how leaders make decisions. We jump too quickly to the conclusion that the leadership must have had poor intentions or lacked the competence to make the right call. This lecture seeks to identify and dispel those myths about leadership and decision making. It explains how decisions actually get made in most organizations, as well as why they tend to go off track. We make the argument that failings at the individual, group, and organizational levels tend to contribute to poor decision making.

Outline

I. Decision making is one of the most essential skills that a leader must possess. In this course, we will look at how leaders can improve their ability to make high-stakes decisions in organizations.

A. We have all witnessed or read about spectacular decision-making blunders.

    1. Why did John F. Kennedy decide to support the Bay of Pigs invasion by a group of Cuban exiles intent on overthrowing communist dictator Fidel Castro?

    2. Why did NASA decide to launch the *Challenger* space shuttle in 1986 despite engineers' concerns about possible O-ring erosion due to the cold temperatures expected on the morning of the launch?

    3. Why did Coca-Cola CEO Roberto Goizueta decide to introduce New Coke in 1985, changing the vaunted formula on the company's flagship drink?

B. When we observe such highly flawed decision making, we often ask ourselves, how could they have been so stupid?

1. We often attribute others' decision-making failures to a lack of intelligence or relevant expertise, or even to personality flaws of the individuals involved. We might even question their motives.
2. We think of our own decision-making failures in a different way. We tend to blame an unforeseeable change in external factors; we don't attribute it to factors within ourselves such as intelligence, personality, or expertise. Psychologists describe this dichotomy as the fundamental attribution error.
3. Perhaps we think of others' failures as the blunders of unintelligent or incapable individuals because we want to convince ourselves that we can succeed at a similar endeavor despite the obvious risks.
4. In most cases, differences in intellectual capability simply do not help us differentiate success from failure when it comes to complex, high-stakes decisions.
5. As it turns out, most leaders stumble when it comes to the social, emotional, and political dynamics of decision making. They also make mistakes because of certain cognitive traps that affect all of us, regardless of our intellect or expertise in a particular field.

II. We maintain a belief in a number of myths about how decisions are made in groups and organizations. By clearly understanding how decisions are actually made in organizations, we can begin to learn how to improve our decision-making capabilities.
A. Myth #1: The chief executive decides.
   1. Reality: Strategic decision making entails simultaneous activity by people at multiple levels of the organization.
   2. We can't look only to the chief executive to understand why a company or nonprofit organization or school embarked on a particular course of action.
B. Myth #2: Decisions are made in the room.
   1. Reality: Much of the real work occurs "off-line," in one-on-one conversations or small subgroups, not around a conference table.
   2. The purpose of formal staff meetings is often simply to ratify decisions that have already been made.

C. Myth #3: Decisions are largely intellectual exercises.
1. Reality: High-stakes decisions are complex social, emotional, and political processes.
2. Social pressures for conformity and human beings' natural desire for belonging affect and distort our decision making.
3. Emotions can either motivate us or at times paralyze us when we make important decisions.
4. Political behaviors such as coalition building, lobbying, and bargaining play an important role in organizational decision making.

D. Myth #4: Managers analyze and then decide.
1. Reality: Strategic decisions unfold in a nonlinear fashion, with solutions frequently arising before managers define problems or analyze alternatives.
2. Decision-making processes rarely flow in a linear sequence, as many classic stage models suggest.
3. Sometimes, solutions go in search of problems to solve.
4. In my research, I found a number of managers who chose a course of action and then engaged their team to conduct analysis of various alternatives. They do so for a number of reasons.
5. Consider the case of Lee Iacocca and the Ford Mustang. Iacocca conducted a great deal of analysis as a tool of persuasion, not of decision making.

E. Myth #5: Managers decide and then act.
1. Reality: Strategic decisions often evolve over time and proceed through an iterative process of choice and action.
2. We often take some actions, make sense of those actions, and then make some decisions about how we want to move forward.

III. To understand how decisions occur, and what can go wrong when we make critical choices, we have to understand decision making at three levels of analysis: individual, group, and organizational.

A. At the individual level, we have to understand how the mind works. Sometimes, our mind plays tricks on us. Sometimes, we make biased judgments. On other occasions, our intuition proves quite accurate.

1. We make poor decisions because of cognitive biases such as overconfidence and the sunk-cost effect.
2. Our intuition can be very powerful, but at times, we make mistakes as we match what we are seeing to patterns from our past.

B. At the group level, we have to understand why teams do not always make better decisions than individuals.
   1. Groups hold great promise, because we can pool the intellect, expertise, and perspectives of many people. That diversity holds the potential to enable better decisions than any particular individual could make.
   2. Unfortunately, many groups do not realize that potential. They fail to realize the synergy among their members. In fact, they make decisions that are inferior to those that the best individual within the group could make on his or her own.
   3. To understand group decision-making failures, we have to examine problems that groups encounter such as social pressures for conformity.

C. At the organizational level, we have to understand how structure, systems, and culture shape the decisions that we make.
   1. We do not make our decisions in a vacuum. Our environment shapes how we think, how we interact with those around us, and how we make judgments.
   2. Organizational forces can distort the information that we receive, the interpretations of those data, and the way that communication takes place (or does not take place) among people with relevant expertise.

IV. Many leaders fail because they think of decisions as events, not processes.

A. We think of the decision maker sitting alone at a moment in time, pondering what choice to make.
   1. However, most decisions involve a series of events and interactions that unfold over time.
   2. Decisions involve processes that take place inside the minds of individuals, within groups, and across units of complex organizations.

B. Many leaders focus on finding the right solutions to problems rather than thinking carefully about what process they should employ to make key decisions.

1. When confronted with a tough issue, we focus on the question, what decision should I make?
2. We should first ask, how I should I go about making this decision?

C. The purpose of this course is to help us understand how to diagnose our processes of decision making, as well as how to enhance those processes moving forward.

V. As we go through this course, we will draw heavily on the case method.

A. A case simply involves a thick, rich description of a series of actual events.

B. In many lectures, we will dive right into a case study to begin our discussion of a particular topic. From that case, we will induce a number of key concepts and frameworks.

C. We also will work deductively at times, starting with theory and then using case studies to illustrate important theories of decision making so as to bring those theories to life.

D. Over time, we will learn by comparing and contrasting case studies as well.

E. Research shows that people learn key ideas more effectively when they can attach those concepts to real-world examples.

F. We hope that the cases will make an indelible imprint, so that you remember the concepts and ideas that we discuss, and so that you will have a deeper understanding of them.

Suggested Reading:

Harrison, *The Managerial Decision-Making Process.*

Roberto, *Why Great Leaders Don't Take Yes for an Answer.*

Questions to Consider:

1. Why do we often hold a distorted view of how decisions actually take place in organizations?
2. Why do we often focus more on the content of a decision than on the process of decision making?
3. What is the value of learning by the case method?

Lecture One—Transcript
Making High-Stakes Decisions

Welcome to this course on critical decision-making. My name is Michael Roberto. I'm the trustee professor of management at Bryant University. In the past I've served on the faculty at Harvard Business School and New York University's Stern School of Business. I teach on the subject to undergraduates, MBA students, and executives. I've conducted research and written books on decision-making, and I work with companies to help their managers improve their decision-making capabilities. I look forward to working with you on this course.

Decision-making is a very complex endeavor, something that we engage in all the time, some decisions more high stakes than others, but oftentimes decision-making can perplex us. It can be quite challenging, and it can, in fact, cause us to trip up and make mistakes. Napoleon once said: "Nothing is more difficult, and therefore more precious, than to be able to decide."

We observe many classic blunders over the years. As students of decision-making, we study these to try to understand what went wrong and to find out how we can improve our own decision-making and the decision-making of others. Let's consider a few examples. Why did President John F. Kennedy decide to support the Bay of Pigs invasion by a group of Cuban exiles intent on overthrowing Communist dictator Fidel Castro? Why did NASA decide to launch the Challenger Space Shuttle in 1986 despite engineers' concerns about possible O-ring erosion due to cold temperatures expected on the morning of the launch? Why did Coca-Cola's CEO decide to introduce New Coke in 1985, changing the vaunted formula on the company's flagship drink?

Sometimes we even see repeat blunders—people making the same mistakes over and over again when they make decisions. Consider the U.S. airline industry, an industry that has been incredibly low in profitability for decades. In fact, over the 30 plus years since the early 1970s, if we actually look at the industry and add up all the profits and losses of all the companies that have come and gone in this industry, we would get a negative number. The industry as a whole has lost money. This has led to some interesting observations on the part of investors in this industry.

Take Warren Buffett. Looking back on the day the Wright Brothers put the first plane in the sky, he once said: "It seems to me it would have been the reasonable financial, if not moral move, to simply shoot down the Wright Brothers on that day." Richard Branson, the British entrepreneur and owner of Virgin Airlines, has another interesting observation about this industry. He once said: "You know, it's very easy to become a millionaire, all you have to do is start as a billionaire and then enter the airline business." Despite all that low profitability, despite so many bankruptcies and failures, we see new entrance into this industry all the time. They keep trying with similar strategies and business models to the companies that failed in the past. We see the same mistakes being repeated over and over again. What's going on with these decisions?

When we observe such highly flawed decision-making, we often ask ourselves: How could they have been so stupid? We often attribute others' decision-making failures to a lack of intelligence, relevant expertise, or even to personality flaws of the individuals involved. We might even question their motives. Of course, we think of our own decision-making failures in a very different way. We tend to blame an unforeseeable change in external factors. We don't attribute it to factors within ourselves such as intelligence, personality, or expertise. Psychologists describe this dichotomy as the fundamental attribution error. In short, we don't attribute correctly when we think about others versus ourselves. We have a bias in the way we attribute the causes of success and failure, particularly failure.

Of course, John Kennedy once asked: "How could I have been so stupid, in the wake of the Bay of Pigs crisis?" He actually, reflecting back, wondered how could he have made such a mistake. As we look at others' mistakes, perhaps we think of others' failures as the blunders of unintelligent or incapable individuals, because we want to convince ourselves that we can succeed at a similar endeavor, despite the obvious risks. In most cases, differences in intellectual capability simply do not help us differentiate success from failure when it comes to complex, high-stakes decisions.

As it turns out, most leaders stumble when it comes to the social, emotional, and political dynamics of decision-making. They also make mistakes because of certain cognitive traps that affect all of us, regardless of our intellect or expertise in a particular field.

We maintain a belief in a number of myths about how decisions are made in groups and organizations. These myths get in the way of our ability both to understand how decisions are made and why failures happen, but also they get in the way of our ability to improve our decision-making. By clearly understanding how decisions are actually made in organizations, we can, in fact, begin to learn and improve our decision-making capabilities. Let's take a look at five myths that many people hold about critical decision-making in organizations.

Myth #1: The chief executive decides. The reality is very different. Strategic decision-making entails simultaneous activity by people at multiple levels of the organization. Political scientist Graham Allison once observed: "Large acts result from the innumerable and often conflicting smaller actions by individuals at various levels of organization in the service of a variety of only partially compatible conceptions of national goals, organizational goals, and political objectives." In short, there are people at multiple points of the organization who are touching that decision. Each have some of their own interest, as well as some shared goals in the organization in mind. We can't look only to the chief executive to understand why a company, or a nonprofit organization, or a school embarked on a particular course of action.

Myth #2: Decisions are made in the room, meaning in some vaunted conference room where the leaders of the company assemble around a table to discuss important topics. The reality is much of the real work occurs "off-line" in one-on-one conversations or small subgroups, not around a conference table. In the academic research there is a whole body of literature that looks actually at the demographic characteristics of the top management team of organizations and tries to predict the decisions they will make, and the quality of their decision-making process, based on their demographic characteristics. For instance, this research suggests that if you have a diverse team that you'll perhaps have more divergent thinking than if you have a homogenous team. There's great merit in that research, but it sort of presumes that there is, in fact, this conference table where those people come together and make decisions. That's, in fact, not the case in many organizations. Decisions aren't simply made in the room. Management scholar James Bryan Quinn is a scholar of decision-making in complex large organizations, and he once reported of an executive who told him:

"When I was younger, I always conceived of a room where all these [strategic] concepts were worked out for the whole company. Later I didn't find any such room."

As it turns out, of course, formal staff meetings do happen in most organizations; however, they're not necessarily the forum where decisions are made. Formal staff meetings often happen simply to ratify decisions that have already been made outside of the room.

Let's take a look at Myth #3: Decisions are largely intellectual exercises. The reality, of course, is that high-stakes decisions are not purely intellectual exercises. In fact, they're complex social, emotional, and political processes. Social pressures for conformity and human beings' natural desire for belonging affect and distort our decision-making all the time. Emotions can either motivate us or at times paralyze us when we make important decisions. Political behaviors emerge all the time, particularly in larger organizations. We see coalition building, and lobbying, and bargaining. All that sort of behavior plays an important role in organizational decision-making. Of course, politics need not always be a bad thing. It sort of has a bad name when we think about decision-making in organizations, that playing politics somehow is a destructive thing. But politics is not always a destructive thing in organizations; some element of political behavior can actually be constructive. Joseph Bower once wrote a very classic book on the way resource allocation decisions are made in organizations. That is to say, how do you take a scarce amount of financial capital and decide what projects you want to invest in as a company, to help the company grow and prosper?

He went in there and did what I would consider something of an anthropological study of how these decisions are made and produced a classic book on this topic in 1970. Joseph Bower went in and lived in the organization and really watched these managers and tried to understand how is it that they decide to put enormous amounts of capital behind particular initiatives, and he came to an interesting conclusion. He said "Look, politics is not pathology. It is a fact of large organization." It's simply there whether we like it or not. He found that decisions rarely were the outcome simply of financial return on investment-type analyses. In school, many business executives are taught to do financial quantifications of key decisions; they're sort of taught let's take the numbers and let's figure out what money you have to put in, what kind of benefit you would get out, and let's figure out if that return on the original investment makes sense for the company. Those models are very useful, in fact, when we look at it from a sort of academic standpoint, but when you look in reality, he found that while these models are sometimes used, they weren't the driving factor behind how capital was actually allocated in companies. He found that behavioral and political aspects of decision processes aren't purely dysfunctional—they can be helpful in making these processes work and helping the company come to these important capital allocation decisions. He found, for instance, that there's a whole set of behaviors around jockeying to present someone's track record so that they can convince people that they're the kind of credible person that should be sort of backed in a particular investment opportunity. In other words, as an executive, you want to convince people "Look, I've done these before, you can trust me with your money; give it to me and I'll make sure I guide us to the right kind of outcome in the future." So it sort of becomes this game, if you will, political game, to sort of convince people that your track record is sufficient enough, so that you can be trusted with the money, and let's not rely only on the financial analysis, because sometimes, after all, it's hard to come up with a financial case in these matters.

Politics is there; it's always there, and Bower sort of makes this distinction and says "Look, when politics is used to get a good proposal through that has benefits for the larger organization, that's okay. It becomes destructive when people are putting their own interest ahead of the organization." But whether it's destructive or constructive, it's there; politics is always part of it. Decision-making isn't purely an intellectual exercise; we aren't simply using some quantitative model to come to these decisions in real life. There's all of this behavioral stuff going on, and it's critical—it's really important to the way decisions are made.

Myth #4: Managers analyze and then decide. The reality, again, is very different. Strategic decisions unfold in a nonlinear fashion, with solutions frequently arising before managers define problems or analyze alternatives. Decision-making processes rarely flow in a linear sequence, as many classic stage models suggest. The classic stage models say, look, we start by defining a problem, then we generate some alternatives, we evaluate those options, we come to a choice, and then we implement. The reality is, in fact, very different.

We don't see that kind of linear progression. Sometimes we even have solutions out in search of problems to solve, a topic that we'll cover later in a subsequent lecture.

In my research, I found a number of managers who chose a course of action and then engaged their team to conduct analysis of various alternatives. They do so for a number of reasons. In part, they might conduct that analysis sort of after they've already come to a judgment, because they're using the analysis to help persuade others of the merits of their decision. At times, they might use the analysis for a very different purpose. Analysis conveys a certain legitimacy on the process. We sort of expect our managers to go through thorough cost-benefit type analysis when they're making key decisions. We expect them to look at a whole bunch of alternatives, to collect a lot of information, and to use formal techniques and perhaps conceptual frameworks to help guide their decision-making. So what we see managers doing is sometimes drawing on a lot of information, bringing out a lot of alternatives, even after they've already made a judgment, because they want to sort of present what they view as a process that will convey legitimacy that will show that they've gone through the right methods for making decisions.

Sometimes they've already made a choice, and then they go through this analysis because they want to sort of check their intuition. They came to sort of a snap judgment based on instincts, and they're not really sure am I right or not, let me go see if I can do some more formal analysis of the options to see if, in fact, that confirms or disconfirms the judgment that I've come to rather instinctively.

So, you see there are a lot of reasons why managers might rely on analysis after the fact. They're essentially deciding and then analyzing before they go forth with implementation. Consider the case of Lee Iacocca and the Ford Mustang. Ford Mustang was introduced in the 1960s, one of the most explosive and successful new car introductions in the history of the United States automobile industry. In fact, Lee Iacocca, who was president of Ford and reporting to Henry Ford II at the time, had a very hard time convincing Henry Ford II to back his project for the new Ford Mustang. He ran into all kinds of opposition in the organization. He conducted a great deal of analysis as a tool of persuasion, not of decision-making. In other words, Iacocca had already decided the Mustang was a good idea, but he needed analysis to persuade others that it was a good idea, and so he went through the process of creating a set of financial calculations, a set of marketing research studies, to sort of back something that he already believed in, that instinctively he had already decided, but the analysis conveyed legitimacy in the process—it gave him another tool of persuasion and influence to get his point across and ultimately convince Henry Ford II that the Mustang should go forward and be marketed to consumers.

The Mustang turned out to be an enormous success, and Lee Iacocca ended up on the cover of many national magazines. Unfortunately, this angered Henry Ford II, who didn't like that "grandstanding." He didn't like that Iacocca was getting all the credit for this great new vehicle. Iacocca had won the battle, but ultimately lost the war. He had gotten the Mustang to market as he desired, but in that effort, he, in fact, had gotten on the wrong side of the Ford family, and ultimately he lost his job at Ford. He went on, of course, to resurrect Chrysler, but his example is important because it shows us that people don't always analyze and then choose. Sometimes they choose and then go through a process of analysis, for reasons other than coming to the right selection of a course of action.

Let's turn to our last myth: Managers decide and then act. Isn't that the reality? Don't we decide and then go do something? Well, no, in fact strategic decisions often evolve over time and proceed through an iterative process of choice and action. A manager at an aerospace firm once described how a critical decision unfolded in his organization. In my research he told me: "The decision to do this didn't come in November of 1996, it didn't come in February of 1997, it didn't come in May of 1997. You know, there was a concept, and the concept evolved." We often take some actions, make sense of those actions, and then make some decisions about how we want to move forward. We go through this iterative process of thought and action. It doesn't linearly move from decision-making process to implementation process.

These, then, are the five myths of decision-making that I think we need to dispel before we can go any further in this course in trying to understand why flawed decisions happen and how we can improve our decision-making capabilities. The fact is that the chief executive doesn't decide alone. Decisions aren't simply made in the room; decisions are not largely intellectual exercises; managers sometimes decide and then use analysis to persuade and influence others, and managers don't simply decide and then act—sometimes they act, make sense of those actions, and then make future decisions.

As we go through the course, as we try to understand how decisions occur and what can go wrong when we make critical choices, we have to understand decision-making at three levels of analysis: the individual level, the group level, and the organizational level. At the individual level, we have to understand how the mind works. Sometimes our mind plays tricks on us; sometimes we make bias judgments. On other occasions, our intuition proves quite accurate. We make poor decisions because of these traps, these tricks that our mind plays on us, and some of these include, for example, the sunk cost effect. The sunk cost effect involves throwing good money after bad, a topic we'll cover in a subsequent lecture. Our intuition can be very powerful, but at times we make mistakes as we match what we're seeing to patterns in the past. We'll look carefully at intuition, how it works, how it helps us in our decision-making, and how sometimes it gets us in trouble.

We'll also turn to the group level of analysis in this course. At the group level, we have to understand why teams don't always make better decisions than individuals. Groups hold great promise because we can pool the intellect, expertise, and perspectives of many people. That diversity holds the potential to enable better decisions than any particular individual could make. None of us is as smart as all of us. We've all heard the expression. Unfortunately, many groups don't realize their potential. They fail to realize the synergy among their members. In fact, they make decisions that are inferior to those that the best individual within the group could have made on his or her own. To understand group decision-making failures, we have to examine problems that groups encounter, such as social pressures for conformity. These kinds of troubles that groups encounter in the group dynamics are essential in our understanding of how decision-making works and how we can improve our capabilities in this area.

Finally we'll have to look at the organizational level of analysis. We have to understand how structure, systems, and culture shape the decisions that we make. The environment is an important factor. We don't make decisions in a vacuum. Our environment shapes how we think, how we interact with those around us, and how we make judgments. Organizational forces can distort the information we receive, the interpretations of those data, and the way that communication takes place (or does not take place) among people with relevant expertise.

Through it all, as we look at these failures, there's going to be an important theme and as we go through all three levels of analysis—this theme is that many leaders fail because they think of decisions as events, not processes. This course has a fundamental process perspective. We think of the decision-makers sitting alone at a moment in time pondering what choices to make, but as we said, most decisions involve a series of events and interactions that unfold over time. Decisions involve processes that take place inside the mind of individuals, within groups of people interacting, and across units of complex organizations. In a study of the foreign investment decision process, Aharoni once said: "Decision-making in complex organizations is a very long social process, not solely an intellectual exercise. The process is composed of many small acts, carried out by different people at different points [in] time."

There's a key theme here though, and that is that many leaders focus too much on finding the right solutions to problems, rather than thinking carefully about what process they should employ to make key decisions. When confronted with a tough issue, we focus on the question: What decision should I make? We should first ask: How should I go about making this decision? See, we don't think in those process terms in most instances. We dive in to solve the problem rather than stepping back to think about what process should I employ? What intellectual process? What group process? What organizational process is necessary for me to make a good decision here? The purpose of this course is to help us understand how to diagnose our processes of decision-making, as well as to enhance those processes moving forward. We want us to look at the way we make decisions, reflect on it, to learn from it, and to be able to improve our decision-making capabilities, and we want to embrace this process perspective as we go through the course. We'll look at the cognitive process, we'll look at the group dynamics and that process, and, of course, we'll look at organizational level of analysis. But through it all, we're trying to make us come to this understanding that, in fact, diving in and focusing solely on content isn't necessarily the answer to coming to better choices.

Let me talk for a moment about the organization of the course. Essentially we're going to follow these three levels of analysis. The course breaks nicely. We'll start with individual level, move to group, and then organization. In the next lecture, we'll begin by diving in at the individual level of analyses. We'll start by talking about the topic of cognitive biases—the notion that we have cognitive limitations, that we're boundedly rational human beings; we don't have some giant super computer in our brains, and those cognitive limits impair our decision-making at times. This is not to say that we always fall prey to these traps, right? Our cognition is incredibly powerful, and we'll look at how it works well in later lectures, but in the next lecture we'll focus on those biases and we'll begin our understanding of the individual level of analysis with regard to decision-making. We'll look inside the mind.

Throughout the course we'll discuss case studies. We'll use those case studies to illustrate the theories and provide practical examples of key techniques and processes. Our first case study will be about Mount Everest, a tragedy that took place in 1996 when five climbers died on May 10 and May 11 of that year, and we'll look at the cognitive biases involved in their decision-making, as they tried for the summit of the world's tallest mountain. We'll use case studies, as I said, throughout the course, and so let me say a few words about case studies. They're not the way that typically many professors lecture; they're not the way that people often present theories and material on particular subjects, so let me talk about my sort of philosophy of the case method and why I think it's important in helping us learn.

A case simply involves a thick, rich description of a series of actual events. Of course, it's a synopsis of those events—it's not going to give us every last detail, but it's going to paint a picture. At first it's purely descriptive, and then on top of that we can layer our analysis, and we want to put ourselves in the shoes of the decision-makers in that case, of the key people involved. We don't do it because we want to attack them, assign blame, point fingers—we do it because we want to understand how we might very well have acted in the same way they did and made the very same mistakes that they did in those cases. We want to empathize with them as we go through these cases, look at their mistakes, and learn with them on how we can improve. We don't go through these cases because we're trying to pick on particular leaders and look at their flaws, expose their flaws;

we do this as a learning opportunity. In many lectures we'll dive right into a case study to begin our discussion of a particular topic. From that case, we'll induce a number of key concepts and frameworks. We won't always work inductively though. We'll also work deductively at times. That means we'll start with theory or concepts or frameworks, and then use case studies to illustrate those important theories of decision-making, so as to bring those theories to life. We'll use cases from a wide range of subject areas; we won't always focus on business—though I am a business professor, and I will draw on many examples from the corporate world as we go through the course, but we'll also look at examples from history and political science, from mountain climbing and firefighting. So, we'll really look at a whole range of domains where decision-making is taking place—some more high stakes than others, some more immediate, some more crisis-like in terms of their atmosphere, others more routine. Mostly we'll focus on high-stakes choices because they really help us really identify key dimensions of critical decision-making. Over time, we'll learn by comparing and contrasting case studies as well. Research shows that people learn key ideas more effectively when they attach those concepts to real world examples. We hope that the cases will make an indelible imprint, so that you remember the concepts and ideas that we discuss in this course, and so that you will come to a deeper understanding of them over time.

I find that with my own students, they will think back after 5 or 7 or 10 years, they'll come back as alumni, and they'll say "You know, I remember that case about Coca-Cola, or I remember that case about Wal-Mart. It's so vivid, even today I can recall the lessons of what that company went through, what that leader went through when they were making those decisions." That's the power of the case method, and so throughout the course we'll sprinkle these cases throughout the lectures.

I do want to say one last thing about case studies as we go forward in the course. I'm using case studies here in sort of a lecture format. When I'm with my students it's much more interactive of course, and the case method is about the professor facilitating discussion among a group of students who've all read a case study and are trying to analyze it. We can't do that here today, but we can still capture some of the benefits of the case method, and I want to point out something that Dean John McArthur, the former dean of the Harvard Business School, once said when asked what students learn when they study all these cases. He said: "How we teach is what we teach." It's a very interesting quote. In other words, yes, we teach a series of theories and concepts and frameworks when we teach about decision-making or strategy or finance, using the case method, but we also are teaching in a different way. We're not simply teaching the theories. "How we teach is what we teach." In other words, we're asking questions, we're diagnosing situations; we're assessing an environment or an organization. That process of critical thinking, in fact, that's what we're teaching. How we teach, the process of asking questions, of thinking critically, of diagnosing and assessing situations, of comparing and contrasting similar or different situations over time, that process of analysis, that's really what we're teaching.

Throughout the course we'll tear these cases apart, we'll look at what went wrong and what went right, and hopefully as we go through that, in fact, what we're learning is not just some theories of decision-making, but we're learning a little bit about how to be more critical thinkers, how to learn from our mistakes, how to diagnose situations more effectively.

With that introduction we're ready to move forward. We're looking at the individual level of analysis; we're going to take a look at this issue of cognitive bias of these traps, these tricks in a way, that the mind plays on us—these things that happen to all of us, whether we're expert or novice in whatever field we happen to be. They don't happen to "stupid people," they happen to everyone. We'll look at the Mount Everest case study to help us understand these traps, to understand these cognitive fallacies in more detail. Thank you very much.

Lecture Two
Cognitive Biases

Scope:

Drawing on the case study of Mount Everest, we explain how human beings tend to make certain types of classic mistakes when we make decisions. We call these mistakes cognitive biases. These biases tend to affect both novices and experts across a wide range of fields. The biases exist because we are not perfectly rational human beings, in the sense of an economist's rational choice model of decision making. Instead, we are fundamentally bounded in our rationality; that is, we do not examine every possible option or every scrap of data before we make a decision. We adopt certain rules of thumb and take other shortcuts when we make choices. By and large, those shortcuts help us make choices in an economical manner, so that we do not get bogged down every time we need to make a decision. However, in some cases, our cognitive limitations lead to poor decisions. In this lecture, the Mount Everest case study illustrates biases such as the sunk-cost effect, overconfidence bias, and recency effect.

Outline

I. One of the most powerful examples of flawed decision making is the 1996 Mount Everest tragedy.

   A. The tragedy occurred when 2 expedition teams got caught in a storm, high on the mountain, on May 10–11, 1996. Both expedition team leaders, as well as 3 team members, died during the storm.

      1. The 2 teams were commercial expeditions, meaning that individuals were clients paying to be guided to the top by a professional mountaineer.

      2. Scott Fischer led the Mountain Madness team. Rob Hall led the Adventure Consultants expedition.

   B. Climbing Mount Everest is an incredibly arduous exercise.

      1. It takes roughly 2 months to climb Everest, because you must spend at least 6 weeks preparing your body for the final push to the summit.

2. During those 6 weeks, you go through an acclimatization routine to allow your body to adjust to the low levels of oxygen at high altitude.

3. During that time, you establish a series of camps along the path to the summit, starting with Base Camp, which is at about 17,000 feet. The summit is at over 29,000 feet (well over 8000 meters).

4. The final push to the summit entails an 18-hour round trip from Camp IV to the summit. You leave late at night and climb through the dark to the summit, reaching it around midday if all goes well. Then you climb down quickly so that you can reach Camp IV again before it gets dark.

5. Supplemental oxygen is critical for most climbers. Even with it, the climbing can be very difficult. As mountaineer David Breashears has said, it can be like "running on a treadmill while breathing through a straw."

C. The 2 expedition teams that encountered trouble on May 10, 1996, violated some of their own rules for climbing.

1. The expedition leaders talked extensively about the need for a turnaround-time rule. The principle was that, if you could not reach the top by one or two o'clock in the afternoon, then you should turn around. The reason is that you do not want to be climbing down in the darkness.

2. On May 10–11, 1996, many of the expedition team members did not reach the summit until late in the afternoon. Some arrived at or after four o'clock. Jon Krakauer, one of the climbers, who wrote a bestselling book about the incident, has written that "turnaround times were egregiously ignored."

3. As a result, they were climbing high on the mountain at a far later hour than they should have been.

4. When the storm hit, they found themselves not only trying to climb down in darkness, but also during a raging blizzard.

5. Five people could not get back to Camp IV, and they died high on the mountain.

II. The Mount Everest case illustrates a number of cognitive biases that impaired the climbers' decision making.

  A. We are not perfectly rational actors.

    1. Economists depict individuals as rational decision makers. By that, they mean that individuals collect lots of information, examine a wide variety of alternatives, and then make decisions that maximize our personal satisfaction.

    2. However, we do not make decisions in a manner consistent with economic models. Nobel Prize–winner Herbert Simon has argued that humans are boundedly rational. We are cognitively limited, such that we can't possibly be as comprehensive in our information gathering and analysis as economists assume.

    3. Herbert Simon and James March have argued that humans satisfice, rather than optimize in the way that economic theory presumes. By satisficing, they mean that we search for alternatives only to the point where we find an acceptable solution. We do not keep looking for the perfectly optimal solution.

    4. In many situations, we take shortcuts. We employ heuristics and rules of thumb to make decisions.

    5. Most of the time, our shortcuts serve us well. They save us a great deal of time, and we still arrive at a good decision.

  B. Sometimes, though, we make mistakes. Our cognitive limitations lead to errors in judgment, not because of a lack of intelligence, but simply because we are human.

    1. Psychologists describe these systematic mistakes as cognitive biases. Think of these as decision-making traps that we fall into over and over.

    2. These biases affect experts as well as novices.

    3. They have been shown to affect people in a wide variety of fields. Psychologists have demonstrated the existence of these biases in experimental settings as well as in field research.

III. The first cognitive bias evident in the Everest case is the overconfidence bias.

  A. Psychologists have shown that human beings are systematically overconfident in our judgments.

B. For instance, research shows that physicians are overly optimistic in their diagnoses, even if they have a great deal of experience.

C. In the Everest case, the expedition leaders clearly displayed evidence of overconfidence bias.

D. Scott Fischer once said, "We've got the Big E completely figured out, we've got it totally wired. These days, I'm telling you, we've built a yellow brick road to the summit."

E. When one climber worried about the team's ability to reach the summit, Rob Hall said, "It's worked 39 times so far, pal, and a few of the blokes who summitted with me were nearly as pathetic as you."

F. Many of the climbers had arrived at very positive self-assessments. Krakauer described them as "clinically delusional."

IV. The second cognitive bias is the sunk-cost effect.

A. The sunk-cost effect refers to the tendency for people to escalate commitment to a course of action in which they have made substantial prior investments of time, money, or other resources.

    1. If people behaved rationally, they would make choices based on the marginal costs and benefits of their actions. They would ignore sunk costs.

    2. In the face of high sunk costs, people become overly committed to certain activities even if the results are quite poor. They "throw good money after bad," and the situation continues to escalate.

    3. Barry Staw was one of the first researchers to demonstrate the sunk-cost effect in an experimental study.

    4. Then in 1995, Staw and his colleague Ha Hoang studied the issue in a real-world setting. Their study demonstrated evidence of the sunk-cost effect in the way that management and coaches made decisions in the National Basketball Association.

B. In the Everest case, the climbers did not want to "waste" the time, money, and other resources that they had spent over many months to prepare for the final summit push.

    1. They had spent $65,000 plus many months of training and preparing. The sunk costs were substantial.

2. Thus, they violated the turnaround-time rule, and they kept climbing even in the face of evidence that things could turn out quite badly. Some have described it as "summit fever," when you are so close to the top and just can't turn back.

3. At one point, climber Doug Hansen said, "I've put too much of myself into this mountain to quit now, without giving it everything I've got."

4. Guide Guy Cotter has said, "It's very difficult to turn someone around high on the mountain. If a client sees that the summit is close and they're dead set on getting there, they're going to laugh in your face and keep going."

V. The third cognitive bias evident in the Everest case is the recency effect.

A. The recency effect is actually one particular form of what is called the availability bias.

1. The availability bias is when we tend to place too much emphasis on the information and evidence that is most readily available to us when we are making a decision.

2. The recency effect is when we place too much emphasis on recent events, which of course are quite salient to us.

3. In one study of decision making by chemical engineers, scholars showed how they misdiagnosed product failures because they tended to focus too heavily on causes that they had experienced recently.

B. In the case of Everest, climbers were fooled because the weather had been quite good in recent years on the mountain.

1. Therefore, climbers underestimated the probability of a bad storm.

2. David Breashears said, "Several seasons of good weather have led people to think of Everest as benevolent, but in the mid-eighties—before many of the guides had been on Everest—there were three consecutive seasons when no one climbed the mountain because of the ferocious wind."

3. He also said, "Season after season, Rob had brilliant weather on summit day. He'd never been caught in a storm high on the mountain."

4. We all can get fooled by recent hot streaks. We begin to get caught up in a streak of success and underestimate the probability of failure. If we looked back over the entire history of a particular matter, we would raise our probability of failure.

C. In the lecture that follows, we will examine a number of other biases that affect decision makers.

Suggested Reading:

Krakauer, *Into Thin Air*.

Russo and Schoemaker, *Winning Decisions*.

Questions to Consider:

1. What are the costs and benefits of satisficing (relative to the optimization process depicted by economists)?

2. Why do humans find it so difficult to ignore sunk costs?

3. What are some examples of "summit fever"–type behavior in other fields?

Lecture Two—Transcript
Cognitive Biases

In the opening lecture, we noted that we would focus on a number of cases of catastrophic failures to help us understand the topic of decision-making more clearly (and specifically the role of leadership in the decision process). One of the most powerful examples of flawed decision-making is the 1996 Mount Everest tragedy. We'll focus on the Everest case in this lecture to begin our discussion of individual decision-making, of how the mind works—and specifically, the topic of cognitive biases. This tragedy occurred when two expedition teams got caught in a storm, high on the mountain, on May 10 and 11 of 1996. Both expedition team leaders, as well as three team members, died during this awful storm. Some of you may know this story; it was popularized by Jon Krakauer in the book *Into Thin Air*, a bestseller. Many books, indeed, have been written by survivors of this tragedy, and documentaries and even feature films have been made about the 1996 events on the world's tallest mountain.

You might ask why study Everest if we're interested in the subject of decision-making. In fact, there's a long stream of research on catastrophic failures, and this has been driven by a desire to learn from past tragedies—and these tragedies have occurred in a wide range of fields, not simply the fields of business or history. We have the Bay of Pigs crisis studied by Irving Janis and many others. We have the Challenger Space Shuttle accident studied by people such as Bill Starbuck and Diane Vaughan, two very famous organizational scholars. We have the Pearl Harbor attacks in 1941, written about in a very famous book by Roberta Wohlstetter, and as well by Irving Janis in his work on the phenomenon known as groupthink. There's one thing to note though about these studies of catastrophic decision failures: There's been this tendency to pit competing theories against one another. Each scholar has his theoretical or her theoretical explanation for why that accident, why that tragedy, why that decision failure occurred, and they want to argue why their theory is more powerful in explaining that situation than some other theory.

Let's take Diane Vaughan's study of the Challenger Space Shuttle accident, for example. Vaughan, a noted sociologist, put forward her theory of normalization of deviance, something we'll cover in a later lecture. It was a sociological theory of the incident; Diane Vaughan argued that other prior studies that had relied on psychological explanations of that accident, in fact, were not valid. Her sociological explanation, her theory, was—in her view—more powerful as an explanation, but this tendency to pit competing theories against one another leads to a series of incomplete explanations of these decision failures. Later in the course, we'll talk about how we can analyze decisions more holistically, how we can put together multiple theories and explanations from these three levels of analysis—individual, group, and organizational—to create a more powerful story, a more complete explanation of a decision failure. But for now, here in this second lecture, we're going to focus only on the individual level of analysis in looking at the Everest tragedy. We're going to look only at these cognitive issues, although clearly there are other issues that explain why this tragedy occurred—including many problems, for example, of group dynamics. They're not our concern at the moment.

Now some background: The 1996 expeditions in question were, in fact, led by two of the world's great mountaineers, Rob Hall and Scott Fischer. Rob Hall led a company called Adventure Consultants. He had been to the top of the world's tallest mountain four times. He had guided 39 paying clients to the summit. He ran a company called Adventure Consultants. Adventure Consultants basically was a service provided to people who wanted to get to the top of the mountain, but who needed some help. So these clients would pay something on the order of $60,000 or $70,000 to essentially procure the services of Rob Hall and his fellow guides, who would assist them in trying to get to the peak of Mount Everest. So, Hall had two guides that he had paid to help him bring 8 clients to the summit that year. Those clients included Jon Krakauer, a journalist for *Outside Magazine*—and notably, Dr. Beck Weathers, a cardiologist who, at one point, was actually left for dead by his colleagues on the mountain, and who then wandered into camp almost a full day later, still alive, a remarkable story that's been captured in books and movies subsequently.

The other team was led by Scott Fischer. He was the leader of a company called Mountain Madness, again charging $60,000 to $70,000 to bring people to the top of Mount Everest and other top high mountains in the Himalayas. He had been to the top of Everest once successfully, but he had also climbed many, in fact, more challenging mountains than the Himalayas many times. He also had

8 paying clients that he was trying to assist to get to the world's tallest mountain summit.

It's incredibly arduous exercise to do this, and it's not like just going for a hike and working from bottom to top. In fact, if I dropped you on the top of Mount Everest, if I could do this, if I could sort of bring you to the top of Mount Everest right now, and you got out of an airplane and walked along the summit, you'd be unconscious in less then a minute—that's how thin the air is. So you've got to go through a process of what we call acclimatization. You essentially have to adjust your body to the low levels of oxygen in the air, and the way you do that is basically spending two months in Nepal, sort of allowing your body to adjust, and you work your way slowly through a series of camps. You essentially start at Base Camp, which is at around 17,000 feet or well over 5,000 meters high, and from Base Camp you establish a series of other camps along the path to the summit, and then you spend your time sort of iterating between and among these various camps. For instance, you might start out one day and move from Base Camp to Camp I, and then return that evening, and then a day or two later you might go up to Camp II and come back that evening. Later you might go up to that camp and spend the night and then return to Base Camp, and you continue doing this, establishing a series of four camps along the path to the summit. Ultimately, when you're ready, after six to eight weeks of acclimatization, you're going to make what's called the final push to the summit, a roughly 18-hour exercise. You leave around midnight one day from Camp IV, and you head for the summit, which is at over 8,800 meters in altitude. Your goal is to get there around midday and then try to scurry back down to Camp IV before nightfall. It turns out it's quite dangerous to be climbing down in the dark, very easy to lose your way. It's a little easier to climb up in the dark, and so that's typically the way it's done; leave at midnight, try to get to the top by midday, and then scurry back down.

It's an incredibly arduous exercise, a long endeavor, and people put a lot of time and energy into it. It's obviously very dangerous. In fact, the last few steps on the mountain have been described to me in some very interesting ways. One climber said it's "like running on a treadmill while breathing through a straw …" Some climbers have said that it may take a half an hour to walk the length of a room when you're in that final push to the summit. How challenging is it to climb the world's tallest mountain? Well, through the end of 1996, if we start with 1953 and Sir Edmund Hillary getting to the top of Mount Everest for the first time, and we look through the end of 1996, the year in which this tragedy took place, we know that there were 846 successful ascents of the world's tallest mountain, yet 148 people died during that time. We also know that particular parts of the mountain are very dangerous, and it's not only that "death zone" as it's called near the summit. There are also some perilous points along the way. One is known as the "Khumbu Ice Fall." This is essentially just beyond Base Camp, and it's a series of skyscrapers of ice. Imagine having to walk across the rooftops of these skyscrapers, and the way you do this is you sort of lay ladders across from one rooftop to the other, and you walk across and essentially make your way across these skyscrapers of ice—and, of course, terrible falls happen at times. Sometimes the ladders move as the ice jostles, particularly in the spring, which is when many people are trying to climb the mountain. You must traverse this area many times when you try to climb Mount Everest, incredibly perilous.

When we look at this particular case, what's interesting about it is that the two expedition teams that encountered trouble on May 10, 1996, violated some of their own rules for climbing. The expedition leaders talked extensively about the need for a turnaround time rule. The principle was that if you couldn't reach the top by one or two o'clock in the afternoon, you should turn around. The reason was that you do not want to be climbing down in the darkness. If a storm hit, you could easily lose your way. On May 10 and 11 of that year, many of the expedition team members did not reach the summit until late in the afternoon, some after four o'clock. Jon Krakauer, one of the climbers who wrote that book about the incident, has written that, "turnaround times were egregiously ignored." As a result, they were climbing high on the mountain at a far later hour than they should have. When the storm hit, they found themselves not only trying to climb down in the dark, but also through a raging blizzard. Five people couldn't get back to Camp IV, and they died high in the mountain, a tragic outcome, including both leaders—two of the world's great mountaineers.

The Mount Everest case illustrates a number of cognitive biases that impaired the climbers' decision-making. The point here to remember is that we are not perfectly rational actors. What do I mean by that? Economists, who often model how we make choices, depict individuals as "rational decision-makers." By that, they mean that individuals collect lots of information, examine a wide variety of alternatives, and then make decisions that maximize our personal satisfaction, what they would call our personal utility. However, we don't make decisions in a manner consistent with those models of economic choice. Nobel Prize-winner Herbert Simon, in fact, questioned those models in groundbreaking work that began in the 1940s. He argued that human beings are boundedly rational. We're cognitively limited, such that we can't possibly be as comprehensive in our information gathering and analysis as economists have long assumed.

Herbert Simon and his colleague James March have argued that human beings, in fact, satisfice rather than optimize in the way that economic theory long predicted. By satisficing, they mean that we search for alternatives, only to the point where we can find an acceptable solution. We don't necessarily—in fact we often don't—keep looking for the "perfectly optimal" solution to the problem we face. In many situations, we take shortcuts. We employ heuristics and rules of thumb to make important decisions. Most of the time, our shortcuts serve us well. They save us a great deal of time. They're efficient, and we still arrive at a good decision. Satisficing works.

Sometimes, though, we make mistakes. Our cognitive limitations lead to errors in judgment—not because of a lack of intelligence, but simply because we are human. Systematic biases impair the judgment and choices that individuals make. That's been concluded from a long stream of psychological research, including groundbreaking work by scholars Tversky and Kahneman. These biases affect experts as well as novices, and they affect individuals in a wide variety of professions.

Now let's take a look at cognitive biases on Everest. There's evidence of at least three biases in this case. There may very well be more, but based on my research, three of them really jump out at me, and I think you'll find them quite powerful. The first is known as the sunk cost effect. Second, we can look and see that there's evidence of overconfidence bias, and lastly, there's something known as the recency effect. I'm going to go through and explain each of these during this lecture.

Let's actually start with the overconfidence bias. Psychologists have shown that human beings are systematically overconfident in our judgment. You know we could look at Scott Fischer and Rob Hall and think that they exhibited hubris or large egos. They may very well have had large egos, and maybe there was some hubris in trying to climb the world's tallest mountain in the way that they did and trying to guide these somewhat less experienced clients to the top of the world's tallest mountain—but let's step back and understand that this is not simply about hubris. In fact, we are hopeful and optimistic by nature, and it usually serves us well. It gets us through the day at times, that optimism, that optimism of the human spirit. But in fact, research shows that many of us are overconfident, and it can become a problem. Research shows that physicians, for example, are overly optimistic in their diagnoses of patients, even if they have a great deal of expertise and experience in their field. Consider, too, students on the first day of class, and this is always an interesting one. When I taught at Harvard Business School, we had a forced grading curve, which meant that no more than 15 percent of the students could get the top grade, and at least 10 percent of the students had to get the bottom grade in that course. And you'd ask on the first day: "Well, how many of you do you think will be in that top 15 percent?" Some years you'd get as high as 75 percent of the students who would report that they thought they'd be at the top of the class. Of course, you think "Well, maybe this is just arrogant Harvard students," often said with a chuckle and a sneer by people, but, in fact, this exercise can be done with classes and with students all around the world in various universities, and you find the same phenomenon. I mean, human beings, we're overconfident in our abilities—and again, that's not always a bad thing. But in the Everest case, the expedition leaders not only displayed the evidence of overconfidence bias, but I think it did impair their judgment in many important ways.

Let's take a look at the overconfidence bias, and let's take a look at some quotes from the people involved in this tragedy and see how it illustrates this bias in action. For example, Scott Fischer, at one point he said: "We've got the Big E completely figured out, we've got it totally wired. These days, I'm telling you, we've built a yellow brick road to the summit." What an interesting way to describe the path to the top of the mountain. He's essentially talking about a yellow brick road, a reference to *The Wizard of Oz*, a famous United States American movie from 1939. Imagine that, the yellow brick road to the summit. At one point, one of the clients was concerned that he couldn't do it, he couldn't get to the top, and he was quite worried—

he was worried about the whole team, whether they could get to the top. And Rob Hall turned to him and said: "It's worked 39 times so far, pal," a reference to the 39 paying clients that he brought to the summit over the years. And he said: "A few of the blokes who summitted with me were nearly as pathetic as you." Jon Krakauer said Rob Hall believed a major disaster would happen on the mountain that year; however, "Rob's feeling was that it wouldn't be him; he was just worried about having to save another team's ass." Krakauer concluded that everyone on the mountain seemed to have incredibly positive self-assessments. He described his fellow clients as "clinically delusional."

Now let's move to the second bias. This is called the sunk cost trap. It's the tendency for people to escalate commitment to a course of action in which they have made substantial prior investments of time, money, and other resources. If people behaved rationally, they would make choices based on marginal costs and benefits of their actions. In other words, what are the incremental benefits and the incremental costs of moving forward? They would ignore sunk cost. They would ignore costs that they could never recover, but in fact, people don't ignore sunk cost. In the face of high sunk cost, people become overly committed to certain activities, even if the results have been quite poor. They have a hard time cutting their losses. Worse yet, they "throw good money after bad," and the situation continues to escalate. Think of some examples: You're at the casino, you're losing money, you promised yourself you wouldn't lose more than $200, but you know it's very easy to double down and say: "Only one more bet and I'm going to turn this thing around." Or in baseball or other major sports when you sign that player to a large guaranteed contract—now that money's sunk; you're not going to get it back if it's a guaranteed contract, even if you cut the player or choose not to play him or her. Yet, what happens? Once you expend that money, you feel compelled to put them on the field, even if they're not performing very well. We see the sunk cost effect in business, too. Take, for example, acquisitions. What do you have, you have a company goes out under the leadership of a particular CEO, and they acquire another company. They have great promise for that firm, but then things don't go well; the unit's losing money. In a perfect world, perhaps they would divest that business unit; they would sell it, understanding that it's not a good fit with that particular company's strategy, and that they simply can't manage it well, at least not manage it profitably. What we find, though, is that the CEO who makes an acquisition rarely is the one who will then sell that company if it's performing poorly. In fact, it takes a new CEO to come into the firm with a fresh set of eyes without sort of an allegiance to those sunk costs, who often is the one who will divest poorly performing units that were acquired under an earlier regime.

Now let's take a look a little further at sunk costs; let's take a look at some of the research behind this. Barry Staw is one of the first researchers to understand this phenomenon through experimental studies. Staw assigned business students the role of a senior corporate manager in charge of allocating resources to various business units. One half of the subjects made an initial resource allocation and received feedback on their decision. Then the subjects made a second resource allocation to the business units. The other half of the subjects did not have to make an initial allocation. Instead, they received information about the previous allocation along with feedback. What did Staw find? He found that the subjects who had to make that initial investment decision chose to allocate a higher dollar amount in the second period, than those who did not have to make the initial allocation themselves. In addition, Staw gave one half of the students' positive feedback regarding the initial allocation, while the other half received negative feedback. Subjects allocated more dollars to the poorly performing business units than to the successful ones. This supported the prediction that individuals would commit additional resources to unsuccessful activities in order to justify past actions, the sunk cost effect in action.

We say is this just a phenomenon that we find in experimental studies with psychology students, or does this happen in real life? Well, in 1995, Staw and his colleague Ha Hoang studied the issue in a real world setting. Their study demonstrated evidence of the sunk cost effect in the way that management and coaches made decisions in the National Basketball Association. They found that high-cost players, and by "high-cost" I mean players who were drafted very high coming out of college—in other words, they were the ones selected first and paid the most money when they finished college. Those players were played more—in other words, they got more playing time in games, and they stayed on their original team longer than low-cost players who performed at the same level in the professional league. In other words, we keep playing those players who are high-cost, even if they're not performing well. I found the same thing in looking to the study of football players, the same tendency to throw good money after bad, or good playing time after bad in that instance.

There are a lot of reasons why the sunk cost effect may take place. For example, some psychologists argue that it's about what we call cognitive dissonance. The idea here is that you make a decision, you think it's a good decision, you purchase an asset, you make an investment, and then it's not going so well, and you experience this sort of mental distress. How could it be that I was wrong in my initial decision, and you want to relieve that mental distress. You don't do that by cutting your losses—you do it by trying to "fix" that prior decision. You try to sort of throw more investment at it to sort of turn it around so as to sort of rationalize your prior choice. That's one theory, the theory of cognitive dissonance that might explain why we have a hard time ignoring sunk costs. But other colleges disagree. They would argue, perhaps, prospect theory—another theory we'll look at in a few lectures—that maybe that's a way to understand why this happens. The idea behind prospect theory is that if we're in a losing situation, we tend to take more risks; we become gamblers, as opposed to when we're in a successful situation, and so that theory would suggest that perhaps we throw good money after bad because we're trying to dig out of a losing situation, and that maybe lies behind the sunk cost problem that we all face.

Hall and Fischer understood the sunk cost problem. It didn't mean that they could avoid it. They established the turnaround time rule. This notion, Fischer called it the "Two O'Clock Rule": "If you aren't on top by two, it's time to turnaround. Darkness is not your friend." Yet, as we mentioned earlier, turnaround times were ignored during this ascent. So they set up a rule to try to combat the problem, and then ignored the rule. That's how powerful this trap is, how powerful this sort of disability of the human mind can be. We have a number of quotes that sort of illustrate this. We can hear the climbers talking in the way that conveys the sunk cost effect weighing on them. Take, for example, Doug Hansen; he said: "I've put too much of myself into this mountain to quit now, without giving it everything I've got." He's talking about the prior investment he made and how that leads to a desire when you're close to the summit to keep going. You've got that summit fever, and you're not going to stop; momentum is building. Jon Krakauer said: "You must be exceedingly driven, but if you're too driven you're likely to die. ...

[The clients] had each spent as much as $70,000 and endured weeks of agony to be granted this one shot at the summit"—$70,000, weeks of agony, he's talking about those sunk costs, they're weighing on the climbers. Lastly, David Breashears, who was on the mountain at the time making the IMAX film about Everest and who helped in the rescue of these climbers. He was on a third expedition team, not one of the teams involved in the tragedy. In fact, he turned around when he sort of saw the weather perhaps becoming more dangerous. He was going down as these climbers kept going up. He said: "So many times on mountains, we get past this point where we don't know how to turn around. ... This ship, this locomotive, is steaming up the mountain, and the only reason to keep [it] going is that the ship is already underway." So there you have it, examples in their own words of how the sunk cost effect does play in these kinds of decisions on Everest in 1996.

The last bias that I want to talk about in this lecture is known as the recency effect. The recency effect is actually one particular form of what's called the availability bias. The availability bias is when we tend to place too much emphasis on the information and evidence that is most readily available to us when we're making a decision. This notion of sort of relying on what's salient to us—well, recent events are salient to us, so in fact we often over-rely on recent events when estimating probability or when thinking about what might happen to us in the near future. In one study of decision-making by chemical engineers, scholars showed how they misdiagnosed product failures because they tended to focus too heavily on causes that they had experienced recently. They weren't looking at the full range of past experience with regard to product failures.

Let's think about this, this notion that we tend to place too much emphasis on information and evidence that's readily available, such as recent events. Again, Breashears, as an observer of these folks, saw sort of this bias, and he thought about it afterwards. He had been on the mountain for two decades—he was an expert on Everest; he had seen good weather and bad over many years, and in most years he'd seen bad weather. But Rob Hall had seen an unbelievable or remarkable streak of good weather through the 1990s, during his time on the mountain. Breashears said:

> Several seasons of good weather have led people to think of Everest as benevolent, but in the mid-eighties—before many

of the guides had been on Everest—there were three consecutive seasons when no one climbed the mountain because of the ferocious wind. Season after season [he said] Rob Hall had brilliant weather on summit day. He'd never been caught in a storm high on the mountain.

So, we all get fooled by hot streaks. What do I mean by that? Well, we begin to get caught up in a streak of success, and we underestimate the probability of failure. If we had looked back over the entire history of a particular matter, we might raise our probability of failure, but we overemphasize those recent sunny events. Consider the dot com boom and then crash. I mean, everyone was caught up in it, and we thought this will never end. Or the real estate boom and crash experienced in 2007 and 2008, or a good run at the casino. You get fooled by that hot streak into thinking that the probability of a downturn, the probability of things beginning to go poorly, well, that must be quite low. You forget instances in the more distant past when terrible failures happen, when bad things occur.

What is the cause of Everest? We've gone over a number of things, but you know, Anatoli Boukreev, he was one of the guides on the mountain that day, and he said be careful about pinpointing one cause. We've mentioned a number of cognitive biases, but they're not the only reason that this tragedy took place. By no means should we conclude that, and I don't mean to suggest that by focusing only on these three particular cognitive biases. Many factors come together to create this tragedy, and that will be true throughout the course. When we look at these failures, it's going to be a whole confluence of events, and mistakes, and problems that lead to decision failures—not one root cause. Boukreev put it well; he said: "To cite a specific cause would be to promote an omniscience that only gods, drunks, politicians, and dramatic writers can claim." Be careful about that. So remember as we go through these cases, we'll use them to illustrate particular concepts, particular reasons why the failure might have occurred, but by no means are we suggesting that that's the root cause, that that's the only thing that contributed to that particular decision failure.

Where are we going from here? In the lecture that follows, we will continue on this subject of cognitive biases. We've only focused on three at this point, but there are many, many others. We won't have time to cover them all in this course, but we will focus on a few that I think are quite important, quite prevalent, and can be quite harmful to us—not just in our business life, but in our personal life. For example, we'll look at the confirmation bias, the notion that we tend to rely on information or search for information actively that will confirm our existing view of the world, our existing hypotheses, and we avoid information that might challenge those or disconfirm our beliefs. We'll look at some interesting cases, such as the Columbia Space Shuttle accident, look at how confirmation bias might have played out in that tragedy, might have factored into why that tragedy occurred—and finally, we'll talk about how to combat cognitive biases. Remember, this course is not just about understanding why failure happens—it's about hopefully finding ways to improve our decision-making capabilities. So we'll talk about how we might become more aware of these biases, but also take some actions to reduce their impact on our decision-making each day.

Lecture Three
Avoiding Decision-Making Traps

Scope:

This lecture continues our discussion of cognitive biases. Drawing on a number of examples ranging from the National Basketball Association to the Pearl Harbor attacks, we examine a range of cognitive biases that can lead to faulty decision making. These biases include the confirmatory bias, anchoring bias, attribution error, illusory correlation, hindsight bias, and egocentrism. We also discuss how one combats such biases. Raising awareness of these potential traps certainly can help individuals improve their decision making, but awareness alone will not protect us from failure. We discuss how effective groups can help counter the failings of individuals, a topic we examine in further depth in the next module of the course.

Outline

I. Many other cognitive biases exist. We will focus on a few more of them in this lecture: first, and in the most depth, on the confirmation bias. This is one of the most prevalent biases that we face each day.

    A. The confirmation bias refers to our tendency to gather and rely on information that confirms our existing views and to avoid or downplay information that disconfirms our preexisting hypotheses.

        1. As Roberta Wohlstetter described in her study of the Pearl Harbor attacks, decision makers often exhibit a "stubborn attachment to existing beliefs."

        2. One experimental study showed that we assimilate data in a biased manner because of the confirmatory bias.

        3. The study examined people's attitudes toward the death penalty and examined how individuals reacted to data in support of, as well as against, their preexisting point of view on the issue.

        4. That study showed that the biased assimilation of data actually led to a polarization of views within a group of people after they looked at studies regarding the death penalty.

B. NASA's behavior with regard to the *Columbia* shuttle accident in 2003 shows evidence of the confirmation bias.

1. There was clearly an attachment to existing beliefs that the foam did not pose a safety threat to the shuttle.

2. The same managers who signed off on the shuttle launch at the flight readiness review, despite evidence of past foam strikes, were responsible for then judging whether the foam strike on *Columbia* was a safety of flight risk.

3. It's very difficult for those people to detach themselves from their existing beliefs, which they pronounced publicly at the flight readiness review.

4. Each safe return of the shuttle, despite past foam strikes, confirmed those existing beliefs.

5. NASA also showed evidence of not seeking disconfirming data.

6. They did not maintain launch cameras properly.

7. The mission manager also repeatedly sought the advice of an expert whom everyone knew believed foam strikes were not dangerous, while not speaking directly with those who were gravely concerned.

II. The anchoring bias refers to the notion that we sometimes allow an initial reference point to distort our estimates. We begin at the reference point and then adjust from there, even if the initial reference point is completely arbitrary.

A. Scholars Amos Tversky and Daniel Kahneman demonstrated this with an interesting experiment.

1. They asked people to guess the percentage of African nations that were United Nations members.

2. They asked some if the percentage was more or less than 45% and others whether it was more or less than 65%.

3. The former group estimated a lower percentage than the latter. The scholars argued that the initial reference points served as anchors.

B. This bias can affect a wide variety of real-world decisions.

1. Some have argued that people can even use anchoring bias to their advantage, such as in a negotiation. Starting at an extreme position may serve as an anchor, and the other side may find itself adjusting from that initial arbitrary reference point.

2. Think of buying a car. The manufacturer's suggested retail price often serves an anchor, or certainly the dealer would like it to serve as anchor. They would like you to adjust off of that number.

3. Some have said that anchoring bias requires the use of unbiased outside experts at times. For instance, does a Wall Street analyst anchor to the prior rating on a stock and therefore not offer as accurate a judgment as someone new to the job of evaluating that company's financial performance?

III. There are a number of other biases that psychologists have identified.

A. Illusory correlation refers to the fact that we sometimes jump to conclusions about the relationship between 2 variables when no relationship exists.

1. Illusory correlation explains why stereotypes often form and persist.

2. One very powerful experience can certainly feed into illusory correlation.

3. Sometimes, odd things happen that show correlation for quite some time, but we have to be careful not to conclude that there are cause-effect relationships. There have been links made between Super Bowl winners and stock market performance, or between the Washington Redskins' performance and election results.

B. Hindsight bias refers to the fact that we look back at past events and judge them as easily predictable when they clearly were not as easily foreseen.

C. Egocentrism is when we attribute more credit to ourselves for a particular group or collective outcome than an outside party would attribute.

IV. How can we combat cognitive biases in our decision making?

A. We can begin by becoming more aware of these biases and then making others with whom we work and collaborate more aware of them.

B. We also can review our past work to determine if we have been particularly vulnerable to some of these biases. After-action reviews can be powerful learning moments.

C. Making sure that you get rapid feedback on your decisions is also important, so as to not repeat mistakes.

D. Tapping into unbiased experts can also be very helpful.

E. Effective group dynamics can certainly help to combat cognitive biases. A group that engages in candid dialogue and vigorous debate may be less likely to be victimized by cognitive biases. We will discuss this more in the next module of the course on group decision making.

F. Overall, though, we should note that these biases are rooted in human nature. They are tough to avoid.

Suggested Reading:

Bazerman, *Judgment in Managerial Decision Making.*

Wohlstetter, *Pearl Harbor.*

Questions to Consider:

1. How does confirmation bias contribute to polarization of attitudes?

2. Why is awareness alone not sufficient to combat cognitive biases?

3. What are some examples of confirmation bias that have affected your decision making?

Lecture Three—Transcript
Avoiding Decision-Making Traps

Last time we introduced the concept of cognitive biases. We focused on three cognitive biases: overconfidence bias, the sunk-cost effect, and the availability bias (and in particular, one form of that bias called the recency effect). In this lecture, we focus on some other prominent cognitive biases, traps that we fall into on a quite regular basis—things like the confirmation bias, the anchoring effect, illusory correlation, the hindsight bias, and egocentrism. We'll close this lecture with some thoughts about how to combat cognitive biases. Along the way, we'll talk about specific things you might do to deal with specific traps, specific biases that we encounter in our decision-making, but at the end we'll try to wrap it up by stepping back and saying okay, what do we do about the fact that we're cognitively limited? What are some strategies we can use to avoid these traps—whether they be the confirmation bias, or the sunk-cost effect, or one of the other biases that we talk about in this lecture. What can we do to counter it? Let me just say, we're not going to be able to fully solve the problem. The power of these biases is they affect all of us; they're part of human nature, and they can't altogether be avoided, but there are some strategies that we could employ to mitigate them at times, and we will look at those as we go through the lecture and at the end.

Let's start with the confirmation bias. It's a very powerful trap that we fall into, and it refers to our tendency to gather and rely on data and information that confirm our existing views, and to avoid or downplay information that disconfirms our preexisting hypotheses. As Roberta Wohlstetter once described in her study of the Pearl Harbor attacks, decision-makers often exhibit what she called a "stubborn attachment to their existing beliefs." One seminal experimental study by Charles Lord, Lee Ross, and Mark Lepper (published in 1979) showed that we assimilate data in a biased manner because of the confirmatory bias. Let's look at what they mean by biased assimilation.

This study examined people's attitudes about the death penalty, and it examined how individuals react to data in support of—as well as against—their preexisting point of view on the issue. These scholars explicitly and very purposefully chose an issue, chose something that's very contentious (where people have quite different views and they often have held those views for many years), and they wanted to see what would happen when they exposed this group of people with disparate views to evidence on the matter. How would they react to that evidence, some in support, some against, what they believed prior to entering the study. This study presented these people with disparate views on the death penalty, identical bodies of empirical evidence. In other words, the people didn't get different evidence; they both got identical bodies of empirical evidence, and specifically, it showed them one study showing evidence confirming their belief that there was a deterrent effect to the death penalty, and another study showed evidence disconfirming that belief. By "deterrent effect," by the way, what we mean is that some people believe that the death penalty actually deters other criminals from committing murders. Others believe there's no such deterrence effect of the death penalty.

What did they find in this study? They actually asked each participant to rate the quality of the empirical evidence, the quality of the study about the death penalty that they had read about, and they found that people rated the studies that confirmed their preexisting beliefs to be much more convincing than the studies that were disconfirming. No surprise there—we like studies, we like evidence, that backs up what we already believe. What else did they find? They actually did something quite interesting. They measured people's attitudes about the death penalty, both pre- and post-study. The question is: When you expose people to evidence both pro and con, do you actually take a group of people with disparate views and bring them closer together in their views, or do their attitudes polarize? What did they find? They found the attitudes actually became more polarized after people with disparate views were shown identical bodies of empirical evidence, both pro and con. They argued that this was evidence of the confirmation bias; people migrated to evidence that supported their preexisting hypothesis, and they migrated to that, they found it more persuasive, more convincing, and they discounted the evidence that contradicted what they already believed. This is very powerful, this confirmation bias, this notion that not only is it something that hurts our judgments in various ways, it also causes our attitudes to become more polarized with others we work with or that we live with. It's a very interesting phenomenon.

Let's step out of an experimental study and into the real world—something that we want to do repeatedly as we go through this course. Let's take a look at NASA and the Columbia Shuttle accident. This occurred in 2003, the second shuttle accident in NASA's history. In January of 2003, the Columbia lifted off, looked like a normal launch to most people observing the shuttle going into space. As the shuttle launched, however, some insulating foam on the external fuel tank dislodged. This was not seen by observers with the naked eye at the time, but was discovered in photographs of the launch that were reviewed the next day by NASA officials. This insulating foam dislodged, came down, and struck the shuttle. As it turns out, it struck the leading edge of the wing of the Columbia. It punctured a hole larger than the size of a human head in the shuttle. The mission went about rather routinely, and no one really knew anything was wrong. While there was evidence, photographic evidence, that, in fact, this foam had dislodged and struck the shuttle, no one had evidence at the time of how large the hole was in the shuttle vehicle. As it turns out, the fact that it was a very large hole caused major issues when the shuttle tried to reenter the earth's atmosphere on February 1 of 2003, at the end of the mission. When it did so, extremely hot gases were able to penetrate into the interior of the shuttle, coming through that hole caused by the foam strike, and essentially those hot gases melted the shuttle from the inside out, disintegrating the vehicle and leading to the death of all involved, of all the astronauts on board.

As it turns out, these foam strikes were happening every year at NASA on many of the shuttle missions. This was nothing new. However, there was a strong attachment to an existing belief that foam did not pose a safety threat to the shuttle. They had seen foam knock off some tiles before. They had repaired the shuttle, and they had gone back into space with that vehicle. They'd never seen anything catastrophic that occurred because of this foam strike. It's interesting to look at how the managers at NASA were dealing with data with regard to these foam strikes over time. As it turns out, there's a very important meeting that takes place before a shuttle is allowed to launch; it's called the Flight Readiness Review. During this meeting, senior officials review all of the outstanding issues with regard to the shuttle, and foam strikes certainly come up at these meetings, because they are something that's not expected, and really that's not supposed to happen during a launch. So, during the Flight

Readiness Review, senior officials, senior managers at NASA, have to judge whether, in fact, this is an acceptable risk. If this issue hasn't been resolved, they have to sort of sign off that, "No, we don't think this will cause catastrophic damage; this isn't a safety of flight issue, and we can go ahead and launch the shuttle." In fact, this review took place before the Columbia went into space in January of 2003, and foam came up. It was an issue that engineers at NASA had not been able to solve. They knew that foam was dislodging; they knew this really wasn't okay, although they didn't think it was going to be catastrophic, but they couldn't figure out a way to avoid it. So, managers and engineers made their best judgment that, in fact, this wasn't a safety of flight issue, and they signed off on allowing the Columbia to go into space.

Note, it's very difficult for those people who've been involved in this Flight Readiness Review to detach themselves from their existing beliefs, which they pronounce publicly at this Flight Readiness Review. In other words, later during the mission, when engineers argued, "You know what, this is the largest foam strike we've ever seen, we could have a real problem here" was the argument made by some engineers while the Columbia was in space. But senior officials who had been at the Flight Readiness Review and who'd signed off and said "No, this is not a safety of flight issue; it's okay to launch," for them to now admit they made a mistake, that's very difficult to do cognitively. They demonstrated an attachment to their existing belief that, "No, this is okay." Each safe return of the shuttle, despite past foam strikes, had been confirming those existing beliefs over time.

If we look more closely, we also see evidence of managers not seeking disconfirming data. For example, over time, NASA was not maintaining the launch cameras. In other words, they had cameras that were taking pictures of each launch, but they hadn't been maintaining these properly—thus while they had some photos that showed foam dislodging, they were grainy photographs, they were fuzzy, they couldn't show exactly where on the shuttle the strike had taken place and how large the hole was. They weren't looking for data that might show how very dangerous the foam strikes were; they had been sort of avoiding it by not maintaining the launch cameras. Also, we know that the mission manager for the Columbia mission in January of 2003 repeatedly sought advice of an expert who everyone knew believed foam strikes were not dangerous, while never speaking directly with those who were gravely concerned and who were involved in an ad-hoc team studying the issue and trying to determine whether, in fact, it was a safety of flight issue on Columbia. That group was meeting during the mission while the astronauts were in space, yet they never got a direct audience with senior NASA officials.

Were senior NASA officials deliberately avoiding the people with disconfirming views? Were they deliberately going only to the person who believed this was not a safety of flight issue? I don't think we can say that. This is the pernicious aspect of the confirmation bias. This was subconscious if you will. We do this without even knowing we're doing it. It's sort of like the people involved in that death penalty study. They aren't necessarily aware that they're engaging in this over-reliance on data that confirms their existing view, and they're not necessarily aware that they're discounting the evidence that might disconfirm their preexisting view. It sort of happens without this awareness, without an understanding necessarily, consciously, that we're doing it—and that's the real danger with the confirmation bias.

What do we do about it? J. Edward Russo and Paul Schoemaker, two scholars who've written books on decision-making and who've looked at this bias, say there are a number of things that we can sort of train ourselves to do. Number one, we ought to routinely, we ought to get into the habit of asking disconfirming questions about conclusions that our experts make, that we make, about various situations. We ought to explicitly entertain and test multiple hypotheses. We shouldn't simply rest our arguments on one hypothesis and get into sort of a discussion of is it right or not; we ought to pose multiple hypotheses, perhaps competing hypotheses, and really get into an exchange, a debate if you will, about which of these hypotheses fits best with the situation we're involved in. Which of them has the most evidence in support? Which of them perhaps has some evidence that disconfirms the hypothesis? They also say we should engage in contrarian analysis. We need to actually assign people to make counterarguments, to poke holes in our hypotheses, to poke holes in our preexisting beliefs, to expose where our preexisting assumptions may not be valid. And, finally, they say we need to be careful about our reliance on the experts in our organizations. Often we defer rather blindly to the experts. We trust their judgment, we put a great deal of faith in their judgment, but we shouldn't take their word for it. They may be too wedded to their existing beliefs, and so we need to probe their decision process and the logic of those experts—not simply rely on their expertise because they happen to have a lot of experience on the matter and because maybe they happen to have been right on many occasions in the past.

I'll tell you an interesting story about Charles Darwin. Organizational learning expert David Garvin, one of my former colleagues at the Harvard Business School, argues the best observers seek out "anomalies, exceptions, and contradictory evidence." He points out that Charles Darwin "went so far as to keep a separate record of all observations that contradicted his theory of evolution." This is very interesting. Darwin essentially is protecting himself against the confirmation bias. He understands that given that he's kind of come to this theory of evolution, that he's come to this set of beliefs, he now knows that is going to sort of distort his view of the world, and that as he continues to study species, he may find himself only migrating to the evidence that supports this nascent theory that he's come forward with. And so he was very careful, keeping separate notebooks of observations both pro and against—both for and against—his theory, very aware of the confirmation bias and aware of how it could lead to some very bad science.

By the way, this notion of confirmation bias rears its ugly head in a wide variety of fields, and when the Merck Vioxx incident happened, we saw some evidence of it. As you might recall, Merck Vioxx, this is a case where Merck had a drug that ultimately had to be pulled from the market; it was an arthritis drug that ultimately ended up with some cardiac side effects that were quite prominent. With worries about the danger to patients, ultimately they pulled the drug from the market. It was interesting what was discovered about the Federal Drug Administration, the regulating body in the pharmaceutical industry. It turns out that the team of people, the unit within the FDA, the Federal Drug Administration, the unit within that agency responsible for deciding whether a drug should go to market is the very same unit that then had to determine whether there was a safety issue and that drug should be pulled from the market. Wow, we had the same exact phenomenon as we saw at NASA, where the same group having to decide whether the shuttle should go up then is the group that had to decide whether there was a safety of flight issue and the mission should be aborted. In both cases, very hard for people to walk away from their existing beliefs, very hard for people to look at data that would disconfirm their preexisting notions, and assumptions, and hypotheses.

Okay. That's the confirmation bias. Let's turn to some other biases. The anchoring bias—anchoring effect refers to the notion that we sometimes allow an initial reference point to distort our estimates. We begin at that reference point and then adjust from there, even if the initial reference point is completely arbitrary. Scholars Tversky and Kahneman demonstrated this with an interesting experiment. Some years ago, they asked people to guess the percentage of African nations that were United Nations members. They asked some people if the percentage was more or less than 45 percent. They asked others whether it was more or less than 65 percent. The former group estimated a lower percentage than the latter. The scholars argued that the initial reference points had skewed their estimates, had served as anchors. Russo and Schoemaker tell an interesting story about their MBA students. They would ask them: What are the last three digits of your home phone number? Suppose they said "781," so then they would ask them whether Attila the Hun was defeated before or after A.D. 781. Then, they would ask them: What specific year do you think Attila the Hun was defeated? Well, the correct answer is A.D. 451, but here's what they found. The telephone number anchor biased the answer to the Attila the Hun question: The lower the telephone number they reported, the lower the estimate they reported of when Attila the Hun was defeated. Wow, talk about arbitrary. You're asking them about their phone number, then asking them about a historical event, and yet their response to the phone number question somehow distorted their answer to something that was being asked about a pure historical fact—the anchoring bias in action.

This bias can affect a wide variety of real world decisions. Once again, this is not simply a product of experiments in laboratories. Some have argued that people could even use anchoring bias to their advantage, such as in a negotiation. It turns out, for example, that starting at an extreme position may serve as an anchor, and the other side may find itself adjusting from that initial arbitrary reference point. Think of buying a car—I mean for many of us, this is a very unpleasant experience. We go to that lot, we have to talk to the sales person, we're going to involve ourselves in all this haggling—I know for me it's a rather unpleasant experience; I don't particularly enjoy it. But, of course, we'd all like to become better negotiators; we'd like to get a better price when we have to buy that car. Let's think about how that negotiation takes place. First of all, you go look at the vehicle, and there's a sticker on the vehicle, a sticker price—the manufacturer's suggested retail price. Hopefully none of you have ever bought a car for the manufacturer's suggested retail price. I mean, we all hope we've gotten cars at well below that price. Why do they put it on the window? Why is it on the sticker if they know they're never going to sell it at that price? Well, the answer is that that price on the window, on that sticker of the automobile, serves as an important anchor for the negotiation. It's often the starting-off point, the launching point, for the give and take between buyer and salesperson. They would like you to adjust off of that number. That's very powerful. So what do you do when you go to the lot? Well, now with the Internet, we have an amazing advantage. Before, we had no real idea of what the cost was to that dealer to buy that automobile from the manufacturer. Now, with a few keystrokes, we go to the web, we know what the invoice price is, we know what the cost to the dealer is of that vehicle. We could print it out, we could go to the negotiation, now we have our own anchor, and we, of course, would like to start from that point, as opposed to the sticker price. In any negotiation then, we have to think about how might we use an anchoring effect to actually help us get a better deal relative to the other party. So anchoring is an interesting thing. It can hurt our judgment; it can help us in multiparty negotiations.

Some have said that combating the anchoring bias requires the use of unbiased outside experts at times, and that's clearly the case. Now, let's take an example. We know that Wall Street analysts, they have to rate stocks. They evaluate their financial performance and decide whether they think the stock is a buy or a sell, and they make recommendations. But the fact is that Wall Street analysts may very well anchor to their prior rating on a stock—and, therefore, not offer as accurate a judgment as someone new to the job of evaluating that company's financial performance. So there we see how an outside expert not anchored to prior judgments they've made, public judgments they've made, might have a better view, might make a better decision. So outside experts clearly can be helpful in combating the anchoring bias, no question about it. Russo and Schoemaker have some other recommendations. First of all, they say it's very important simply to be aware of this bias; awareness alone is an important weapon against it. They also say we should provide a range first, not a single point value, if we have to have a reference point in making a particular decision. We also should work with multiple anchors. Let's take an example from the business world. Often we have to forecast future sales; we have to think about where are we today and what do we think revenue for our company or for a particular product line will be in the future. How should we make those estimates? Well, they would argue that if we start with, say, today's revenue figure, this year's revenue figure and forecast next year's, that this year's revenue figure will produce, will become, an important anchor, and that may distort our future forecast. In fact, we may stay close to the current year and only forecast incremental change and not see a dramatic change that might be coming down the road. So they say we should have several different bases for estimating future revenue. We might use last year's revenue as a reference point; we might use our competitors' revenues as a reference point; we might look at five-year rolling averages; we may do a whole series of analyses, finding different ways to anchor. Once we have multiple competing anchors, we've sort of combated the possibility, we've mitigated the possibility, that one anchor could be extremely distortionary and really lead us down the wrong path.

Finally, they say we need to avoid only considering incremental scenarios. The anchoring bias really is all about the fact that we're adjusting only slightly off of some reference point, and sometimes the world changes discontinuously, and we need to be aware of that—we need to remember that when we're making estimates. And we always need to remain open to new data, data that may suggest that reference points have become outdated, no longer relevant to our judgments and choices.

Okay, a couple of others. Illusory correlation; illusory correlation refers to the fact that we sometimes jump to conclusions about the relationship between two variables when no causal relationship actually exists. Illusory correlation explains why stereotypes often form and persist. One very powerful experience can certainly feed into illusory correlation. Now here's the thing, sometimes odd things happen that show correlation for quite some time, but we have to be careful not to conclude that there is, in fact, a cause-effect relationship there. For example, for many years there was a link made there was a correlation between which conference won the Super Bowl in the National Football League, and stock market performance for that year. Clearly there's no causal relationship between a football game and our equity markets—yet for awhile there, there was this correlation, and it was illusory, and we have to be careful about making any judgment about cause and effect. Now, that's a sort of preposterous example, but I use it because we do get fooled by correlations at times. Similarly, there was for awhile a correlation between the performance of the Washington Redskins (a football team here in the nation's capital in the United States) and the presidential election results in that same year, and sort of the Redskins' performance would predict which political party tended to win in that current year—again, no cause and effect, a total illusory correlation. These exist, though, and we get fooled by them at times—clearly not in these examples; they're sort of extreme, but there are much more subtle examples where we get fooled by correlations where no cause-effect relationship indeed exists.

Hindsight bias: This is what Russo and Schoemaker call the "we knew it all along phenomenon." The more time passes, the more that we think we predicted, or could have predicted, the eventual outcome to a situation. Let me give you an example. Prior to Richard Nixon's trips to China and Russia in 1972, two researchers asked students to consider 15 possible outcomes of those journeys, and to assign a probability to each of those possible outcomes. After the trip, students were asked to remember their estimates. Two weeks after the trip, 67 percent of students thought their original estimates were more accurate than they actually were. Four to eight months later, 84 percent of the students thought they had predicted the outcome of those trips more accurately than they actually did; hindsight is 20-20. How do we combat this? Well, start with writing down agreements. You know, if you've been involved in a negotiation with someone, write down what you've agreed on; otherwise, it's very easy to find people believing that they actually agreed to something quite different than they did, and this can happen even without malicious intent. Record your predictions as a manager or as an individual, and then review your predictions later—learning why or why not you may have been accurate, and why and how you might improve your accuracy in the future. In business, for example, we might look back at the assumptions we made and the forecasts we made in a prior year or in an analysis where we were trying to justify a particular investment. We might then look at the real results, look at how they diverge from that forecast we made some year or two earlier, and then say what can we learn from the fact that, in fact, reality diverged quite a bit from our forecasts—How can we improve? And that kind of recording of predictions and then reflection and review can help combat hindsight bias.

The last bias that I want to talk about in this lecture is known as egocentricism. Egocentrism is when we attribute more credit to ourselves for a particular group or collective outcome than an outside party would attribute. Some argue that this is a variation of the availability bias, which we talked about in the last lecture. The idea is that our actions are more readily available to us than the actions of others are, and so we may sort of look to our own actions and put too much credence in them, put too much emphasis on them. If it's only about claiming credit, then we would simply label this behavior as self-serving bias. What psychologists have found is sometimes this egocentrism involves instances where we attribute more blame to ourselves for a collective outcome than an outside party would attribute. In that case, we're not seeing self-serving behavior; we're truly seeing what they describe as egocentric bias, putting more emphasis on our own actions than on the actions of others.

Okay, so there's our story, there's a number of biases, all traps that we fall into, all products of human nature. How do we combat them beyond some of the steps that we've already noted, for example? We certainly could begin by becoming more aware of them, and that's one reason for including them in these lectures, to bring that awareness to you so that you can begin to sort of think about how these biases may be affecting you in your day-to-day lives or in your professional careers. We could also review our past work to determine if we've been particularly vulnerable to some of these biases. After-action reviews, as the U.S. Army calls them, can be powerful learning moments. Making sure that you get rapid feedback on your decisions is also important so that you don't repeat past mistakes, and tapping into unbiased experts can be very helpful, because they can sort of look at things with a fresh perspective. They won't have the same reference points, the same confirmatory bias, the same preexisting hypotheses; they don't have the egocentrism thing working against them, so outside experts are very important. Effective group dynamics can help. A group that engages in candid dialogue and vigorous debate may be less likely to be victimized by cognitive biases, and we'll discuss this more in the next module of the course, where we focus on group dynamics and group decision-making in some detail.

Overall though, I would caution you. These biases are rooted in human nature, and they're tough to avoid. I cannot give you an elixir, a simple strategy for how you can avoid them at all times. Remember, we started by talking about these blunders at the start of the course, and we said, look, they're not about a lack of intelligence in many cases, and when we see those blunders, now we can look back and say: Was there cognitive bias? Were there traps that leaders fell into when making key decisions? And remember, these same biases affect our own decision-making. When we look at the failures of others, I think now we might say, "There but for the grace of God go I"; I might be vulnerable to the very same traps.

So where do we go from here? We're going to talk about the impact of framing on our decision-making, particularly with regard to risk-taking. When I'm talking about a frame, I mean the mental models that we hold and how those models shape our behavior and our choices. We'll see that how we frame a problem actually drives the kind of solutions that we select, and this can be a dangerous thing at times.

Lecture Four
Framing—Risk or Opportunity?

Scope:

Drawing on case studies of the September 11 attacks, the automobile and newspaper industries, and the Vietnam War, we discuss the concept of framing. Frames are mental structures—tacit beliefs and assumptions—that simplify people's understanding of the world around them and help them make sense of it as they decide and act. For instance, many national security officials viewed the threats facing the United States at the start of this century through a cold war frame, even though we had moved well beyond that era by the time of the 9/11 attacks. Frames can help us, because they enable us to deal with complexity without being overwhelmed by it. However, the frames we adopt also can be quite constricting. This lecture explains how powerful frames can be and how the way that a problem is framed can, in fact, drive the types of solutions that are considered. We examine the difference between framing something as a threat versus an opportunity, as well as how framing affects our propensity to take risks. We conclude by discussing how one can encourage the use of multiple frames to enhance decision-making effectiveness.

Outline

I. Frames are mental models that we use to simplify our understanding of the complex world around us, to help us make sense of it. They involve our assumptions, often taken for granted, about how things work. How we frame a problem often shapes the solution at which we arrive.

    A. Economists believe that we estimate expected values when confronted with risky situations and that framing of the situation should not matter.

        1. Economists would argue that we weight different possible outcomes with probabilities when faced with a risky situation and then determine what the expected value will be.

        2. Most of us are slightly risk averse, meaning we would rather take an amount slightly less than the expected value, if given to us with certainty, rather than take the risk of a high or low outcome.

3. Economists do not believe that how we frame the situation should matter in terms of our decision making in risky situations.

B. Prospect theory suggests that framing matters. Even small changes in wording have a substantial effect on our propensity to take risks.

    1. According to prospect theory, framing does matter a great deal. If we frame a situation in terms of a potential gain, we act differently than if we frame it in terms of a potential loss.

    2. Amos Tversky and Daniel Kahneman argued that framing situations in terms of a loss causes us to take more risks.

    3. In one famous experiment, they showed that we act differently if a decision is framed in terms of the probabilities that lives will be saved from a particular medical regimen versus in terms of deaths that will be prevented.

    4. Their work shows that we make different decisions given alternative frames, even if the expected values in both situations are identical.

C. Prospect theory may be one explanation for the escalation of commitment that occurs when there are high sunk costs.

    1. The Vietnam War was a tragic example of the escalation of commitment. We gradually kept increasing our involvement, despite poor results.

    2. One could argue that we poured more resources into the war because we framed the situation in terms of a loss. Thus, we had a propensity to take more and more risk to try to avoid the loss.

II. Management scholars have extended this early work by arguing that we act differently when situations are framed as opportunities versus threats.

A. According to this theory, organizations act very rigidly when faced with threats, and they act more much flexibly and adaptively if they frame those same situations as opportunities.

    1. In particular, scholars have argued that we tend to simply "try harder" using well-established routines and procedures when we frame something as a threat.

2. However, we may not think differently, or find new ways of working effectively. We may be doing more of what got us in trouble in the first place.

B. More recent work suggests that framing a situation as a threat may be useful in that we do allocate more resources to the problem, but we need to frame it as an opportunity to use those resources effectively.

1. In other words, we need to balance these 2 competing frames.

2. One study examined how the newspaper industry responded to the threat of the Internet.

3. The study found that those who exclusively examined it as a threat were responding by pouring dollars at the Web. However, they tended to simply replicate their hard copy online; it wasn't a creative use of the technology.

4. Those who framed it as an opportunity did respond more adaptively, but they didn't necessarily allocate sufficient resources to the situation.

5. The most effective organizations initially assessed the threat, but then reframed the Web as an opportunity to do exciting new things.

III. Framing is a general phenomenon, not simply about binary categories.

A. We've always adopted mental models that shape our way of looking at situations. Sometimes, though, those mental models become outdated.

1. In the case of the September 11 terrorist attacks, the 9/11 Commission found that many government agencies were still operating with a cold war frame at the time.

2. The cold war mind-set viewed threats as emanating primarily from nation-states.

3. The cold war mind-set emphasized conventional warfare and arming ourselves to protect against military attacks by the armies of other nations.

4. The various arms of the federal government were all still organized based on this cold war model of national security. They were not organized to defend against these so-called asymmetric threats.

B. Mental models ultimately come down to our taken-for-granted assumptions about how the world works. These assumptions can easily get outdated, and yet we don't make them explicit and challenge them.

   1. USC professor James O'Toole once identified the core assumptions of the management team at General Motors in the 1970s.

   2. His analysis suggested that GM was unable to recognize how and when these assumptions had become outdated.

   3. When the threat of Japanese imports arose, they first dismissed it. Then, having framed it as a threat, they acted very rigidly in response.

IV. What should individuals do about the fact that framing can have such a powerful effect on our decision making?

   A. First, leaders need to be careful about imposing their frame on their management team. In some situations, leaders may want to hold back on offering their assessment, because their framing of the situation may constrict the range of advice and alternatives brought forth by their team.

   B. We also should consider adopting multiple frames when we examine any particular situation. In other words, we ought to define our problems in several different ways, because each definition naturally tilts us toward one kind of solution.

   C. Finally, we need to surface our implicit assumptions, and then probe and test those presumptions very carefully.

Suggested Reading:

Kahneman and Tversky, *Choices, Values, and Frames.*

O'Toole, *Leading Change.*

Questions to Consider:

1. How does framing of a situation shape the risks that we take and the amount of resources that we expend?

2. Why do we find it so difficult to shake old mental models?

3. How can we reframe situations to encourage more divergent thinking?

Lecture Four—Transcript
Framing—Risk or Opportunity?

Consider these two questions: Could the way that I present and define a problem for you actually shape the solution that you select? Does the way that a leader frames a problem actually narrow the range of alternatives that his advisors might consider and discuss? In the last two lectures, we talked about cognitive bias. Today, we'll talk about the distortions that could be created based on how problems are framed or defined for us. Moreover, we'll look specifically at the relationship between how we frame problems and the level of risk that we take. What is a frame? Frames are mental models that we use that simplify our understanding of the complex world around us. In other words, frames are mental models that help us make sense of the world around us. They involve our assumptions—often taken-for-granted assumptions—about how things work. How we frame a problem often shapes the solution at which we arrive. Let's think for a moment about how economists think about choice, and we've gone back to that a number of times in this course, because economists have some pretty sophisticated models of how we make decisions. In particular, they're interested in the decisions we make about purchasing goods, for example.

For years, economists believed that we estimate expected values when confronted with risky situations, and that framing the situation in one way or the other really shouldn't matter. Economists would argue that basically we weight different possible outcomes with probabilities, and when faced with a risky situation, we then determine what the expected value will be. In other words, we take the probability of outcome A times the result of outcome A, plus the probability of outcome B, times the result of outcome B, and that yields some expected value. Most of us are slightly risk averse, meaning we would rather take an amount slightly less than that expected value if it was given to us with certainty, rather than take the risk of a high or low outcome. In other words, we like that certainty equivalent rather than the gamble—most of us, not all of us; some of us love risk. In the field of business we often look at entrepreneurs and say, they seem like they enjoy taking risk, they're more risk-seeking than the average person; they're tolerant of the fact that they're going to face a lot of ambiguity that they might fail. Most entrepreneurial ventures do fail, and most entrepreneurs go into it understanding that, and they're willing to take the risk, but most of us are risk averse.

Economists for many years didn't believe that how we framed a situation, the language we used in presenting a problem to someone, they didn't believe that mattered in terms of the decision-making we would undertake in risky situations. It turns out that wasn't correct. Tversky and Kahneman, two scholars we've mentioned before, experts in decision-making, put forth an interesting theory some years ago; they called it prospect theory, and their theory suggests that framing matters. In fact, even small changes in wording have a substantial effect on our propensity to take risks. According to prospect theory, framing does matter a great deal, and if we frame a situation in terms of a potential gain, we act differently than if we frame it in terms of a potential loss. So this notion, then, of loss versus gain turns out to have a great impact on our risk-seeking or risk aversion. Tversky and Kahneman argue that framing situations in terms of a loss is what causes us to take more risks, much more risks than if we frame it in terms of a potential gain.

How did they show this? Interestingly, they conducted some experiments that I'd like to actually walk through with you. Let me paint a scenario for you, and then I actually want you to answer, as the subjects in Tversky and Kahneman's experiments were asked to answer. Here's the scenario: Imagine that the United States is preparing for the outbreak of an unusual Asian disease that is expected to kill 600 people. Two alternative programs to combat the disease have been proposed. Assume that the exact scientific estimate of the consequences of the program are as follows: If program A is adopted, 200 people will be saved. If program B is adopted, there is a one-third probability that 600 people will be saved and a two-thirds probability that no one will be saved. Which of these two programs do you favor? And I would ask you right now to sort of take a mental note of which program, A or B, you favor. If you have a paper and pencil, write it down because I'm about to present you a second scenario, and I'm going to compare your answer to that situation to the answer you just gave in this situation about program A and B.

Okay, let's turn to that other scenario. Once again, imagine that the United States is preparing for the outbreak of an unusual Asian disease expected to kill 600 people. Again, we have two alternative programs to combat the disease, and assume again that we know the exact scientific estimates of the consequences of these two programs. Here they are—in this case, we have program C and program D. If program C is adopted, 400 people will die; we know that with certainty. If program D is adopted, there is a one-third probability that nobody will die; however, there's a two-thirds probability that 600 people will die. In comparing programs C and D, which of these two programs do you favor? Please make a mental note of your response, or again, if you have a pencil and a pad, write down which program you favor.

Let's think about your responses. What happens when this is done with a large group of subjects? Here's what Tversky and Kahneman found: With regard to problem number one, comparing programs A and B, people tend to be risk averse. The average person, at least in their response, tends to be risk averse. In problem two, people exhibit risk-taking tendencies. What's going on there? I mean, the two situations are identical; the only difference is that the first problem focuses on the number of lives that can be saved, while the second one focuses on the number of lives that can be lost, and what happens is when we frame it in terms of a loss, we see people engaging in risk-seeking or risk-taking behavior. When we frame it in terms of a gain, we see people being much more risk averse—on average, not everyone, of course. The point is that we see people flipping from risk aversion to risk-seeking behavior just because we define the problem a different way, and that's quite interesting because, in fact, most studies found, of course, that people are pretty consistent; they either tend to be in terms of their personality and character sort of risk averse or not. That's what we thought at least, but now here, Tversky and Kahneman are showing us that language matters—how we define the problem actually dictates the choices that we make, and this is really an amazing conclusion. Small changes in wording matter a great deal—language matters. Definition of problems dictates, or at least drives towards, the kind of solutions we come up with, with regard to those problems.

We talked several lectures ago about the sunk-cost effect, the escalation of commitment. Prospect theory may be one explanation for the escalation of commitment that occurs when there are high sunk costs. Let's take an example. You know, tragically, the Vietnam War may be an example of the escalation of commitment. As you might recall, or you might have read about in the history books, the Vietnam War was not an instance where we sort of went in completely into a battle, into a war, all at once. Instead, we sort of dipped our toe in. We started out by sending advisors to South Vietnam; we then begin to introduce troops into combat there, and over time we added more and more troops and escalated our commitment. We gradually kept increasing our involvement, despite a series of very poor results. One would argue, drawing on prospect theory, that perhaps we kept pouring more resources into the war because we framed the situation in terms of a loss. Thus, we had a propensity to take more and more risk to try to dig out of the loss position.

That framing of the situation as a loss really started way back at the beginning when the whole thing was sort of defined or put forth for the American people and for the president as "we don't want to lose South Vietnam to the communists." It wasn't about sort of gaining a victory to accomplishing objectives; it was sort of this defensive posture that said we're very worried about the Soviet threat. We're very worried about Soviet expansionism. We don't want to see communism run rampant in various parts of the world—so we need to sort of draw a line in the sand. We want to sort of avoid the loss of another nation-state, of another region, to communism. In fact, there was this sort of so-called domino theory that if we lost the state, the country, of South Vietnam to communism, then other nation-states in South Asia and East Asia might fall like dominos to Soviet expansionism into communism. So, we had framed this as sort of this loss, this potential loss, and maybe that led us to take a number of risks and to escalate our commitment to what was a failing course of action—a very sad circumstance where prospect theory might help us explain the behavior of our leaders in that case.

From this body of work, this early body of work, largely laboratory studies looking at framing and its impact on decision-making, we have management scholars who extended the research by arguing that we act differently when situations are framed as opportunities versus threats, and now they're making an interesting dichotomy, and in the field of management and business we often do think about what might happen to the firm, as there may be a threat coming from the external environment from a competitor, or from a regulatory change, or from a change or shift in consumer tastes, or there might be an opportunity. So, if you're a chocolate manufacturer, then all of this emphasis on health and wellness might be framed as a serious threat; people are worried about obesity, and they're going to consume less candy and chocolate—that could harm our business. Or that same issue of health and wellness could be framed as an opportunity. There's some scientific research showing that, for example, there's some health benefits to dark chocolate, and so as a management team you might look at the health and wellness trend and say, here is an opportunity for us to actually bring out a line of products that have some health benefits that play into that trend, that play into that growing consumer preference. So this notion that managers all the time are sort of framing things in terms of this sort of dichotomy of opportunities and threats seems quite real. According to this theory, organizations act very rigidly when they're faced with threats, and they act much more flexibly and adaptively if they frame those same situations as opportunities—very different behavior depending on how they've defined the problem, how they've defined the situation. In particular, scholars have argued that we tend to simply "try harder" using well-established routines and procedures when we frame something as a threat. However, we may not think differently. We may not find new ways of working very effectively if we frame it as a threat. We may be doing more of what already got us in trouble in the first place. That's threat rigidity, and it can be a real problem.

What's interesting about this work is it has been extended by various scholars who began to dig into this in more detail, and one of those scholars is named Clark Gilbert, a former colleague of mine at the Harvard Business School. He was doing his graduate work in the field of management around the time the web really started to take off, and he became very interested in what was going on in the newspaper industry at the time. We all know that the newspaper industry has been seriously disrupted by the web. Circulations are down across the board, newspapers in the United States. Advertising revenue has dried up dramatically with the emergence of things like Craigslist, and Monster.com, and all sorts of other online advertising avenues—Google search ads, et cetera. So he became very interested in how will traditional newspapers react to the emergence of the web, and what he did here is say, might it matter how they frame the situation, how they define what is going on with regard to the web. His work suggests that framing a situation as a threat may actually have some usefulness. Why? Because if we frame it as a threat, we may actually allocate more resources to the problem; it may sort of wake us up and say, we have to do something. But we might need to frame it as an opportunity to use those resources effectively, because framing as an opportunity leads to more divergent thinking, less rigidity in our behavior, more openness to new ideas. In other words, what Gilbert is saying is it's not as simple as: Opportunity framing is better than threat framing. In fact, what the best organizations do is balance two competing frames, and this is what he looked at in the context of the newspaper industry and its response to the Internet. His study found that those newspapers who exclusively examine the web as a threat responded by pouring dollars at their websites. However, they tended to simply replicate their hard copy online. Their paper copy became a PDF that was posted on a URL, on a website that people could download and read—not a very creative use of the technology—in fact, a use of the technology that bore a striking resemblance to what already existed, not fully taking advantage of what the web had to offer.

Those who framed it as an opportunity did respond more adaptively, but they didn't necessarily allocate enough resources to the situation to implement their strategy as well. Here's what those organizations did. They, by framing it as an opportunity, they saw the web as a chance to do things you can't do with a hard copy of a newspaper that gets dropped at someone's door at 6 am. These are the kinds of organizations (those who framed it as an opportunity) who started blogs, podcasts, who had forums for discussion and bulletin boards, who started doing things with their website that they couldn't do with their hard copy. This was much more divergent thinking, more creative, more open to new ideas—so there are the benefits of the opportunity framing, but they didn't allocate enough resources to really fully capitalize on the technology and on the opportunity. The most effective organizations in the study initially assessed the web as a threat, and in response to that they woke up—they sort of jostled the organization out of its slumber, and they poured some resources at it. They often set up a separate organization, a unit that was told, go get this thing, go study it, go figure out what's going on, but then they quickly reframed the web as an opportunity and they said wait, wait, wait, the web isn't going to just destroy our business, there might be an opportunity to really grow new streams of revenue, to do exciting new things, and so the best organizations were able to sort of manage these competing frames—a very interesting body of work that's shown us not just the power of framing, but how we might use framing to our advantage as leaders in organizations.

Framing is a general phenomenon, not just a binary thing. Framing is not always about sort of A versus B, threat versus opportunity, loss versus gain. We have always adopted mental models that shape our way of looking at situations. Now sometimes, though, those mental models become outdated. Let's take the case of the September 11 terrorist attacks. What the 9/11 Commission found in their report on these attacks is that many government agencies were still operating, in 2001, with a "Cold War" mindset, with a Cold War framing of the world and the threats around them. The Cold War mindset viewed threats as emanating primarily from other nation-states. The Cold War frame emphasized conventional warfare and arming ourselves to protect against military attacks by the armies of other nations. The various arms of the federal government were all still organized based on this Cold War model of national security. They weren't organized to defend against these so-called asymmetric threats (i.e., threats that came from things other than nation-states, threats that came from things other than conventional armies, threats that involved networks of people in various places—not world leaders of countries, threats that involved different kinds of ways of attacking people—and not attacking their armies, but perhaps attacking its civilians). The government and its various agencies were not organized. Their mental model caused them—because they were in that Cold War mind frame, that Cold War mindset—to be sort of predisposed to a very different set of defensive tactics than were called for to be able to be prepared to defend against something like the terrorist attacks of 9/11. So what we see here is that a mindset that worked quite well for 40 or 50 years after World War II became outdated. New kinds of issues arose in the environment, and new kinds of threats arose, and a certain model, certain frame of the world, still persisted in the organization in its culture and structure, and that meant that when new threats and new things emerged, they were still operating in a sort of old model.

The Federal Aviation Administration also had this sort of issue as they sort of experienced the 9/11 terrorist attacks. The Federal Aviation Administration had developed a lot of procedures to try to sort of promote and preserve aviation security. Many of those procedures were born during the '60s and '70s, during a time when there were two main concerns to aviation security. One was hijacking, of course. There were a number of very prominent hijackings, particularly in the 1970s, and the second threat they were worried about was someone somehow putting a bomb in checked luggage and that bomb going off in the cargo bay of a plane and taking it from the sky. They weren't at all sort of considering the notion of someone being a suicide bomber, in a way, on a plane and killing themselves and taking the plane down with them—so their frame, sort of their whole model of security, was based on the fact that they had this deep experience in an era in the '70s where hijackings and bombings were sort of the norm for terrorists. So again, we can get caught in a way of framing the situation and a certain mental model, and it can become outdated, and it's hard to shake it.

Speaking of hard to shake mental models, mental models ultimately come down to our taken-for-granted assumptions about how the world works. These assumptions can easily get outdated, and yet, we don't make them explicit and challenge them in our organizations. Let me ask you a question: What was the most successful (the largest and most profitable) company in the world in 1972? General Motors. General Motors, with more than 50 percent market share in the United States in the automobile market, with incredible profits, with revenue growing every year; on top of the world. USC Professor James O'Toole once identified the core assumptions of the management team at General Motors in the 1970s, when they were on top of the world. He developed a list of sort of the 10 fundamental shared basic assumptions at General Motors, c. 1972. It's a bit of a stylized list, it may be a little extreme. I'm sure that some of the managers at General Motors would quibble with some of these, but it's illustrative. He said, one: GM is in the business of making money, not cars. In his belief that was sort of one of the fundamental shared basic assumptions, one of the fundamental faccts of the mental model-driving behavior and decision-making at GM. Two: Success comes not from technological leadership but from being able to quickly adopt innovations successfully introduced by others. Three: Cars are primarily status symbols. Styling is, therefore, more important than quality to customers, who, after all, are going to trade up every other year anyway. That was the model in the automobile industry in the '60s and '70s: Get people to trade up as incomes rose in the post-World War II era.

Next: The U.S. car market is isolated from the rest of the world. Foreign competitors will never gain more than 15 percent of our domestic market. Energy will always be abundant and cheap—the fifth poor assumption (1972 note, just before the first OPEC embargo, the first dramatic spike in oil prices that occurred during the 1970s). Okay, five more assumptions that O'Toole identified. Workers have no important impact on production or product quality; that's the purview of inspectors, of engineers. Seven: Consumer, environmental, and other social concerns are unimportant to the U.S. public. Eight: Government is the enemy. It should be fought tooth and nail every inch of the way. Nine: Strict, centralized financial controls are the secret to good administration. And the final assumption: Managers should always be developed from the inside; managers should be promoted from within.

Those were the 10 assumptions O'Toole identified in looking back at the management team at GM; that was their mental model in 1972. His analysis suggested GM was unable to recognize how and when these assumptions had become outdated. Many of them became outdated right then in 1973, like the assumption about energy prices. Some took more years, even a decade or more, to fundamentally become flawed and outdated. When the threat of Japanese imports really began to build steam during the 1970s and early '80s, General Motors first dismissed it. Then they framed it primarily as a threat, and they acted very rigidly in response. It's very interesting to watch how calcified mental models can become—how hard it can be for a team to shake itself from that model, from that frame of a situation, and that becomes even harder when there's very little turnover in that management team, when everyone has worked in the industry for a long period of time and in that particular company for a long period of time. That lack of exposure to other ideas and outside perspectives can make it hard to sort of frame it in any other way than the way it has always been framed by a particular organization and its leaders.

How can we improve the way we frame things? What should individuals do about the fact that framing can have such a powerful effect on our decision-making? First, leaders need to be careful about imposing their frame on their management team. In some situations, leaders might want to hold back on offering their assessment of a situation, because their framing of a situation may constrict the range of advice and the range of options brought forth by their team. That's an important lesson with regard to framing that every leader should heed. How else can we improve the way we frame? We should consider adopting multiple frames or multiple definitions of any particular situation. In other words, we ought to define our problems in several different ways—some more broad than others—because each definition naturally tilts us toward one kind of solutions, toward one range of options. We need to think about our metaphors, too. We use them all the time. We make metaphors in our speech and in the way we sort of describe situations to others, and those metaphors are very powerful, but metaphors can also constrict our thinking; they're part of how we frame problems and situations. We need to surface our implicit assumptions, what are those taken-for-granted assumptions that are part of these mental models that we take around with us. We need to probe, and validate, and test those very carefully.

And finally, we need to think about the reference points and yardsticks that we use when we define problems. Let me give you an example. Prior to Jack Welch becoming CEO of General Electric in 1981, GE looked at each of its business units and said: Is it growing its revenue; is it growing its profit; how's it doing relative to last year? Is it doing better? If it's doing better than last year, then, hey, that's a good thing. If it's doing worse, then that's a bad thing, and that's a pretty basic way of looking at their businesses. Welch took over and said we need a different reference point and a different yardstick because all we're doing is comparing ourselves to ourselves, to our past, and hey, the Japanese are coming, and all kinds of other challenges are coming in our markets, and this inward focus and self-comparison will do us harm. So he established new reference points and yardsticks. He said we want to be number one or number two in the markets we serve, and if we're not number one or number two, we ought to fix it, sell it, or shut it down. Wow, all of a sudden the benchmark, the yardstick, the reference point became how we're doing relative to all these competitors. It no longer became an internal reference point. He's providing a whole different frame on performance of his business units, and in so doing he unlocked all kinds of opportunities for the company. They did divest some units. They shut some things down, but they also realized what their real gems were, and they grew those businesses very aggressively, and Welch went on and GE went on to great success during his two-decade tenure at the company.

We have to remember throughout this that frames are models. Models are, by definition, simplified abstractions of reality. These models aren't "right" in the sense that they don't capture all the complexities of reality, but they can be useful to us. They help us cope with all that complexity and ambiguity in the world around us. They help us make decisions, but we have to be careful of oversimplification, and that's one of the things that we often do. We do oversimplify situations as we sort of model them, as we sort of come up with a way of defining or framing a situation in order to help us make decisions.

Through it all, we have to remember this notion that better off we will be if we have competing frames, if we have multiple ways of defining the problems we face, so that we don't sort of force ourselves down one path by virtue of the definition we've started with of a problem or situation. F. Scott Fitzgerald, author of *The Great Gatsby*, once said, "The test of a first-rate intelligence is the ability to hold two opposite ideas in mind at the same time and still retain the ability to function." The power of competing frames, it's hard to do, but a first-rate intelligence has the ability to do it—that's what Fitzgerald said, and I think it's true. I think the ability to hold those multiple frames in our mind and not allow one definition of a situation to constrict the range of options we consider is absolutely critical. Now where are we going from here? At this point we've talked about how our cognitive limitations can distort our decision-making, but we don't want to make it seem like we always get it wrong due to bounded rationality, that we always fall into traps. We want to understand the power of the human mind—and particularly, the power of intuition. We don't have to do tons of formal analysis to get the right answer to tough problems. We can use our instincts, and our instincts are often correct.

So, in the next lecture, let's take a closer look at how our intuition works. What is the process by which we seem to make these snap judgments, using our instincts to assess situations and make choices? We'll learn at times, also, how our intuition can lead us astray, but most importantly we'll get an understanding of what intuition is all about.

Lecture Five
Intuition—Recognizing Patterns

Scope:

What is intuition? How does it work? What are the classic mistakes that we make when employing our intuition? Can one develop intuition? How do we combine rational analysis and intuition effectively? Drawing on case studies from healthcare, the military, firefighting, and the video-game industry, this lecture seeks to answer these questions. Intuition, fundamentally, represents an individual's pattern-recognition abilities based on their past experience. When we use intuition, we do not go through a rational analysis of multiple alternatives, with deep evaluation of the consequences of each option. Yet our intuition often leads to good decisions. This lecture explains how the intuitive process works, a process whose steps we often are not aware of as they unfold. As it turns out, intuition is more than simply a gut instinct. It involves powerful cognitive processes that draw on the wealth of experiences that we have stored in our brains. Of course, intuition can lead us astray in certain predictable ways, and we will explore those pitfalls as well.

Outline

I. What is intuition? How does it affect the way we make decisions?

   A. Intuition is fundamentally about pattern recognition and pattern matching based on our past experience. Psychologist Gary Klein's work has been informative on this matter.

   B. When we use our intuition, we do not evaluate a whole series of alternatives, as many decision-making models suggest that we should.

   C. Instead, we assess a situation, and we spot certain cues.

   D. From these cues, we recognize patterns based on our past experience. We match the current situation to these past patterns.

   E. As part of that pattern matching, we often reason by analogy to past situations that seem similar to the one we currently face.

F. Based on that pattern recognition, we then embark on a course of action. We adopt certain "scripts" from our past experience.

G. We don't explore a wide range of options; instead, we tend to mentally simulate our initial preferred action. We envision how it might play out. If it seems feasible, we go with it. If not, then we might explore other options.

II. How does intuition work for actual decision makers facing challenging situations?

   A. Firefighters use intuition when determining how to fight a blaze. They often do assess a wide range of options, but they don't have time to do so in many cases.

      1. Klein gives an example of a firefighter who assessed a situation that appeared to be a simple kitchen fire.

      2. However, certain cues (or features of the situation) did not match the pattern of experience that the firefighter had had with kitchen fires.

      3. From that, he concluded that something did not seem right. This didn't seem like an ordinary kitchen fire.

      4. He ordered his men out of the building right away. The floor collapsed shortly thereafter. As it turned out, this fire was actually emanating from the basement. It was far more serious than a simple kitchen fire.

   B. Nurses and doctors use intuition all the time, despite all the data that you might think drive their decision making.

      1. Here, you see a clear distinction between novices and experts. Novices don't have the experience to engage in the pattern recognition that an expert can employ.

      2. Nurses often report that they took action simply because they didn't think things felt right. Something told them that the patient was in more trouble than the data suggested.

      3. In one study, we examined a mechanism called rapid response teams in hospitals.

      4. These teams were designed to pick up on early signs of a potential cardiac arrest and to trigger intervention to prevent such an outcome.

5. Nurses were given a set of quantitative criteria to look for in assessing patients at risk. They were also told to call the team if they simply felt uncomfortable about a situation.

6. Many hospitals reported that a substantial number of calls came when experienced nurses felt uncomfortable but the vital signs appeared relatively normal.

7. One hospital reported to us that nurse concern (without vital sign abnormalities) was the best predictor that intervention was required to prevent a bad outcome from unfolding.

C. In a case study on Electronic Arts, the leading video-game publisher, we found that intuition played a very large role in decision making.

1. The leaders of the development process did not have a formal method for evaluating games under development.

2. Instead, they relied on their intuition to determine whether a game appeared viable.

3. They often drew parallels to past situations.

4. The Electronic Arts case illustrates one of the challenges of organizations that rely heavily on intuitive decision making. The question there was, how do you pass on this wisdom to newer managers? It's hard to codify that knowledge.

5. Hospitals face the same issue with nurses. How do you pass along that intuition? They find that much of it occurs through apprenticeship and the way that expert nurses communicate their thought process to novices.

6. Thinking out loud turns out to be a key practice that expert nurses employ. Such behaviors work much more effectively than trying to write down intuitive wisdom.

III. What are the dangers of intuition? How can it lead us astray?

A. We are susceptible to cognitive biases, as described in the 2 prior lectures.

B. Research has shown that we sometimes misuse analogies.

1. We do not make the right match to past situations in our experience.

2. We draw the wrong lessons from those analogous situations.

3. We will explore this important issue more in the next lecture.

C. In highly complex, ambiguous situations, sometimes the complexity obscures our pattern-recognition ability.

D. We sometimes have outdated mental models, particularly regarding cause-and-effect relationships.

E. We fail to question well-established rules of thumb. For instance, many industries adopt simple rules of thumb; they become the conventional wisdom. However, they can become outdated.

F. Intuition can lead us astray when we move outside of our experience base. Then, the new situations don't fit nicely with the past patterns we have seen.

G. Finally, it's very hard to communicate our intuitive judgments and choices. Thus, it can be hard to persuade others to commit to our intuitive decisions or to get them to understand how and why we made that choice. This can have a detrimental effect on decision implementation.

IV. How can we communicate our intuition more effectively?

A. Often, when a leader uses intuition, people misinterpret the leader's intent, and therefore implementation suffers.

    1. Gary Klein has shown this in his research with military commanders.

    2. The idea is that people need to understand your rationale and your intent, because in a large organization, they will then have to make their own decisions out in the field during the execution process. You want them to make decisions consistent with your original intent.

    3. Klein works on exercises with military commanders where they try to issue orders with clear intent and then subordinates feed back to them what they perceive the intent to be.

    4. Military commanders then learn how to clarify their explanations so as to make their thinking more transparent.

B. Organizational scholar Karl Weick has proposed a simple 5-step process for communicating intuitive decisions and garnering feedback so as to ensure clear understanding on the part of a team.

1. Here's what I think we face.
2. Here's what I think we should do.
3. Here's why.
4. Here's what we should keep our eye on.
5. Now, talk to me.

V. Leaders should find ways to combine intuitive judgment with formal analysis. Here are a number of ways to effectively do so.

A. Use analysis to check your intuition, but not simply to justify decisions that have already been made.

B. Use intuition to validate and test the assumptions that underlie your analysis.

C. Use analysis to explore and evaluate intuitive doubts that emerge as your prepare to make a decision.

D. Use the intuition of outside experts to probe the validity of your analysis.

E. Use mental simulation (and premortem exercises) to enhance your analysis of alternatives.

F. Do not try to replace intuition with rules and procedures.

Suggested Reading:

Benner, *From Novice to Expert.*

Klein, *Sources of Power.*

Questions to Consider:

1. What are the positive and negative effects of utilizing intuition to make key decisions?

2. How can we integrate intuition and analysis more effectively in our decision making?

3. What can we do to refine our pattern-recognition capabilities?

Lecture Five—Transcript
Intuition—Recognizing Patterns

In our last lecture we talked about framing, the impact that mental models have on our decision-making—and specifically, we talked about how frames can impact our propensity to take risks. Today we go into the mind, and we really look at what does it mean when we say we use our gut to make decisions, our instincts? We're going to look at intuition in this lecture. When researchers and consultants talk about decision-making, they often describe a multi-stage process that begins with how we define a problem; then generate alternatives; evaluate those options, perhaps with formal analytical methods; and then, finally, the stages of choice and implementation. Of course, many decisions don't follow the stage model of decision-making. In part, that's because the process doesn't move in a linear fashion through these phases, as we discussed in Lecture One during our discussion of myths that many people hold about decision-making. But many decisions also don't follow this model because people use intuition, rather than formal analysis, to make key choices. They don't necessarily generate and evaluate many options. They seem to assess a situation and come to a solution without that comparative analysis of alternatives.

Robert Graves, the English poet, once talked about intuition. He said: "Intuition is the supra-logic that cuts out all the routine processes of thought and leaps straight from the problem to the answer." Researchers, of course, want to know more than just how we might somehow come to that decision; they want to know what's going on inside the mind as we use intuition. This sixth sense, this gut instinct, we've all experienced the phenomenon, but what precisely does it mean? How does the intuitive process work? Perhaps most importantly, researchers are interested in this fundamental question: Can we actually harness and enhance our intuition so as to become better decision-makers? For a long time, many people believed that this is just something that happens; we can't improve it; it's just there. But researchers more recently have begun to look and say, no, if we understand the process inside the mind, perhaps we can harness it—perhaps we can improve it with time. We might even be able to teach people how to refine their intuition, and we certainly can help people share their intuition with others, as we'll discuss later in this lecture.

Let's go back to some seminal research in the field. In 1985, psychologist Gary Klein set out to study how firefighters made life-or-death decisions. In the process, he learned (unexpectedly) about the intuitive process. In his very first interview, Klein asked a fire commander to describe a very challenging incident in which he had been involved. The commander insisted that "ESP" had been a critical factor in making a good choice. Extrasensory perception? Was the commander kidding? The commander explained how he had once arrived at the scene of a seemingly small and straightforward kitchen fire. His men began spraying water at the fire from the living room, but "the fire just roared back at them." After a few repeated attempts, the commander was puzzled. Why wasn't the water effective in fighting the fire? Then, his "sixth sense" kicked in, according to the commander, and he became very concerned. He immediately ordered his men out of the house, despite not actually knowing precisely why these alarm bells were going off in his head. Soon thereafter, the living room floor collapsed. If the firefighters had remained in the house, they could have been seriously injured or killed.

As Klein asked probing questions, the commander described what he was thinking back at the time of the fire. He recalled being surprised that the water had virtually no impact on the fire. He remembered being puzzled by how hot it was in the living room. A small kitchen fire should not have emitted that much heat. Meanwhile, he heard very little noise when he was standing in the living room. That seemed odd to him as well, given that a hot fire such as this one should have been rather noisy. As it turned out, the floor collapsed because the main fire was located in the basement and not in the kitchen, directly beneath where he had been standing. That explained the ineffectiveness of the water; it explained the extreme heat and the low noise level. The commander did not know that at the time, but he did know that the situation didn't quite feel right. His intuition had helped him detect a serious problem.

Klein explained his interpretation of the commander's thought process. He said:

> The whole pattern did not fit right. His expectations [the commander's expectations] were violated, and he realized that he did not quite know what was going on. That was why he ordered his men out of the building. … The commanders

experience had provided him with a firm set of patterns. He was accustomed to sizing up a situation by having it match one of those patterns. He may not have been able to articulate the patterns or describe their features, but he was relying on the pattern-matching process to let him feel comfortable that he had the situation scoped out.

Over time, Klein studied the decision-making of a variety of experts in other fields, not just fire commanders. He looked at pilots, military leaders, and nurses. He concluded that intuition plays a powerful role in the way that experts size up a situation and make decisions. According to Klein, intuition is fundamentally a pattern recognition process.

Let's look at that process in a little more detail. Let's walk through its major stages or phases—though remember, these are all happening rather instantaneously. We're not talking about a phase model, something that proceeds over minutes, or hours, or days. This is something we're not even really aware of, yet Klein's research has been able to tease out some of the key steps, some of the key phases of thinking that are going on in that instant inside of the mind. Let's begin, intuition is fundamentally about pattern recognition and about pattern matching based on our past experience. When we use our intuition, we do not evaluate a whole series of alternatives, as many decision-making models suggest that we should. In fact, almost all prescriptions for improving our decision-making prior to Klein's work talked about the importance of generating lots of options and comparing and contrasting those alternatives. There's much merit in that approach, and it's certainly true that when you get together with a group or a larger organization to make a decision that you should generate a lot of options and compare and contrast them. But as an individual, when making decisions, when you rely on your instinct, that simply isn't what many people do. Instead, we assess a situation, and we spot certain cues, certain things in the environment—in the circumstance—that begin to trigger sort of our thinking. From those cues, we recognize patterns based on our past experience. We seem to match that current situation to these past patterns, something in our body of expertise—in our body of experience—that looks like the current situation or looks quite different, but somehow has triggered us to begin a comparison that's useful to us.

As part of that pattern matching, we often reason by analogy to past situations that seem quite similar to the one we currently are facing. Based on that pattern recognition, we then embark on a course of action. We adopt certain "scripts" from our past experience. In other words, we say, look, this happened to work in the past in a situation that looks eerily similar to the current one, so we'll adopt that set of actions, that script that worked well in the past, and we'll use them here. Of course, if we look at the situation and say, this does look like a past circumstance, but a set of actions didn't work in that past circumstance, then we might say those are actions we know we should reject this time around. So, we don't explore a wide range of options; instead, we tend to mentally simulate our initial preferred action. We envision how it might play out. If it seems feasible, we go with it. If not, if for some reason our mind feels uncomfortable, then—and only then—might we explore other options. That's how the process of intuition seems to work.

So let's go back to our firefighter again to understand how this process works in a real example, the example of the kitchen fire. Klein argued that intuition gradually develops as someone begins to develop deep expertise in a specific field. As an individual encounters more and more situations, he or she develops a more sophisticated ability to identify, recognize, and match patterns. In other words, though we are not always aware of it, the mind is constantly hunting for patterns in all the situations that we encounter, and it uses pattern matching to spot problems and guide us to solutions.

Let's go back to that fire commander in our example. We see that he could not match the kitchen fire with the patterns from his past experience. He had seen many kitchen fires in the past, and based on that experience, he expected to see certain patterns in terms of the noise level, the heat, and the way that water affected the fire. However, in this case, the cues that he observed in his environment, in that house, did not match those patterns. Thus, his intuition told him that he was not experiencing a simple contained kitchen fire. He could not rely on the actions, the scripts, that he was used to using quite automatically and instinctively in that circumstance. So the lack of a pattern match led him to conclude that he might be facing a much more serious problem than he first envisioned. He knew he wasn't facing a simple kitchen fire. It caused him to seek a different solution than the one he normally would have chosen quite automatically in a normal kitchen fire. So we see that pattern matching doesn't mean simply doing what worked in the past. Sometimes pattern matching, and the identification of a mismatch, enables us to reject a set of actions, to reject a script that did work in the past, because we understand in our mind that we're actually facing a rather novel situation.

Of course, firefighters are not the only ones who use intuition in high-stakes decision-making, and Gary Klein and others have studied people in other fields. As we mentioned, he looked at nurses and doctors, and many others have as well. Nurses and doctors use intuition all the time—despite all the data that you might think drives their decision-making. Clearly they look at medical tests. They look at all sorts of quantitative data that they gather from vital signs and the like. We understand that data plays an important role in the medical field, but so does intuition. Here you see a clear distinction between novices and experts. Novices, that new nurse who has just begun to work in a hospital or just come out of her undergraduate experience, or perhaps a doctor who is an intern or a resident, again relatively inexperienced—they don't have the base of patterns, the experience, to engage in pattern recognition that an expert can employ.

Nurses often report that they took some actions simply because they didn't think things felt right. Something inside their mind told them that the patient was in far more trouble than the data suggested. We have looked at this in a study. My colleagues Jason Park, Amy Edmonson, and David Ager, and I went to look at an important new innovation in the medical field—something called Rapid Response Teams. As you may know, in a typical hospital there are Code Blue Teams. What is a Code Blue Team? Well, sometimes in a hospital, someone unexpectedly goes into cardiac arrest. Unfortunately, when this happens, you have what is called a code blue, and immediately you have a team of experts come to that patient's bedside to try to resuscitate them. They go through a whole set of procedures to try to bring that patient's heart back to normal function. These are heroic people, and they do save many people, but code blues, unfortunately, have a low success rate. Many of those people don't make it. Even if they survive that particular incident, they end up in much worse health over time, and sometimes they die in later weeks. So, Code Blue Teams are really important, but an important innovation has happened in hospitals. They have come to realize that in the hours, six to eight hours prior to one of those cardiac arrests, in fact, there are subtle signs that a patient is beginning to deteriorate, and the question is: Can we detect those signs and move to the patient's aid proactively, so as to preempt a cardiac arrest? This is the notion of a Rapid Response Team.

Scholars, and researchers, and practicing doctors identified what are some of these early warning signs that happen in the six to eight hours before an unexpected cardiac arrest, and they posted lists of these warning signs—what they called triggers—in each unit of hospitals. Frontline nurses were told if you see these signs, call a Rapid Response Team, a small group, a cross-functional team of people who could come in and assess that patient to try to understand if they truly are in trouble and then try to intervene to preempt cardiac arrest. This was an important innovation begun in Australia and the United Kingdom and now has spread like wildfire throughout the American healthcare community, with tremendous results: Mortality rates are down; unexpected cardiac arrest rates are down; time spent in intensive-care units is down—tremendous progress because of the ability to pick up these early warning signs.

Nurses were given this set of criteria, largely quantitative criteria, to look for in assessing patients at risk in their normal day-to-day work on a floor in a hospital. They were also told, though—importantly— to call the Rapid Response Team if they simply felt uncomfortable about a situation. Note this important additional criteria, this additional warning sign that they are told to be aware of. What they're being told is, if the quantitative criteria look okay, but if your instincts, your intuitions, say, this patient is sliding down, this patient is in trouble, still pick up the phone and call—still page that Rapid Response Team. The healthcare community here is respecting intuition of expert nurses and understanding that simply looking at the quantitative data is not enough to treat patients well.

Well, what happened? Many hospitals reported that a substantial number of calls came from experienced nurses who felt uncomfortable, but the vital signs appeared relatively normal in many of those cases. One hospital, in fact, reported to us that nurse concern, nurse discomfort, (without vital sign abnormalities) was the single best predictor that intervention was required to prevent a bad outcome from unfolding. So, Rapid Response Team calls became opportunities to not only capitalize on intuition but also to help patients prevent terrible outcomes, but there is even more. When these experts on these Rapid Response Teams were called to the bedside of patients, what we now had often was the ability to bring experts and novices together to care for a patient. Here, what we discovered in our research was that people, in fact, can share their intuition with others—that experts can, in fact, help develop the intuition of novices, those novices who don't have the experience base to engage in the kind of pattern recognition that experts are able to do.

I've talked about nurses and firefighters—these are all situations where people are in sort of emergencies or crises, but does intuition play a role in sort of more normal day-to-day organizational life? Well, I wrote a case study several years ago on Electronic Arts, the leading video game publisher, and I found that intuition played a very large role in decision-making at that firm. For those who are not familiar with Electronic Arts and their business, they produce video games—things like the Madden series of National Football League video games, which are then used along with video game consoles, things like the Microsoft Xbox or Sony Playstation, to play these games. They're a software company, by and large, and they produce rather innovative games in a whole wide range of areas—from sports, to military games, to various action hero-type games and the like. I looked very carefully at their product development process, and here is where I saw intuition at work. The leaders of the development process did not have a formal method for evaluating games under development. Instead, they relied on their intuition to determine whether a game appeared viable. They often drew parallels to past situations. Does this particular game look like one we've developed in the past? Did that past game actually have success in the marketplace? Why or why not? Is this game somehow different than anything we've done in the past?

Over and over I saw executives there leading the product development process, drawing these parallels in contrast to past circumstances, to past games that had come through the development process. The Electronic Arts case, though, illustrates one of the challenges of organizations that rely heavily on intuitive decision-making. The question there was: How do you pass on this wisdom to newer managers? It's hard to codify that knowledge. They were very worried: Could they sustain their success if the leaders of the product development process, who had been at the firm for many years, suddenly left? What happens when all that tacit knowledge walks out the door? This is a concern, same concern that the hospitals had: How do the expert nurses pass on that wisdom to the novices? You can't do it in a classroom. You can't teach intuition in a lecture; that is certainly the case that was discovered in healthcare and at the video game publisher that I studied, but you can pass on this knowledge.

How do you do it? Well, hospitals, as I said, face this issue with nurses, and they found that much of this occurs through apprenticeship, much of this passing on of wisdom. The way that expert nurses communicate their thought process to novices is critical. It turns out "thinking out loud" is a key practice that expert nurses employ. In other words, they go to the bedside of a patient, and as they're trying to help that patient in the presence of a novice nurse, they're talking through their thought process, and they will sort of explain their reasoning: Why am I calling for this test? Why am I concerned about this patient? Why do I think that this particular vital sign might be telling us something about this patient that maybe the novice doesn't understand? This process of thinking out loud is a way to share the intuitive process that is going on in the mind of the expert. Such behaviors work much more effectively than trying to write down intuitive wisdom. In fact, the other thing we found is that experts often use a Socratic method when they're working with that young apprentice, with that novice. In other words, they're asking questions of the novice and teaching them how to assess situations through that process of asking questions and eliciting answers. Through that Socratic method, they're teaching how they assess the situation and how they match patterns based on their past experience, a very powerful process.

Mentoring, then, is how intuition is shared and developed. It requires astute observation and active listening on the part of the inexperienced, as well as empathy and communication skills on the part of the expert. Here is what one healthcare leader told me about how this mentoring and apprenticeship worked at their hospital, with regard to the Rapid Response Team process. They said:

> We encourage the Rapid Response Team to share a past experience, to show empathy with the floor nurse, to say something like: "I was scared when I first encountered this type of situation too ... let me tell you about it." We also

want the Rapid Response Team to share what they did in that past experience, what they thought it was, and how they might not have perceived a situation correctly when they first encountered it. In other words, show that they too were a novice once, and were surprised by something quite different than they expected and unfamiliar to them.

So that empathy is very important as the expert works with the apprentice. To develop your intuition, as you talk through situations with others and watch them handle those circumstances, you should keep asking yourself: What are they seeing that I'm not seeing? How would they fit this situation into a pattern of their past experience? What cues are they attending to in the current situation? So can we learn intuition? Can we develop it? I certainly think we can, but it's not through textbooks, it's not through a lecture—it's through this model of mentoring and apprenticeship, and through the communication that takes place between expert and novice, that the novice is able to mind that experience base of the expert and learn how to spot patterns, to look for cues, to reason by analogy.

So far I've talked largely of the benefits of intuition, how intuition actually saved lives in the healthcare field or in firefighting, or how it helped develop better video games in a business like Electronic Arts, but, of course, there are dangers to intuition. Let me talk about those for a moment now. As we mentioned in prior lectures, we are susceptible to cognitive biases, and when those cognitive biases happen naturally in the intuitive process, we aren't even aware really of what's going on, and we may very well fall victim to these traps without having time to realize that this trap has affected us. Research has also shown that sometimes we misuse analogies. As I said, that reasoning by analogy to past experience is an important part of the intuitive process, but sometimes we pick the wrong analogies, the subject of our subsequent lecture.

We also don't make the right match to past situations in our experience. We draw the wrong lessons from those analogous situations, and we'll explore that more in the next lecture, but there are other dangers of intuition as well. In highly complex, ambiguous situations, sometimes the complexity obscures our pattern recognition ability. We can't see through the fog of war to understand what actually is the pattern there. There is too much noise in the environment as we assess the situation. We also sometimes have outdated mental models, particularly regarding cause-and-effect relationships. We remember how it used to work in our particular industry, or our particular field, but new technological innovations and changes in the way humans interact, or the preferences of consumers, cause those mental models to be outdated—but we haven't fully come to that understanding—that realization—yet, and, therefore, our intuition can lead us astray.

Let's talk about a few other dangers of intuition. As part of our intuitive process, we often rely on well-established rules of thumb, but we may not question those from time to time and seek to understand whether those rules of thumb still apply. For instance, many industries adopt rules of thumb as they go about making decisions, and they become sort of conventional wisdom throughout the industry, or they can become outdated. For example, many technological industries used to have rules of thumb with regard to how fast a new consumer innovation would diffuse throughout a society—how fast would it spread. For many years, the rate of diffusion of the video-cassette recorder used to be used to predict the rate of diffusion for new consumer technological innovations. So, for example, they understood, these companies understood, how long it took for 10 percent of the American population to have a VCR, and then they understood how much longer it took for the population to have, 20 percent of them, to have a VCR; and 30 percent; and the like. So they had this sort of graph that could tell them how fast VCRs penetrated American society. In fact, some subsequent technologies for consumers in their home followed a very similar path, a very similar rate of penetration into households over time. That, then, became a rule of thumb. Let's use those penetration rates to predict technological diffusion, technological spread, to American households. But with the Internet and with all sorts of other changes in the 1990s, those old rules of thumb didn't apply anymore, and so the old intuition became outdated. Things moved faster. Households adopted technology at far more rapid rates than they did the VCR, and so the rule of thumb that worked for a long time had become something that, in fact, could lead firms astray, far astray.

Intuition can also lead us astray when we move outside of our experience base, when we encounter novel situations, new circumstances that don't fit nicely with the past patterns we have seen. Novelty becomes a problem because intuition is based on looking for similar things in our past experience. Finally, and perhaps most importantly, it's very hard to communicate our intuitive judgments and choices. Thus, it can be hard to persuade others to commit to our intuitive decisions, or to get them to understand how and why we made that choice. Thus, sometimes the intuitive process can have a detrimental impact on our ability to get decisions implemented with a broader team or organization.

How can we effectively communicate our intuition? Often when a leader uses intuition, people misinterpret the leader's intent—and, therefore, implementation suffers. Gary Klein has shown this in his research with military commanders. The idea is that people need to understand your rationale and your intent, because in a large organization they will then have to go out and make their own decisions out in the field during the implementation process. You want them to make decisions consistent with your original goals, your original intent. Klein works on exercises with military commanders where they try to issue orders with clear intent and a clear statement of their goals and objectives, and then subordinates feed back to their commanders what they perceive the intent to be. From this exercise military commanders learn how to clarify their explanations of their intuitive choices so as to make their thinking more transparent. This turns out to be a very powerful process—not so much for refining how intuition works in coming to the choice, but refining how we then explain our intuitive choices so that we can get them implemented with our team or with our organization.

Researcher Karl Weick, a famous scholar of organizations, has proposed another method, a simple five-step process for communicating our intuitive decisions and garnering feedback so as to ensure clear understanding on the part of our teams. He says we should go through these five steps: First: Here's what I think we face—that's what the leader should tell his team: Here's what I think we face (i.e., his or her assessment of the situation). Then: Here's what I think we should do. Third: Here's why (i.e., here's my rationale). Here's what we should keep our eye on as we move forward. Finally: Now, talk to me. Now, talk to me—tell me what you've understood of what I've said; tell me where you see flaws in my thinking. This simple process is a way to communicate your intuition, get feedback, and ensure that you have alignment between what you believe, what you want people to do, and what they think you want them to do.

Finally, I want to close this lecture by pointing out that I am not suggesting that analysis, formal analytical methods, have no role in decision-making. In fact, the best decision-makers are the ones who can combine intuition and analysis. So, how do you do that? First, you can use analysis to check your intuition, not simply to justify decisions that have already been made. You can use intuition to validate and test the assumptions that underlie your formal analysis. Third, you can use analysis to explore and evaluate intuitive doubts that have cropped up as you prepare to make a decision. Fourth, you can use the intuition of outside experts to probe the validity of your analysis. Finally, you can try to use rules and procedures at times to help refine and improve your decision-making, but don't try to replace intuition with rules and procedures; the two should go hand in hand.

Where are we going next? I'm going to close by pointing out that we're going to dive in, in the next lecture, into one specific dimension of the intuitive process—reasoning by analogy. Of course, reasoning by analogy is key to intuition, but it's also part of the analytical process that many people use. We'll look at analogies both in terms of intuition and formal analysis, we'll look at the power of analogies, and we'll look at the dangers that decision-makers sometimes face when they reason by analogy.

Lecture Six
Reasoning by Analogy

Scope:

Reasoning by analogy represents one powerful dimension of the intuitive process. This lecture explains how analogical reasoning works. Put simply, when we assess a situation, we often make references or analogies to past experiences. Often, these analogies prove very helpful to us as we try to make sense of an ambiguous and challenging problem or situation. However, analogical reasoning can cause us to make flawed decisions as well, largely because we tend to overemphasize the similarities between 2 situations when we draw analogies. Moreover, we tend to underemphasize key differences, or ignore them altogether. Drawing on case studies such as the Korean War and business examples in industries such as beer and chocolate, we explain how and why analogies lead us astray, as well as how you can improve your analogical reasoning capabilities.

Outline

I. Whether making decisions intuitively or analyzing a situation more formally, we often rely on reasoning by analogy to make key choices.

   A. What is reasoning by analogy?
      1. Analogical reasoning is when we assess a situation and then liken it to a similar situation that we have seen in the past.
      2. We consider what worked, as well as what didn't work, in that past situation.
      3. Then, based on that assessment, we make a choice about what to do—and what definitely not to do—in the current situation.

   B. Why is it so powerful?
      1. Analogical reasoning can save us time, because we do not necessarily have to start from scratch in search of a solution to a complex problem.
      2. Analogical reasoning enables us to look back historically and avoid repeating old mistakes.
      3. It also enables us to leverage past successful choices to identify best practices.

4. Research also shows that some of the most innovative ideas come when we think outside of our field of expertise and make analogies to situations in completely different domains. The analogy thus can be a powerful source of divergent thinking.

C. Why can analogical reasoning be troublesome?
   1. Research shows that we tend to focus on the similarities between the 2 analogous situations and downplay or ignore the differences.
   2. We also become overly enamored with highly salient analogies that have left an indelible imprint on us in the past, even when those analogies may not fit the current situation.
   3. We do not surface and seek to validate our underlying assumptions that are embedded in the analogical reasoning.

II. What are some examples of faulty reasoning by analogy?

A. Richard Neustadt and Ernest May have done some of the groundbreaking work on analogical reasoning. They refer back to the Munich analogy, which so many political leaders refer to time and time again.
   1. The Munich analogy refers to Neville Chamberlain's appeasement of Hitler in the late 1930s.
   2. Whenever a dictator engages in an aggressive maneuver, we hear leaders hearken back to the Munich situation. They argue that we should confront, not appease, the dictator given the lessons of Hitler in the 1930s.
   3. Neustadt and May argue that we overuse the analogy.
   4. They give an example of one leader who used it well but did not fully explore the analogy, leading to later errors. Their example is Truman with regard to Korea.
   5. Analogical reasoning, with reference to Munich, led Truman to rightfully stand up and defend South Korea, according to these 2 scholars.
   6. However, failing to completely vet the analogy led Truman to later endorse a move to try to unify the Korean Peninsula—not an original objective of the war effort.

7. This miscalculation led to Chinese entry into the war and the long stalemate that followed.

B. Many business leaders also have fallen down when they have reasoned by analogy.

    1. There is the example of Staples founder Tom Stemberg and early Staples employee Todd Krasnow, who launched the dry-cleaning chain called Zoots.

    2. They explicitly drew analogies to the office supplies market back before Staples and other superstores were formed.

    3. The analogy proved not to be a perfect match, and Zoots struggled mightily.

    4. Another example is when Pete Slosberg, founder of Pete's Wicked Ale, tried to move into the specialty chocolate market.

    5. Finally, we have the Enron example. The company reasoned by analogy as part of their new business creation strategy.

    6. Enron drew analogies to the natural gas market, where they originally had success with their trading model. Poor use of analogies led them far afield, eventually even taking them to the broadband market.

    7. In the Enron case, we see what scholars Jan Rivkin and Giovanni Gavetti describe as "solutions in search of problems." The Enron executives did not reason by analogy because they had a problem to solve. Instead, they started with something that had worked in the past, and they searched for new venues that they deemed analogous.

    8. The temptation with such efforts is to seriously downplay differences and to focus on similarities, particularly given the incentive schemes at Enron.

III. How can we improve our reasoning by analogy?

A. Neustadt and May have argued that there are 2 key things that we can do to refine our analogical reasoning.

    1. We can make 2 specific lists: one describing all the likenesses between 2 situations we deem to be analogous and another describing the differences.

2. Their second technique is to write down (and clearly distinguish), that which is known, unknown, and presumed in the situation. The objective is to clearly separate fact from assumption and to then probe the presumptions carefully.

B. Writing these lists down is critically important.
   1. We need to be very methodical in writing down these lists, because it forces us to be much more careful in our thinking. We protect against sloppy analogical reasoning this way.
   2. Moreover, by writing these lists down, we help others conduct careful critiques of our thinking.

C. We can accelerate and enhance our analogical reasoning capabilities.
   1. Certain types of learning experiences can help us refine our analogical reasoning abilities. For instance, one benefit of the case method is that it exposes us vicariously to many, many different situations.
   2. Over time, we can compare and contrast those situations and try to apply past experience to new case studies we examine.
   3. We become better and better at recognizing patterns, and we refine our ability to distinguish useful analogies from dangerous ones.
   4. In a way, business education is as much about refining our intuition, and specifically our analogical reasoning capabilities, as it is about learning formal analytical frameworks.

Suggested Reading:

Neustadt and May, *Thinking in Time*.

Salter, *Innovation Corrupted*.

Questions to Consider:

1. What are some of the dangers of reasoning by analogy?
2. What types of analogies are most salient?
3. How can we sharpen our analogical reasoning?

Lecture Six—Transcript
Reasoning by Analogy

Throughout the history of business, we see leaders reaching back to the past and trying to apply successful business models that have worked for them in a prior "life," in a prior industry, or prior corporation—it's only natural. We see them drawing comparisons between past circumstances and current ones, and we try to apply what works so well for us in those past situations. We also see people trying to invent new businesses, to be entrepreneurs by applying a model from one industry to another, and it's very successful in many instances. It's how many new businesses are invented in America and around the world—a wonderful catalyst for brainstorming and invention, and we often see this behavior in waves. Let's take, for example, the surge of what's called "big box retailing" in the United States in the 1980s. By "big box retailing" I mean the emergence of these superstores in a variety of fields where we had home improvement superstores, and office supply superstores, and electronics superstores. Some called them category killers, because these superstores were not broad in their product lineup but, instead, intensely focused on one particular product category.

What role did analogies and reaching back to the past play in development of the business models of these superstores? Interestingly, I both researched and actually worked at Staples, the office supply superstore. It was founded by Thomas Stemberg. Tom Stemberg founded Staples in the mid-1980s, based on some past experience in another industry. He had worked in the supermarket business for many years after his graduation from Harvard Business School. He understood the supermarket business, and he knew that there had been a great deal of consolidation in that business and the emergence of larger supermarkets over time. After, for many years, of course, in the mid-20th century, we had smaller sort of groceries and markets in towns across America. The emergence of these superstores happened as people realized there were economies of scale, benefits of being big in the business. What Stemberg did when he invented Staples was, in fact, draw from that experience and understand how the supermarket model of doing business could apply to office supplies. He drew an analogy from office supplies to groceries and applied a business model that had worked quite well, and invented a whole new industry, the office supply superstore business.

In the previous lecture, we spoke about the role of intuition in decision-making. We argued that intuition is fundamentally a process of recognizing patterns based on our past experience. We match the current situation to these past patterns. As part of that pattern matching, we often reason by analogy to past situations that seem quite similar to the one we're currently facing. Whether making decisions intuitively, or analyzing the situation more formally, we often rely on reasoning by analogy to make key choices. What is reasoning by analogy? Analogical reasoning is when we assess a situation, and then liken it to a similar situation we have seen in the past. We consider what worked and what didn't work, and then based on that assessment, we make a choice about what to do, and what definitely not to do, in the current situation. Clearly, Stemberg drew an analogy from office supplies to groceries, and he was able to understand what had worked and what didn't, and he was able to sort of revolutionize a business where largely we bought our office supplies from small stationary stores across America. Within a few years he had come up with a whole new business model that allowed, unfortunately for the small stationary stores, many of them to go out of business, but meanwhile, a whole new industry, a very profitable industry, of office supply superstores to emerge. An analogy had led to entrepreneurship, invention, innovation, and a great deal of value for the American consumer because, of course, office supplies became much cheaper over time with the emergence of the superstore concept.

Why is analogical reasoning so powerful? How can it help decision-makers? Reasoning by analogy can save us time, because we don't necessarily have to start from scratch in search of a solution to a complex problem. Reasoning by analogy enables us to look back historically and avoid repeating old mistakes. It also enables us to leverage past successful choices, to identify the best practices from our past. Research also shows that some of the most innovative ideas come when we think outside of our field of expertise. Make analogies to situations in completely different domains, and then bring it back to the domain in which we're working. The analogy, thus, in those situations, can turn out to be a powerful source of divergent thinking. It can help people who perhaps have been totally immersed in one domain, not fall into the trap of becoming sort of like-minded. They've been in this domain together for a long time, and they think one way, and by reaching outside of that domain and making analogies to totally different industries and totally different fields, they can perhaps bring a whole new level of perspective and divergent thinking to their own domain.

Reasoning by analogy unfortunately doesn't always work so well. It can be troublesome, even dangerous at times. Why? Research shows that we tend to focus on similarities between two analogous situations, and we downplay or ignore the differences. We also become overly enamored with highly salient analogies that have left an indelible imprint on us in the past, on our minds, even when those analogies may not fit the current situation. In other words, there are certain events that happen to us in life, whether it's in business or our personal life, that leave that imprint, that sort of put a scar in our brain, whether it's a good thing or a bad thing. They sort of really leave such an important and enormous impact that we migrate to those. When we see a situation, we kind of look back to those very important moments in our life, and we draw analogies even when they're not relevant. We also don't surface and seek to validate our underlying assumptions that are often embedded in analogical reason. Of course, not everything is a fact. We have to make assumptions in ambiguous situations, but sometimes we draw a series of implicit assumptions when we reason by analogy, and we don't validate, probe, and test those assumptions very carefully.

And finally, there's one last way that reasoning by analogy can be dangerous. Pointed out by strategy scholars Jan Rivkin and Giovanni Gavetti of the Harvard Business School, they have argued that sometimes what we see is solutions in search of problems. In other words, something worked for us quite well in the past, and we take that particular model, that framework, that solution that worked well, and we kind of go out and look actively for other situations where we can apply it. In other words, we're not starting with a problem that we have to solve and then looking for an analogy. We're starting with the analogy and kind of going out and looking for new problems. The problem with that is it's sort of like we've got a hammer, and everything looks like a nail to us. We've got that hammer we love, and we're out hunting, and we're just applying the analogy because we love the analogy, rather than letting the situation and the problem dictate how we should go about solving them, and we'll talk more about that when we talk about Enron later in this lecture.

Two scholars, Richard Neustadt and Ernest May of Harvard's Kennedy School of Government, have done groundbreaking work on the use of analogies—and, in particular, they focused on American presidents and their decision-making. How have American presidents reached back into history to look back at other situations and then used those past situations to inform their current choices? One example in their research is President Harry S. Truman's decisions during the Korean War, and it's an example I want to walk you through today because it's very important. Truman used analogies in that case. He used an analogy both effectively in certain ways, but also ineffectively in other ways, and we'll walk through and understand why that was. By the way, Neustadt and May point out not just that there are problems with analogical reasoning—they're not only showing you the flaws, but they also advise decision-makers on how to improve their reasoning by analogy.

How do they do that? What advice do they have for decision-makers? Neustadt and May have argued that there are two key things we can do to refine, to improve, our analogical reasoning. In fact, they say we can make two specific lists: one describing all the likenesses between two situations that we deem to be analogous, and another describing the differences. Making those two lists, they would argue, is very powerful because it ensures that we're not only talking about the things that look the same; that we're looking for distinction actively. The second technique, they would argue, is that we should write down (and clearly distinguish) what is known, what is unknown, and what is presumed about a situation. The objective here is to clearly separate fact from assumption, and then to probe the assumptions carefully to see are they, in fact, valid? Can we collect more information to sort of test and validate assumptions? Perhaps most importantly, though, it's making the distinction between what is fact and assumption, because it's often the case that decision-makers confuse the two. We make implicit assumptions, but then we sort of take them as fact. We assume all sorts of things in ambiguous situations; that's just what we have to do. We can't always resolve all uncertainty, but we can be careful about not allowing ourselves, not allowing our mind, to come to believe that those assumptions are, in fact, truths.

What kinds of analogies did they study when they looked at Harry Truman and other presidents? One analogy came up over and over again—the Munich analogy. What is the Munich analogy? This

Munich analogy refers to British Prime Minister Chamberlain's appeasement of Adolf Hitler in the late 1930s. That was the case, you remember, when Hitler was beginning his expansion in eastern Europe, beginning to invade and take over other countries. At the time many of the other western European countries did not want to enter another war, and so they appeased Hitler. They tried to come to some resolution with him, but in so doing, they sort of granted him additional lands and additional power over other parts of Europe, and so they allowed him to continue to expand his influence and move his army into other territories. Of course, many people today look at that as a huge mistake—that we, in fact, encouraged his expansionism, and that led to the broader war. No one wants to repeat Chamberlain's appeasement.

Today, in fact ever since then, ever since the late 1930s, whenever a dictator engages in some aggressive maneuver, we hear leaders hearken back to the Munich situation. They argue that we should confront—not appease—the dictator, given the lessons of Hitler in the 1930s. Clearly, political leaders overuse this analogy. Not all acts of aggression and not all dictators are the same—yet whenever we see a dictator, a totalitarian regime, an authoritarian regime, moving into another country or engaging in some aggressive action, we hear people all around the world invoke the Munich analogy.

Richard Neustadt had an interesting perspective on Truman's decision-making, because not only is he a presidential historian and political scientist who has written and done research on these subjects, but he was an advisor to Harry Truman. He was there when these decisions were taking place. He understood what was going on. He has a very interesting perspective. So, they looked at how the Munich analogy played out with regard to the Korean War. They argued that Truman actually used the Munich analogy quite well at first, but he didn't fully explore the analogy, leading to later errors. Let's go over some basic facts about the Korean War just to acquaint yourself with the circumstance and situation before I walk through the analysis that Neustadt and May have done.

At the end of World War II, a time when the Japanese occupied Korea, the Soviets and the U.S. then went in and it became divided along the 38th parallel, north and south. In June of 1950, the communist regime of North Korea invaded the south in an effort to reunify the country, and this led to great international concern, including in the White House. North Korea had great success at first. They moved deep into the south. The United Nations came together, led by U.S. forces, and moved in to come to the aid of South Korea to help them repel this North Korean attack. By mid-September, General Douglas MacArthur had led a daring amphibious invasion at Inchon that was very successful in pushing back and coming to some actual momentum in not only getting the north out of South Korea, but actually moving U.S. and other Allied Forces into the north. But, then, the U.S. forces went further, and they decided to probe even deeper into North Korean territory, a crucial decision by MacArthur and Truman that actually led to Chinese troops coming into the war to the aid of North Korea. The Chinese troops and the North Koreans then threw the U.S. back midway into the south, and after that we had a long stalemate that went on until finally, the new president, Dwight Eisenhower, was able to bring peace to the Korean Peninsula. Two years of stalemate—it was a very, very difficult time.

But what happened in this case? Analogical reasoning, with reference to Munich, led Harry Truman to rightfully stand up and defend South Korea, and to bring the Allies in to help him, to get the north out of the south, and to preserve this regime of collective security that was first sort of envisioned with the emergence of the United Nations toward the end of World War II. However, failing to completely vet the analogy led Truman to later endorse a move to try to unify the Korean continent, and the scholars, Neustadt and May, point out this was not an original objective of the war effort. This miscalculation led to Chinese entry into the war and the long stalemate that followed. They point out that the China situation was fundamentally different than anything related to Hitler, Chamberlain, and the 1930s with appeasement—a crucial difference that was not really identified and explicitly discussed when Truman used the Munich analogy to come to the aid of South Korea. The key point here: Standing up to Hitler in the late 1930s almost certainly would have not meant invading and occupying Germany at that point of time. It might have meant coming to the aid of other nations, such as Poland and Czechoslovakia, and pushing Hitler back to preserve the sovereignty of those nations, but it probably didn't mean invading and occupying Germany—not in the late 1930s at least. So, very important: The analogy to Munich really would not have suggested going in and pushing deep into North Korea to try to "punish" them in some way for what they had done, although it clearly would have meant, and might have meant, that it made sense to go in and defend South Korea. So, Truman strayed from his initial goal. He strayed, the scholars argued, because he wasn't exactly clear about what the Munich analogy was telling him, and what it meant he should do.

Let's look at that methodology that was offered to us. What are the similarities and differences, the likenesses and differences? What if Truman had written those down? Well, what are the similarities? We have armed aggression both in the '30s and in 1950, when the north invaded south of Korea. We have a victim seeking outside aid, we have a treaty violation, we have expansionist dictatorships in the world, and we have a number of democracies who really aren't interested in going to war because a recent war has really scarred them and led to many, many deaths. But there are clear differences. The two Koreas are not clearly separate sovereign nations; we have collective security, something very different with the United Nations than we had with the weak League of Nations in the 1930s. We have little U.S. domestic support for a policy of isolationism and appeasement, but we also have nuclear weapons, and we have an aggressor who has the backing of a much larger, more powerful nation—China. Of course, we have the Cold War raging, something quite different than the 1930s. [There are] many crucial distinctions that tell us that simply applying, in a very sort of stark and simple way, a lesson from appeasement in the 1930s to the Korean situation is not the right thing to do.

There are many assumptions, of course, also, and we could go through and list those. Things like there was an assumption that the Russians had deliberately instigated the North Koreans, and that China and Russia would not want to broaden the war for fear of instigating a broader world conflict. Of course, that assumption proved out to be incorrect: China did enter the war, did come to the aid of the north, though they didn't want a broader world conflict— they didn't want the U.S. coming that close to their own borders. So, drawing these lists, Neustadt and May have argued, coming up with what are we assuming, what's similar, what's different, might have helped Truman understand that, yes, the Munich analogy might suggest that we should confront the north and come to the aid of South Korea, but the Munich analogy doesn't logically lead to a decision to invade the north and try to reunify the country. There is no reason why we would come to that conclusion based on the Munich analogy, if we vetted it in a more thorough and rigorous way. So, it's interesting. It's a wonderful example because it shows us a president using analogies in a very powerful and effective way, at least initially, but then straying from his initial goals, initial intent, because, perhaps, he didn't vet that analogy and really think through it in as rigorous a way as he could have. Those simple methodologies offered by Neustadt and May might help in doing so.

Let me give you some business examples because this is not just something that President Truman did or other American presidents have done. Businesses, as I mentioned at the beginning of the lecture, do this all the time. We said Tom Stemberg did this when he so successfully built the office superstore business in the 1980s, but I want to take you to another example involving Tom Stemberg and an early employee of Staples named Todd Krasnow, who ran marketing for the firm. They reasoned by analogy, again in the late 1990s, after a decade or more of great success in office supplies. They said: What is like office supplies? Is there another business where we can see much fragmentation and much opportunity for a large player to go in, build a supermarket-like concept, and consolidate the industry and deliver greater value for consumers? They made an analogy to dry cleaning. They explicitly drew analogies from the office supplies market back before Staples and other superstores were formed. They saw a fragmented market with opportunities for someone to achieve scale economies and to use professional management to deliver a better experience and more value to consumers. This analogy between office supplies before Staples and the dry cleaning market as it stood in the 1990s proved not to be a perfect match, and this company they founded named Zoots struggled mightily.

Zoots eventually folded in 2008, with the name bought by some employees who kept open some stores under the name, and other stores were sold off to rivals. Why wasn't this analogy correct? Why couldn't we take this industry that was littered with mom and pop dry cleaning shops around America, looked a lot like those mom and pop stationary stores littered across America in the 1970s? What was different here that allowed them not to apply the superstore concept effectively? As it turns out, they went with the notion that they could build centralized production facilities. In other words, they would do all the dry cleaning in a central location, and then simply have small storefronts to actually listen to the customer, pick up their laundry, etcetera, but all of the actual cleaning could happen in centralized production facilities. This would be like the large distribution facilities that the superstores were using in office supplies. Stationary stores, they got their supplies through wholesalers and distributors in a very inefficient logistics network. The creation of superstores allowed the creation of large distribution centers owned by the store, owned by Staples, that could process and distribute the items in a much more efficient way. Couldn't we centralize production of dry cleaning and have these facilities and central locations that could process all the cleaning of shirts, and suits, and dresses more effectively? It turns out that couldn't happen. This notion that we could have centralized production and economics of scale, it wasn't quite like office supplies, and the reason is there is much more need for local customization in the dry cleaning business than there is in the stationary business. That customer really needs to interact, talk through how they want it cleaned, what kind of stains are there. There is all of this customization in terms of how they like their suits, and shirts, and dresses that doesn't exist in the stationary business, and that meant centralization and going after economies of scale wouldn't work quite as well. The analogy was not a perfect match.

We've seen this in other businesses as well. Let me tell you the story of another very successful entrepreneur. Pete Slosberg was the entrepreneur who invented Pete's Wicked Ale, one of the most famous and successful microbrews that existed in the 1980s. Remember, microbrews emerged when American people, managers, and entrepreneurs interested in making better beer, better beer than some of the mass market beers that existed, started small firms and started advertising in quirky ways to appeal to people who wanted a better beer, a better domestic beer than was available at the time. Slosberg had a great deal of success in the business, and after selling the business off he decided: Can I use this business model again? Can I find another industry that kind of looks like the state of the beer market back in the 1970s, before I began my business, and can I apply my business model, what I know well? Again, as we mentioned at the start of the lecture, this is the way many entrepreneurs have built great businesses in America and around the world over the years—but again, sometimes we get the analogies wrong because we don't look enough at the differences and, of course, this is what happened with Pete Slosberg. He decided to launch a chocolate business, if you will, a micro-chocolate business—a small, higher-end, domestic chocolate business. More premium than Snickers, and Kit Kat, and Hershey bars, and the like, but not an import either, to be made here in the United States, and it would sort of be quirky in its advertising and marketing, much like Pete's Wicked Ale was. But there were key differences between beer and chocolate, and the business model didn't fit.

For instance, the target market for craft brews, such as Pete's Wicked Ale, consisted of males aged 18 to 34. The target market for premium chocolate tended to be wealthier, more-educated females. He knew that, but he didn't fully understand the implications of the difference in the customer base for how he might be able to apply the business model he used in beer to chocolate. Not understanding how the difference played out and what impact it would have is one of the problems that we encounter when we reason by analogy. We might see a difference, but not understand fully its implications as we go forward with a new decision. Of course, he saw other things, too, like outsourcing production was a key part of the business model in the beer business. He understood that he would need to find excess capacity at larger brewers and use them to help him make the beer. He thought he could do the same thing in chocolate, but it turned out it was more difficult because chocolate manufacturing and product packaging is a bit more complex than in craft brewing, and that turned out to be a major hurdle in his efforts.

Let me take you to one last example. It illustrates the notion we introduced at the earlier part of the lecture, of solutions in search of problems. An example is Enron. The company, if we all recall, was very successful and made all the headlines back in the 1990s, listed for many years as the most innovative company in America; then, of course, it collapsed. Many of its leaders ended up going on trial; some of them went to jail. Enron was an oil and gas pipeline company that in the late 1980s and early 1990s discovered an opportunity. They discovered and invented a new business, the ability to create markets for natural gas—in other words, that we could write contracts, and we could trade those contracts in ways much like we trade stocks, or bonds, or the like. So, this was a very, very successful thing—trading for a specific amount of gas, at a specific location, at a specific price, and if you could do that and buy and sell contracts, you could, in fact, create a much more efficient natural gas market in the United States. Enron did this and was very successful at creating a market, and creating contracts, and introducing all sorts of new efficiencies to the market in doing so.

But what did they do? They wanted to invent new businesses. They wanted to expand, and so what they said is: Can we take this (what they called template) model that works in natural gas, and can we find other fields where we can apply it? This template essentially became what are the characteristics of the natural gas market—and can we now, with this list of characteristics that eventually they actually wrote down, can we use that to go on the hunt for new business opportunities, and can we take the young, smart people in our organization and give them that template and send them off and incent them to go find opportunities where this template applies? And they actually did. They created an incentive system—a skewed incentive system—where, in fact, there was more reward for inventing new businesses than there was for running old businesses in a profitable way.

So, now you've incented people to actually go out and really use those analogies and really go out and maybe stretch those analogies too far. Initially, they went into things that were rather similar to natural gas—things like electricity—but over time they kept stretching the analogy further and further. So, they didn't make one big leap way away into something totally different than gas; they did it in small incremental steps—that's what often happens with analogies. We start with analogies that are close to home, but we go down the slippery slope, and they did it as well. What was their template? It was a series of questions: Was the product a fungible commodity that could be divided into indistinguishable units? Did it have a complex and unique logistics system? Were there many buyers and sellers, all of whom lacked market power? Could one create standard contracts and product offerings, etcetera, etcetera? Ultimately, that list led them to some markets like broadband, quite different than natural gas. Note one important thing: That list, that template, that set of questions—that was descriptive of the gas market, but in answering it, in looking for other markets that had those same characteristics, they were only focused on similarities. Never were they focused on the differences, and therein was the problem.

So, in the Enron case we see this notion, solutions in search of a problem, a great business model, and let's go figure out other places we can apply it. There is a temptation here, and it's to seriously downplay differences and to focus on similarities, particularly given those incentive schemes at Enron. They could have benefited—go back to Neustadt and May—from that advice, to make those lists, to identify not just the likenesses but also the differences. That template (that list of the characteristics of natural gas), that was all about what are the similarities between that and the new businesses we're going to enter. They also didn't separate fact from assumption very well—and again, those lists of known, unknown, and presumed could have really helped.

It's important to note that Neustadt and May say we need to write these lists down. It's critically important. We need to be methodical in writing down lists, because it forces us to be much more careful in our thinking. We protect ourselves against sloppy analogical reasoning. They site Lee Iacocca, the former chairman and CEO of Chrysler Corporation, who once said about writing things down: "In conversation, you can get away with all kinds of vagueness and nonsense, often without realizing it. But there's something about putting your thoughts on paper that forces you to get down to specifics. That way, it's harder to deceive yourself—or anybody else," very, very important.

Rivkin and Gavetti, these two strategy scholars who have pointed out this problem of "solutions in search of problems," have said there are a number of things we can do in addition to what Neustadt and May have prescribed, and they say one of the most important things to do is to really understand that we can use analogies in multiple ways. We don't always simply use them to come to a solution. Sometimes we can ask others to reason by analogy with us, simply to generate a more wide range of alternatives to encourage more divergent thinking. Sometimes we can use analogies to sort of test whether a solution we've already come up with actually makes sense. We can do all sorts of things besides simplistically coming up with choices based on a reference to a past situation. They also say, look, it's really important that we understand the environmental context around a past situation before we leap and make an analogy—that we really need to understand that past choice as it sat in its environment, as it sat in the context at the time. Finally, they point out we need to translate, decide, and adapt—that we can't take solutions from the past whole cloth and apply them to the present day, that we need to recognize and think carefully about what the adaptations need to be when we draw that analogy and we make current choices.

I'm going to close by saying that we can accelerate and enhance our analogical reasoning capabilities. Certain types of learning experiences can help us refine our analogical reasoning capabilities. For instance, one benefit of the case method of learning and teaching is to expose us vicariously to many, many different situations. Over time, we can compare and contrast those situations, and try to apply past experience to new case studies we examine. We become better and better at recognizing patterns in doing so, and we refine our ability to distinguish between useful analogies and dangerous ones. In a way, any case study education is as much about refining our intuition and improving our ability to reason by analogy, as it is about learning formal analytical frameworks, and that's something important to remember. I hope in this course we can actually expose you to many situations so that you also can begin to think about how you match patterns and how you reason by analogy—and expose you to, perhaps, a broader experience base than you already have.

In the next lecture, we'll turn to sense-making, the notion that sometimes we act and then we decide. In other words, we look at a series of actions, and we try to make sense of them and use those sense-making procedures to inform our new choices.

Lecture Seven
Making Sense of Ambiguous Situations

Scope:

Until now, we have treated decision making as a fairly linear process (i.e., we think and then we decide). However, Karl Weick coined the term sensemaking to describe how we do not always think and then decide. Instead, we sometimes decide and then think about how we have behaved, which then leads to further decisions. Action becomes an iterative process of decision making and sensemaking. This sensemaking process, which we engage in all the time, shapes how we behave. Drawing on 2 fascinating cases of wildland firefighters—in the Mann Gulch and Storm King Mountain fires—we examine how sensemaking processes can unfold in ambiguous situations and how poor decisions and actions can transpire.

Outline

I.   What is sensemaking, and how does it affect our individual decision-making capabilities?

    A. Traditional models of decision making suggest that we decide, and then we act. As we noted in our discussion of myths during Lecture One, decision-making processes are not always as linear as the models suggest.

        1. Sometimes we take actions—we try things—and then we try to make sense of those behaviors.

        2. We also make a number of choices through a process of trying to make sense of the actions of those around us—particularly those who lead us.

        3. Sensemaking becomes a powerful tool for decision makers particularly in highly ambiguous situations. In those cases, we cannot choose and act unless we can assess the situation properly.

        4. Sensemaking, in those ambiguous situations, often involves trying to sort out conflicting signals, as well as trying to separate the key signals from all the background noise.

B. We use certain mental models to make sense of ambiguous situations.

1. The use of those mental models helps us identify cause-effect relationships more readily. Ultimately, sensemaking is about understanding the connections among various actions and events.

2. Making connections and identifying cause-effect relationships helps inform our further action.

3. Sensemaking, then, is really about how we reflect and learn from experience and then use that learning to inform further action.

4. As we noted earlier, however, we can get into trouble when the mental models become outdated. In those cases, we may have a hard time comprehending novel situations.

II. Sometimes, our sensemaking capabilities can break down and lead to serious failures. Scholar Karl Weick has described this as the "collapse of sensemaking." It can lead to poor decisions and flawed actions.

A. Weick first described the collapse of sensemaking in reference to a famous forest fire that took place in 1949. Initially, the smokejumpers made sense of actions around them and concluded that it was a routine fire.

1. In the summer of 1949, 12 smokejumpers died fighting a seemingly routine fire that suddenly transformed into a deadly blowup at Mann Gulch in Montana. Only 3 men survived.

2. Karl Weick has argued that as time passed on the mountain, the smokejumpers' initial assumptions about their situation slowly began to unravel.

3. Originally, the smokejumpers assessed the situation as quite routine. They did not see this as a novel or dangerous situation. They thought that they would have the fire under control by midmorning.

4. Numerous early actions by their leader reinforced this initial situation assessment.

5. For instance, their leader, Wag Dodge, stopped to eat his dinner when the smokejumpers landed on the ground. The smokejumpers "made sense" of this action by concluding that he must not have thought the fire was too serious.

6. At one point, one smokejumper stopped to take photographs of the fire. Again, this reinforced the initial situation assessment.

B. The collapse of sensemaking began when Dodge's attitude about the fire suddenly changed.

1. Shortly after he stopped eating dinner and began working on the fire, Dodge expressed concern about the fire. Suddenly, his attitude shifted.

2. The crew could not reconcile his earlier actions with the sudden alarm in his voice.

3. In the midst of the crew's confusion, with the roaring fire at their heels, Dodge yelled for them to drop their tools. When nothing around them appeared rational, holding on to their tools—which symbolized their identity as firefighters—seemed the only thing that *did* make sense.

4. Of course, holding onto the tools slowed them down, thereby heightening their risk of not being able to outrun the fire.

5. Finally, Wag Dodge decided to light a small fire in front of the raging blowup, amid a grassy area.

6. He lay down in the ashes, and he called out to his team to join him.

7. That behavior made no sense at all to the smokejumpers, most of whom were very inexperienced. Their intuition, which was not rooted in as much experience as Dodge's, told them to run.

8. Running proved to be the wrong move. Dodge survived, because the fire went right over him. His escape fire had burned all the grass in that small area, depriving the main blaze of fuel in that area.

9. Weick argued that the inexperienced crew, who did not have Dodge's intuition, lost their ability to make sense of the situation very quickly, and this hurt their ability to act effectively.

III. We saw the sensemaking breakdown again in a fire that took place in 1994, called the Storm King Mountain, or South Canyon, fire.

  A. Again, we had firefighters refusing to drop their tools amid a blowup.

  B. Tools are a symbol of firefighting. They are embedded in the firefighter's identity. Dropping your tools means you are admitting that you can't fight the fire. That is a very difficult judgment to make.

  C. In fact, when a blowup is going on, and many homes are in danger, it doesn't seem to "make sense" to give up these most important tools.

  D. Some smokejumpers at South Canyon likened dropping their tools to running up a white flag.

  E. One firefighter was actually found dead still holding his saw in his hands.

IV. These fires, especially the Mann Gulch blaze, remind us of the important link between intuition and sensemaking.

  A. Dodge came to believe very quickly that the fire was very dangerous, and he knew to light the escape fire because of his ability to recognize patterns. He was matching what he saw to his past experiences, making sense of what he saw.

  B. Dodge could do this because he had much more experience than most of the smokejumpers on his team.

  C. Dodge had never started or seen the escape fire tactic before in his life.

  1. He invented it on the spot—in the midst of the blaze.
  2. He noticed cues in the situation that suggested this was not a routine fire.
  3. He recognized that he could not outrun the fire, again based on his experience.
  4. He had seen a backfire tactic used, and he adapted that concept to this situation, recognizing that a backfire would not work here.

  D. Unfortunately, Dodge could not communicate his intuition in the midst of the blowup.

  1. He was described as a poor communicator.

2. He also didn't have much time to explain his thinking to his crew.

3. They had already "made sense" of the situation, and his actions ran completely contrary to their assessment. Thus, he had a huge obstacle there in terms of persuading them.

4. It's a great example of how intuition can be hard to communicate.

5. It also shows how there can be conflict between how you make sense of a situation and how others make sense of it. That can lead to problems.

V. Many have taken important leadership lessons from the Mann Gulch fire.

A. Michael Useem has argued that Dodge made critical mistakes long before the blowup occurred that made him less credible and effective as a leader. Thus, his crew was not as amenable to understanding or going along with how he came to make sense of the situation.

B. Dodge was not considered an effective communicator.

1. He was described as an individual of few words. People said it was "hard to know what he was thinking."

2. Thus, his crew members had a hard time understanding his intuitive reasoning and sensemaking. They couldn't understand his rationale.

C. Dodge also lost credibility over time during the blaze, having not done enough to build up a base of credibility prior to the fire.

1. Dodge did not attend the 3-week summer training with his men. His credibility relied on his reputation and positional authority, as many of the crew members had never worked with him.

2. The team did not train as a team. It had never worked together as a unit on prior fires. People worked on a particular blaze based on a rotation system.

3. His credibility eroded during the early stages of the fire. There was a rough landing, a broken radio, and no ground crew. This did not impress his crew members.

4. He left the crew several times during the early stages. His departures, coupled with his poor communication skills, eroded his credibility further.

5. By the time he set the escape fire, his crew lacked confidence in him. Thus, they did not follow him.
6. Even if there was no time for communication, his intuition and sensemaking, a huge base of credibility, and a well-designed team structure might have helped him persuade others to join him in the escape fire. It could have made up for the sensemaking challenges.
7. For all leaders, the lesson is clear. You must build trust, spend time designing and bringing together your team, and then communicate your intuition and sensemaking clearly if you want to succeed in highly risky and ambiguous situations.

Suggested Reading:

Useem, *The Leadership Moment*.

Weick, *Sensemaking in Organizations*.

Questions to Consider:

1. Why do leaders sometimes find themselves in Wag Dodge's predicament?

2. How can leaders encourage collective sensemaking that results in a shared understanding of a situation?

3. Does sensemaking always lead to better future decisions? Why or why not?

Lecture Seven—Transcript
Making Sense of Ambiguous Situations

So far we've been talking about the cognitive process that leads to a decision. Traditional models of decision-making suggest that we decide—then we act. As we noted in our discussion of myths during Lecture One, decision-making processes are not always as linear as the models suggest. Sometimes we take actions, we try things, and then we try to make sense of those behaviors. We also make a number of choices through a process of trying to make sense of the actions of those around us, particularly those who lead us. Sense-making, then, is about coming to an awareness, an understanding, of an ambiguous situation. It's a critical part of the way we make choices. In highly ambiguous situations we cannot choose and act unless we can assess the situation properly. Sense-making, in those ambiguous situations, often involves trying to sort out conflicting signals, as well as trying to separate key signals from all the background noise in the situation. By background noise, I mean all the irrelevant information that really won't help us in making the choice. It may actually confuse us in making the choice. In many cases, sensemaking is a process of shared cognition. In other words, we aren't alone. We are coming to this cognitive understanding of an ambiguous situation through close interaction with our colleagues. In other words, we are trying to arrive at a shared mental map when we look at that uncertain circumstance.

Sense-making doesn't always work out so well. Sometimes we have a very hard time making sense of a situation. Karl Weick—noted organizational scholar, really the father of sensemaking theory—has described this kind of situation where things don't seem to make sense anymore. He said:

> Things seem inexplicable. And to make it worse, many of our ways of making sense of the inexplicable seem to have collapsed. Our weaknesses come rushing to the forefront. The first impulse is to grasp for some explanation, any old explanation. And what we get hold of are the automatic explanations that we have lived with the longest and evoked most often.

This notion of reaching for the old explanations—it's very important. What Weick is saying is, sometimes we do grasp, because we look at a situation, we're trying to assess it, it doesn't make sense to us, and we're looking, we kind of know those old explanations, those old ways of assessing the situation, probably won't work, but they're all we have. In those instances, sensemaking seems to break down, and our ability to make decisions becomes problematic. We may end up sort of in paralysis in those instances.

So, we use mental maps, mental models, to make sense of ambiguous situations, and the use of those mental models certainly helps us identify cause-effect relationships more readily. Ultimately, sensemaking is about understanding connections among various actions and events. Making connections and identifying cause-effect relationships help inform our further action. Sense-making, then, is really about how we reflect and learn from experience—not only our own, but those of others—and then we use that learning to inform further action. As we noted earlier, however, we can get in trouble when our old mental models become outdated. When we face novel situations, we have a hard time. Sometimes we can't make sense of them anymore.

This notion of our sensemaking capabilities breaking down can lead to serious failures. Scholar Karl Weick has described this as the "collapse of sensemaking." Sometimes we go from really thinking we have a read on a situation to suddenly having no ability to really make good choices at all, and we see some very flawed actions in those situations. Weick first described this notion of the collapse of sensemaking in reference to a famous forest fire that took place in 1949. In the summer of 1949, 12 smokejumpers died fighting a seemingly routine fire that suddenly transformed into a deadly blowup at Mann Gulch in Montana. Only 3 men survived in that fire. It was a deadly day that was really an important seminal moment, though, in the history of forest fires because we learned from that, and we did improve. But at the time, it really was an amazing day because when those smokejumpers arrived at the fire they really did think it was just a routine forest blaze.

Smokejumpers—what is a smokejumper? We should probably say something about this before moving on with this story. A smokejumper is someone who is trained to fight a forest fire. They're trained to do so by actually riding in an airplane and then parachuting down right into the spot where the fire is raging, and being able to fight it in remote areas where you can't get there with the typical vehicles that firefighters would use. Smokejumpers allowed us to go get at fires before they became big—before they got close to houses, and buildings, and towns, and cities, where they could inflict a great deal of damage. Go to places, remote places, when the fire is small and stop it in its tracks, that's what smoke jumping was all about, and that's what these men were trying to do (and they were all men at the time). That is what they were trying to do by jumping from a plane into Mann Gulch and stopping this fire in Montana before it threatened people's homes, and communities, and schools, and churches.

The U.S. Forest Service trained these smokejumpers, a highly select outfit. They created this cadre of smokejumpers in 1940, nine years before the Mann Gulch fire. Again, they were there to attack fires quickly by parachuting onto them while they were still small. The Forest Service expected the smokejumpers to attack what they called "class C fires," fires that were only 10 to 99 acres in size, and they were going to put them out fast, before they became large blazes that were threatening. These smokejumpers, then, who fought at Mann Gulch were not greatly experienced. They ranged from having been on the job only a few months to at most eight years. Remember, the service only invented this concept in 1940, and the Mann Gulch fire took place nine years later. They fought in rotating crews. What does that mean? That means this is not an intact team that had worked together on many fires. Instead, these smokejumpers were at a base in Missoula, Montana—and from there what did they do? They would go out on fires and be called on fires based on a list. So, if they needed 5 firefighters, they would draw the top 5 names on a list. Then, for the next forest fire, they would take the next 10 people on the list, depending on the size of the fire. Then, you then went to the bottom of the list once you got back from the fire you had just fought. So you weren't working with an intact team, and that's an important concept, because we said sensemaking is about shared cognition. It's about coming to an understanding, an awareness, of the situation with others—and when you're not part of an intact team, that can be difficult, as we shall see in this story.

Norman Maclean wrote about this fire in a famous book called *Young Men and Fire*, and I'm going to draw from that tremendous book, as well as from Karl Weick's research as I tell this story. And Maclean wrote at one point that these were "a hardened set of individuals this group was; a hardened combat platoon it was not," because they hadn't worked together before. In fact, many crew members had never worked with Wag Dodge, their leader that day on the Mann Gulch fire. In 1949, the Forest Service had put Wag Dodge in charge of base maintenance at Missoula, Montana; therefore, he had even missed the three-week summer training session, which most of these smokejumpers had taken part in. He had not trained with the crew he was now leading on that day in the middle of this very serious blaze. They didn't know him well.

Many smokejumpers considered Wag Dodge to be a man of few words. Interestingly, Norman Mclean reports that his wife concurred. She said "He said to me when we were first married, 'You do your job and I'll do mine, and we'll get along just fine.' … I loved him very much, but I didn't know him very well." A wonderful anecdote—sad in a way, but very, very useful in understanding what happened to sensemaking as this team worked with its leader in Mann Gulch in 1949. Mrs. Dodge also knew none of the smokejumpers in Missoula, because her husband never spoke of them nor invited them home for dinner. At Mann Gulch, Dodge did not even know the names of all the men on his crew. After the fire, Walter Rumsey, one of the survivors, told the Investigative Review Board: "Dodge had a characteristic in him. … It is hard to tell what he was thinking." And that can be a dangerous thing, as we shall see.

Karl Weick has argued that as time passed on the mountain, the smokejumpers' initial assumptions about their situation slowly began to unravel. Remember, I said originally the smokejumpers assessed the situation as quite routine. In fact, they used to call these "10 o'clock fires," meaning that by 10 am the next morning they'd have the whole thing wrapped up, they'd be back at their base, relaxing and waiting for the next fire that they had to go fight. This to them looked like a 10 o'clock fire. They did not see it as a novel or dangerous situation. They thought that they would have it under control. Numerous early actions by their leader reinforced this initial situation assessment, reinforced their way of making sense of what they saw when they arrived on the scene. For instance, their leader, Wag Dodge, stopped to eat his dinner when the smokejumpers landed on the ground. The smokejumpers "made sense" of this action by concluding he must not think the fire is too serious. At one point, one smokejumper stopped to take photographs of the fire. Again, this reinforced to everyone else on the team this initial situation assessment that said, it's routine, it's a 10 o'clock fire, we're not certainly going to be putting our lives at risk here—this is simply a matter of executing what we know, what we've done before, and we'll be fine.

What happened? The initial assessment began to unravel. By the way, all of this happened within an hour. The fire went from seeming routine as they jumped from the plane to an hour later blowing up into a massive blaze that killed many of them. So, this collapse of sensemaking took place very quickly, and this was very challenging. It began when Dodge's attitude about the fire suddenly changed. Shortly after he stopped eating dinner and began working on the fire, Dodge expressed concern about the fire. Suddenly, his attitude shifted; he seemed to be taken aback—startled and very worried. The crew could not reconcile his earlier actions with the sudden alarm in his voice. It didn't make sense to them.

In the midst of the crew's confusion, with the roaring fire at their heels, Dodge yelled at them to drop their tools, the axes and other devices they use to fight a forest fire. When nothing now appeared rational to them around them, holding onto their tools seemed to be the only thing that did make sense. The tools really symbolized their identity as firefighters. These were what they used to fight fires. It was part of them, part of their identity; this is what it meant to be a firefighter is to hold that axe and the other techniques and tools they used. Of course, holding onto them, though, slowed them down—thereby heightening the risk of not being able to outrun the fire. When Wag Dodge told them to drop their tools, he's signaling to them that he didn't think they could outrun the fire, and that they needed to move fast, but this didn't make sense. Just five minutes earlier, Wag Dodge was having dinner; this was routine. People were taking photographs, and they were jokingly calling it a 10 o'clock fire. Everything had changed so quickly, and dropping their tools just didn't make sense—you never did that, certainly not on most of the fires they were used to fighting. Remember, many of them were rather inexperienced. They had never seen a blowup, a large blaze suddenly emerging from something that looked so routine.

Finally, they made their way. They started running for the ridge, trying to escape the blowup, and Wag Dodge suddenly stops. He decides to light a small fire in front of the raging blowup, amidst a grassy area. Literally, he took out a match and lit the grass. Then, after the grass burned for a moment, he lay down in the ashes, and he called out to his team to join him. Remember, the rest of the smokejumpers are running for the ridge, trying to escape the fire with all their might. Some of them are dropping their tools, some not—but they're running out of fear, and Wag Dodge has stopped. He has dropped all that he has, he has lit a match, and he is literally lying down in the ground just a few feet ahead of a raging blowup. This behavior made no sense at all to the smokejumpers, most of whom were very inexperienced. Their intuition, which was not rooted in as much experience as Wag Dodge's, told them to run and run with everything they had. Running, though, proved to be the wrong move; Wag Dodge survived that day because the fire ran right over him. His escape fire had burned all the grass in that small area, depriving the main blaze of fuel. The fire, thus, sort of stopped when it got to that little burnt-out grassy area and went around and over him—and Dodge, who had laid flat on the ground, managed to survive. In fact, the fire went past him, and then he got up and dusted himself off, and he was virtually unscathed.

Weick argued, Karl Weick, the scholar, argued that the inexperienced crew, who did not have Dodge's intuition, lost their ability to make sense of the situation very quickly, and this hurt their ability to act effectively. They didn't really know what Dodge was doing. They couldn't make sense of his actions—going from eating a meal, to telling them to drop their tools, to lying down in the grass ahead of a raging blowup. Dodge's eroding credibility and lack of knowledge of his team had made it tough to develop that shared cognition where people could make sense together of this ambiguous, novel, and unexpected situation. So, instead, what you had was a team with very different assessments of the same situation, and so some ran, and others didn't know what to do—some dropping their tools, others not—and Dodge lying in the grass. So we had a total fragmentation of the team, a collapse of sensemaking.

We have seen these sensemaking breakdowns in other situations as well. Fortunately, after Mann Gulch, we had very few fires like it, at least very few fires that had killed smokejumpers. No smokejumper had actually died in the line of duty in a blaze since 1949, until a very serious fire on Storm King Mountain in 1994. Norman Maclean, who had written that book about the Mann Gulch fire, his son John Maclean wrote a book about this Storm King Mountain Fire—sometimes known as the South Canyon Fire—in Colorado, in 1994. On July 6 of that year, 12 smokejumpers perished in a fire on Storm King Mountain. Again, we had firefighters refusing to drop their tools amidst a blowup. These were, as I said, the first smokejumper deaths since Mann Gulch. In the investigation, they found that these firefighters violated some key rules. They made some risky choices, but beyond that we see again a very interesting example of this struggle to make sense. Tools, remember, we said are a symbol of firefighting. They're embedded in the firefighter's identity. Dropping your tools means you're admitting you can't fight the fire. It's a very difficult judgment to make. In fact, when a blowup is going on and many homes are in danger, it doesn't seem to "make sense" to give up these most important tools. No firefighter, no smokejumper, is trained to sort of give up. It's not really part of who they are. Some smokejumpers at that South Canyon fire likened dropping their tools to running up a white flag, but sadly that day, the Investigative Board found that one firefighter actually was found dead still holding his saw in his hands. He could not come to drop the tools, even when the blaze had caught up with him and was leading him to his death.

These fires, especially the Mann Gulch blaze, remind us of the important link between intuition and sensemaking. Wag Dodge came to believe very quickly that the fire was very dangerous, and he knew to light the escape fire, because of his ability to recognize patterns. He was matching what he saw to his past experiences, making sense of what he was seeing. Wag Dodge could do this because he had a much broader and deeper experience base than most of the people on his crew. It's important to point out Dodge had never started or seen the escape fire tactic before in his life. In fact, there was no such tactic. It had been written about in a novel—something like it, at least, had been written about in a novel many, many years earlier—but Dodge had never read that novel, and so really he, nor any other smokejumper, even knew about this thing called an escape fire. The name "escape fire" wasn't even coined until after Wag Dodge saved his own life that day at Mann Gulch. He invented it, on the spot in the midst of the blaze. How did he do it?

He noticed cues in the situation that suggested this wasn't a routine fire. He recognized that he couldn't outrun the fire—again, based on his experience. He had seen another tactic used called a "backfire," and he adapted that concept to this situation, recognizing that that technique known as a backfire wouldn't work here. He invented it on the spot by adapting from past experience—by looking and trying to match patterns and seeing that this blaze was going to be more serious but that past techniques that were used in training would not work. Unfortunately, Dodge could not communicate his intuition in the midst of the blowup. He did try to yell to the team and tell them to join him in lying down in the grass, but he couldn't explain the rationale behind this novel technique that no one had ever heard of or seen and that seemed so bizarre while everyone else was running for their lives. Remember, he also was described as a poor communicator. He didn't have much time to explain his thinking to the crew. They had already "made sense" of the situation, and his actions ran completely contrary to their assessment. So, he had a huge obstacle there in terms of persuading them. It's a great example of how intuition can be hard to communicate, but it also shows how there can be conflict between how you make sense of a situation and others make sense of it, and that can lead to problems.

Remember, we said at the beginning of the lecture that great teams and organizations develop collective sensemaking—a shared mental map—and they update that continuously by looking at the situation and seeing if their mental map is correct. They revise, and revisit, and improve it, and refine it, and they work together to make sure everyone is revising their mental map in a similar way as they go through a situation.

Karl Weick has studied some interesting teams in his career. He's looked at the teams on aircraft carriers, and he's looked at aviation flight crews. He said the best of them develop what he calls "collective mind," meaning they're constantly updating their sensemaking as new cues emerge from the environment around them. They're working together to make sure that they're updating in unison. It's not that they always agree. Sometimes they disagree how they make sense of a situation, but they talk it out, and they're constantly working to make sure that they've got a common mental map that they're referring to as they make further choices. This ability to refine, and sharpen, and build a collective mind, he would argue, is key to safety in those very dangerous professions, like working on an aircraft carrier or flying a commercial airline. There are many lessons from Mann Gulch, and many people have taken those lessons and applied them to leadership more broadly in other fields.

Wharton Business School Professor Michael Useem has made an interesting study of what the lessons are for business leaders from

Wag Dodge's mistakes. He's argued that Wag Dodge made critical mistakes long before the blowup occurred that made him less credible and effective as a leader. Thus, his crew was not as amenable to understanding or going along with him now that he came to make sense of the situation. Dodge was not considered an effective communicator. He was, as we said, described as an individual of few words. People said it was "hard to know what he was thinking." Thus, his crew members had a hard time understanding his intuitive reasoning and sensemaking, and they couldn't understand the rationale of his actions. But it's important to note that he had lost credibility over time during the blaze, having not done enough to build up a base of credibility prior to the fire. He hadn't trained with the crew. He didn't learn their names. His credibility relied on his reputation and his positional authority. The team didn't train together. It had never worked as a unit or with him, and as his credibility eroded, he got into trouble, and that credibility erosion began in the early stages of the fire. There was a rough landing, a broken radio, and no ground crew there to help them. This didn't impress his crew members. They wondered how good was Wag Dodge at what he did. He left the crew several times during the early stages of the fire. His departures, coupled with his poor communications skills, eroded his credibility further. By the time he set the escape fire, his crew lacked confidence in him. Thus, they did not follow him. Even if there was no time for communicating his intuition and sensemaking, a huge base of credibility, of trust—and a well-designed team structure—might have helped him persuade others to join him in the escape fire, even if they didn't really know exactly what he was doing. It could have made up for the sensemaking challenges.

For all leaders the challenge is clear. One must build trust, spend time designing and bringing together your team, and then communicating your intuition and sensemaking clearly, if you want to succeed in highly risky and ambiguous situations. That's the lesson here of Wag Dodge. If he had built up the trust and credibility, if his crew had great faith in him and knew him well, and if they had worked together as a team, then even though sensemaking had collapsed, even though they didn't understand what is this man doing lying in a grassy fire, they might have followed him. They might have gone along. We put great faith in leaders sometimes; this crew did not. He didn't have the base of trust and credibility.

It's important, Useem and Weick and others have pointed out, that we need the trust and credibility with our team as leaders because sometimes we won't be able to make sense of novel, difficult, ambiguous situations. That's when we need the trust of our team the most, when we won't be able to come to that collective mind, that shared mental map. When the novelty and the ambiguity will overwhelm us, we need them to follow us, to have faith in us, and Dodge hadn't built that kind of credibility. He allowed it to erode, in fact, in his early choices during that fire.

So, let's conclude. Sense-making is a shared cognitive process—not simply going on in one person's head. Constantly updating our mental models to build collective situational awareness is very important. Not being wedded to old models in novel situations is critical in coming to that alignment where everybody has a shared understanding of the situation. If they disagree, they're talking out their disagreements; they're talking out why they see the situation differently, why they're making sense differently—it's so important. A lack of alignment in the mental models can be dangerous.

Commercial airlines have learned this so, so well over the years. They put their pilots—in fact, they put their entire crews—through some very important training. They call it "crew resource management training" (or CRM), and the whole point of this training is to get the teams working together to build shared situational awareness. When someone sees something that doesn't make sense, they're taught to communicate it with the rest of the team, and then to work out how it might make sense, what's going on here. And if the team, if members of it are seeing a situation differently, then they work that out, and they work—very importantly—on making sure that if a junior subordinate member of the team sees something that doesn't make sense, disagrees with the direction a leader is going, they're encouraged to speak up, and talk about it, and talk through the sensemaking process as a group. This is very, very critical—something that was not really done with Wag Dodge. He hadn't worked with that team very well.

With this lecture, we're done with the individual level of analysis—the first major module of the course. The topic of shared cognition is a wonderful transition from individuals to groups. Remember how individuals make choices to how groups make decisions. Remember, we hear much promise of the synergistic potential of groups. We hear the phrase "none of us is as smart as all of us," and, of course, there is a wonderful power in groups. We bring together a diverse group of people, and we think that that diverse group of people can do a better job than an individual in many cases. We hold great promise for them. But are groups better than individuals? Do groups always do better than we could do on our own? Why is it that sometimes groups falter? We will see many examples in the next module of why sometimes groups don't do so well. We will call these "process losses." We'll say that groups don't always achieve their synergistic potential. Sometimes they really do falter because the dialogue and the dynamics between them breaks down, and that's what we plan to study in the next module.

Lecture Eight
The Wisdom of Crowds?

Scope:

Up until now, we have examined individual decision making, largely focused on cognition. Of course, most of us make many decisions as part of a group or team. The question then arises, are groups better decision makers than individuals? Do teams achieve synergistic benefits by blending together the talents and expertise of various members? In this lecture, we begin by talking about James Surowiecki's book, *The Wisdom of Crowds*. In that book, the author shows how often a large "crowd" of people actually seems to be more intelligent than any particular individual. In this lecture, we will look at how and why crowds tend to have such wisdom, using examples ranging from game shows to business cases. However, we will also examine the major conclusions from the literature on small groups and teams. We will see why many teams do not achieve their potential. They suffer so-called process losses (i.e., the interaction of team members actually does not yield synergistic benefits). We will examine several factors that contribute to process losses, such as the information-processing problems that tend to occur in groups.

Outline

I. We now shift from individual decision making to group decision making, which will be the topic of the next 9 lectures.

  A. We will begin by considering how teams can be more effective than individuals—how 2 or more heads can be smarter than one.

  B. Then we will begin looking at why groups often do not achieve their potential, why they actually do worse at times than the best individual decision makers.

  C. Ultimately, we will spend a great deal of time talking about how to improve group decision making and avoid many of the classic team decision-making pathologies.

II. Are groups better decision makers than individuals?

    A. The conventional wisdom is that groups can make better decisions than individuals because they can pool the diverse talents of a team of individuals.

    B. The notion is that groups can achieve synergistic benefits. Merging ideas from diverse perspectives creates the potential for new ideas and options that no individual could create on their own.

    C. Unfortunately, many groups do not realize those potential synergies; they experience process losses. By that, we mean that the groups fail to capitalize on the diverse talents of the members, and they actually do worse than the best individual in the group could do on his or her own.

III. In some situations though, we do see that groups do better than individuals.

    A. In his bestselling book *The Wisdom of Crowds*, James Surowiecki argues that a large "crowd" of individuals can actually be more intelligent than any individual expert.

        1. Surowiecki explains this phenomenon by describing what happened on the popular game show *Who Wants to Be a Millionaire?*

        2. As you may recall, participants had several techniques that they could employ to help them answer a difficult question. For instance, they could "ask the audience," in which case the audience would vote on which of the 4 possible answers was correct.

        3. At the time of Surowiecki's book's publication, the audience had answered correctly an astounding 91% of the time!

        4. The point is that the aggregation of all those individual judgments leads to a good answer, even though we haven't handpicked the group to include a bunch of experts.

        5. Surowiecki provides many examples of how the aggregation of information in this manner provides better-quality decisions than most individual experts can make.

B. Surowiecki and others have shown many other examples of this pooling of intellect, where a crowd does better than most individuals could.

    1. For instance, a Canadian mining company created a contest whereby people around the world could examine their geological data and offer a recommendation as to where to search for gold on their properties. The contest yielded solutions that had eluded their in-house experts.

    2. Many other companies are trying to leverage the power of this mass collaboration. Even the U.S. federal government has done this.

    3. Many people are using wiki technology to pool the intellect and judgments of many individuals.

    4. Prediction markets are also an example of this phenomenon. Examples include the Iowa Electronic Markets, which tries to predict elections, and the Hollywood Stock Exchange, which tries to marshal the judgments of thousands of people to predict how well particular films will do.

C. Surowiecki argues, however, that there are several critical preconditions for making the crowd smarter than individuals.

    1. You need to have diversity within the crowd: Many different disciplines, perspectives, and areas of expertise must be represented.

    2. You have to have decentralization, meaning that the crowd is dispersed, and people with local and specific knowledge can contribute.

    3. You have to have some effective way of aggregating all the individual judgments.

    4. Finally, and most importantly, you must have independence. In other words, you can't have individuals being able to sway others, or situations in which pressures for social conformity can impact people. This is the key condition that usually doesn't hold in actual teams within organizations. They are interacting closely, and they are interdependent.

IV. What are some of the process losses that hinder groups whose members are interdependent, unlike the crowds in Surowiecki's examples?

   A. Certainly, pressures for conformity arise within groups. We will talk about that in depth in the next lecture.

   B. We also have schisms that develop within teams. Scholars have described how negative outcomes result when "fault lines" emerge within teams.

      1. Fault lines are schisms that often emerge based around natural demographic subgroups within a team.

      2. We can see in-group/out-group dynamics emerge in these situations, which leads to dysfunctional conflict.

   C. In some groups, they exhibit an inability to manage air time, such that a few individuals dominate the discussion. Others are not able to get their ideas on the table.

   D. Free riding is another process loss. Some members may not feel personal accountability, and they may loaf, expecting others to carry the load.

   E. Information-processing problems also arise in many groups, such that pooling and integration of individual knowledge and expertise does not occur.

      1. For instance, Gary Stasser's research shows that team members tend to discuss common information quite extensively but often fail to surface all the privately held information that group members possess.

      2. Moreover, group members tend to discuss private information less than common information, even when privately held information does surface.

      3. The lack of adequate information sharing is one of the most perplexing challenges that teams face, and that hinders their decision-making effectiveness.

   F. Finally, information filtering can occur in many groups, whereby some individuals funnel data as it moves up the hierarchy. They prevent a leader (or a team) from having access to key data that may help them make a better decision.

V. We close this lecture with an example of a group process loss, with particular emphasis on the problem of information filtering.

    A. The case is the Son Tay incident during the Vietnam War.

        1. This was an operation designed to free prisoners of war in North Vietnam during the Nixon administration.

        2. During the summer of 1970, intelligence indicated the location of a camp with American prisoners of war.

        3. The United States prepared a special rescue operation, and Nixon approved it.

        4. During the fall, information arose that suggested that perhaps the prisoners were no longer at the camp.

        5. Key officials chose to withhold that information from the president.

        6. Some have argued that Nixon's behavior caused his advisers to think that his mind was already made up and that he didn't want to hear this new information.

        7. The mission went ahead, and the soldiers performed brilliantly. However, there were no prisoners at the camp. It was a major blunder.

    B. The Son Tay incident demonstrates to us how groups can fail to capitalize on all the information and expertise of their members. We do not always find the ways to pool expertise effectively, despite the clear promise that teams hold.

Suggested Reading:

Steiner, *Group Process and Productivity.*

Surowiecki, *The Wisdom of Crowds.*

Questions to Consider:

1. In what circumstances is a team likely to outperform individuals working on their own?

2. In what circumstances are individuals likely to outperform teams?

3. How and why do people filter information, and what can be done to reduce the negative impact of filtering?

Lecture Eight—Transcript
The Wisdom of Crowds?

We now shift from individual decision-making to group decision-making, which will be the topic of the next nine lectures. We will begin by considering how teams can be more effective than individuals—how two or more heads can be smarter than one. Then, we will begin looking at why groups often do not achieve their potential, why they actually do worse at times than the best individual decision-makers among them. Ultimately, we will spend a great deal of time talking about how to improve group decision-making and avoid many of the classic team decision-making pathologies that researchers have discovered and described over the years.

Are groups better decision-makers than individuals? We've always heard the expression: None of us is as smart as all of us. The conventional wisdom is that groups can make better decisions than individuals, because they can pool the diverse talents of a team of people. The notion is that groups can achieve synergistic benefits, that we can bring together diverse perspectives, merge them, and that this creates the potential for new ideas and options that no individual could create on their own. Unfortunately, many groups do not realize these potential synergies; they experience what is called "process losses." By that we mean that groups fail to capitalize on the diverse talents of their members, and they actually do worse than the best individual in the group could do on his or her own.

In his best-selling book, *The Wisdom of Crowds*, James Surowiecki argued that a large "crowd" of individuals, a large group, could actually be more intelligent than any individual expert. He gives a very interesting example about this from *Who Wants to Be a Millionaire?*—which I will share with you shortly. The point that Surowiecki is trying to make is that the aggregation of a whole series of individual judgments can lead to a very good answer, even though we haven't hand-picked the group to include a bunch of experts. Surowiecki provides many examples of how the aggregation of information, in this manner, provides better-quality decisions than most individual experts can make.

Let's talk about *Who Wants to Be a Millionaire?* This is a famous game show brought to the United States from Britain several years ago, hosted by Regis Philbin, when it first went on in primetime, made famous by his question he would always ask: "Is this your final answer?" As you may recall, participants on that game show had several techniques that they could employ to help them answer difficult questions. For instance, they could "ask the audience," in which case the audience would vote on which of the four possible answers they believed was correct. The computers quickly tallied the votes of all the audience members and reported those results to the participant in the game show, who was sitting there across from the host, ready to answer the question. Did the audience—the team, if you will, the crowd—do better than the individual? Did it help to employ a team on these problems? Remember, the audience is not made up of a bunch of experts who happen to know a lot on the subject of that particular question. It's just a general cross-section of the American population. During the first years of the show, Surowiecki went and actually calculated how often the audience was correct. In other words, the top vote-getter among the four answers, how often was that top vote-getter the correct answer to the question at hand? He discovered that the audience had answered correctly in an astounding 91 percent of the questions for which the participant in the game show had asked for their assistance. The wisdom of crowds, that was the name of his book, *The Wisdom of Crowds*, that how could they always be so right even when that crowd, that group, was not composed of a group of experts.

Surowiecki and others have shown that many other examples exist of how this pooling of intellect can take place, where a crowd does better than most individuals could. For instance, there's the example of a Canadian mining company that created a contest where people around the globe could examine geological data that the mining company had compiled, and look at it, analyze it, and offer a recommendation as to where to search for gold on the company's properties. The contest, as it turned out, yielded solutions that had eluded the in-house experts of the Canadian mining company. The mass collaboration of many people around the globe had produced an answer that no one expert in-house could have produced. Many other companies are trying to leverage the power of this mass collaboration. They're trying to figure out ways to pool the intellect of diverse people from not just inside their organizations, but from around the globe, bringing that together to come to judgments that are far better than any individual expert could make. Even the federal government of the United States has begun to try to do this. Many people, including the federal government, are using "Wiki" technology to pool the intellect and judgments of many individuals.

What is Wiki technology? Some of you may have heard of Wikipedia. This is an online encyclopedia. It's not built, though, by professors, and historians, and experts in science, and history, and math, and the like; it's built by average people all around the globe. How do they do it? How do they get it right? And Wikipedia is fairly accurate—not perfect, but it is, in fact, fairly accurate. What happens? Well, someone will go on the website, and they'll post their knowledge on a particular subject, and then other people are able to go in and edit that input. They're able to offer their knowledge of that instance and that situation, and over time—through hundreds and thousands of people who are looking and refining the knowledge and information on that subject—we come to something that no one expert could have actually written. We come to this powerful group answer. Wikipedia is now this online encyclopedia with millions of entries on all sorts of subjects, and it has been found, in fact, by some researchers to be more accurate than some published encyclopedias. It is rather incredible, the power of mass collaboration.

What is the federal government of the United States doing to capitalize on this kind of technology, this ability to have this sort of online site where people can constantly edit and improve what is written? Well, they're doing the same thing with internal information about key aspects, for example, of the war on terror. There are internal secure websites where multiple people, from various agencies of the federal government, can contribute what they know about the intelligence they're gathering about various threats to the United States. So, no one person in the Central Intelligence Agency, or the Federal Bureau of Investigation, or the Federal Aviation Administration may know everything about the threat posed by some terrorist group in another part of the world. If you pool together all that knowledge through the use of this technology, you get to a better answer than any one expert can come to. It's very interesting that they're able to do this, because, remember, we talked after the 9/11 attacks in this country of how the agencies weren't collaborating very effectively. They weren't sharing knowledge. The difficulty, despite all the best efforts, is that one person at the Central Intelligence Agency doesn't know who it is that's working on the same subject over at the FBI, or at the FAA, or some other part of the government. It's very hard to know who else has the relevant information, because technology allows people to come together virtually in a way where they don't need to know who is collaborating with them even. They can be anonymous to one another, but they can work together. The power, the wisdom of crowds, describes Surowiecki. He also points out that there are prediction markets that have emerged. What is a prediction market?

One example is the Iowa Electronic Markets, and what happens here is that people can go on and actually trade what essentially is like a commodity, a financial instrument, in which what they're essentially doing through trading is trying to predict the outcome of future American elections. It turns out that these electronic markets, where lots and lots of people are offering their predictions, can offer outcomes, predictions that are more accurate than leading pollsters sometimes can offer. We also have the Hollywood Stock Exchange, again a prediction market where people go in and essentially—through trading—are placing their bet on the judgment of how well a particular film will do, how popular will it be, how large will the box office revenue be for that film. Thousands of people go to the Hollywood Stock Exchange and try to predict, and it turns out, again, that they can be quite accurate in their predictions of how well feature films will do when they hit movie theaters around the country—the power of mass collaboration.

But wait, what do we know? We know from decades of research on teams that many teams fail. This kind of mass collaboration, this synergy of bringing people together, it doesn't always work. Often it doesn't work. Ivan Steiner, a famous team dynamics scholar, has said that too often there are process losses, meaning when we bring groups together in a decision-making process, instead of that process producing synergy, there's a certain something [that] drops out. It's like a leaky bucket. There are losses. Tremendous opportunities to bring knowledge together don't happen, and the groups stumble. Richard Hackman—Harvard's leading scholar on teams, a social psychologist who studied groups for decades—has said many teams fail to realize their potential. While he thinks teams can do great things, he's rather pessimistic on how well the average team can do.

What's going on? When does the crowd have wisdom, and when doesn't it? Is there a systematic way to identify the instances in which a team may prevail over the individual? Surowiecki argues there are several critical preconditions for making the crowd smarter than individuals. He says, first you need to have diversity within the crowd—many different disciplines, perspectives, and areas of expertise must be represented. Second, you have to have decentralization, meaning that the crowd has to be dispersed, and people with local and specific knowledge can contribute. Third, you have to have some effective way of aggregating all the individual judgments. That Wiki technology is a powerful way to do it. Finally, and most importantly, you must have independence. In other words, you can't have individuals being able to sway one another, or situations in which pressures for social conformity can impact people's judgments. You must have independent judgments that you're pooling together. Ah, but now we come to the key issue. Surowiecki's crowds don't look like the teams that we all work in, in organizations. Most teams, particularly in an organizational setting, violate these preconditions—and, in particular, they violate the independence precondition.

Independence doesn't hold in actual teams within organizations. They are interacting closely, and the members are fundamentally interdependent. In the close interaction in which they engage in, social pressures emerge that often distort group decision-making. People are trying to build consensus; they're trying to persuade and influence one another—that can be positive, but often it's negative. People aren't making independent judgments because of persuasion and influence, because of pressures for conformity—people's judgments get distorted by those around them. Sometimes we're working together and we're improving our judgments, but many times we're swaying one another in a negative way. Sometimes people actually dismiss their own doubts; they're afraid to go against the crowd. They suppress their own descending view because of pressures that emerge. We'll talk about those kinds of pressures in the lectures that follow. They're important, and they explain why teams don't always pool individual expertise in the way that Surowiecki explains ideally they can and should.

So, what are some of these process losses that hinder groups whose members are interdependent? What happens? Certainly, pressures for conformity—they constitute one of the most important elements, one of the most important pressures or dynamics that distort group decision-making, and we will talk about that in depth in the next lecture. We call these pressures for conformity, we often term them "groupthink," a phenomenon where groups end up prematurely converging on an alternative, suppressing dissent, and not engaging in the vigorous dialogue and debate that's necessary to make good decisions. But there are other process losses as well, and I'd like to introduce a few of those in this lecture, before we dive deep to understand conformity pressures and groupthink in the lectures that follow. For example, we have schisms that develop within teams. Scholars have described how negative outcomes often result because "fault lines" emerge within teams.

What is a fault line? It's something quite similar when we think of faults that lead to earthquakes. Faults also happen within groups in organizations. Fault lines are schisms that emerge based around natural demographic subgroups within a team. For instance, if you had a group of people, and half of them are engineers and half of them are marketing folks, sometimes a fault line emerges between the two groups, and that creates a lot of dysfunctional conflict—such that they're not actually pooling their expertise and creating an outcome that's better than any individual could produce. Instead, they end up really faltering as a team because of this schism. We see this on a variety of demographic characteristics. It can happen on gender, on race; it can happen on age; it can happen on the functional background, or even educational background, of the members involved. We see in these kinds of situations that a sort of in-group/out-group dynamic emerges, where people are sort of staying with their own crowd and really denigrating, perhaps, the people in the other subgroup. This leads to a lot of dysfunctional conflict. It's one of the fundamental process losses that researchers have discovered in trying to understand why teams don't always do so well.

In some groups, we see an inability to manage airtime, such that a few individuals dominate the discussion, and others aren't able to get their ideas on the table. This notion of sort of a few people dominating a group, that can be very destructive because, again, if we believe that the group is coming together, that its powers are in being able to bring synergy from all these people with diverse perspective, you're not going to get that if some people simply aren't talking, if a few people are dominating the discussion—yet that happens in many groups. Why does it happen? Hierarchy gets in the way. Status gets in the way. The people who sit at the top of the organization chart, the people who have the power, the people who have the professional status—they crowd out others, and they hog up all the airtime, and that, of course, diminishes the group's ability to achieve a synergy, to achieve the ideal that we think of when we say there's wisdom in crowds.

Free-riding is another process loss. Some members may not feel personal accountability. They may loaf, expecting others to carry the load. Certainly, we monitor one another in groups and, in fact, there's peer pressure to sort of make sure everyone is carrying their load, and that helps to mitigate free-riding. Many organizations put in incentives to deter free-riding. For instance, in my own classroom at the university, at the end of a group project, I ask each of the students to rate the contributions of everyone on their team. I ask them to take 100 points and to spread them among the team members—allocate them so as to represent to me how much each person contributed on a project. If there are 100 points and five members on a team, if they believe that all five members contributed equally, they ought to allocate 20 points to each member. But if they feel someone has been a free-rider and that they haven't contributed much, then maybe that person ought to get far less than 20 points. That little reporting mechanism, where people are asked to evaluate their peers on a team, that can be a powerful incentive system to deter free-riding. But monitoring, peer pressure, and incentives—they're not enough; it still does occur. Some free-riding will happen simply due to the diffusion of responsibility that naturally occurs within groups. The phrase has often been said: "When everyone is responsible, no one is responsible," and that is a feeling, a diffusion of responsibility, that sometimes emerges within groups. Free-riding will always be there, despite the best of incentives and the best monitoring mechanisms we can put in place.

Information-processing problems also arise in many groups, such that the pooling and integration of individual knowledge and expertise does not occur. For instance, Gary Stasser's research shows that team members tend to discuss common information quite extensively, and they often fail to service all the privately held information that group members possess. Stasser's discovery about the failure to actually leverage information probably turns out to be one of the most important process losses that we have discovered that explain why groups don't achieve their potential.

What do I mean by shared information or unshared information, or common information and private information? Let's suppose we had a group that was in a consumer products company, and they were discovering, or discussing, what they knew about consumer research and what consumers thought of a particular new product they had brought to market. Suppose they were here in the United States and they were having this discussion. Could be that all members of the team have a certain common body of knowledge, shared information. They all know precisely what focus groups have said, what surveys have shown about what customers believe about the product, what they like and dislike. That's common or shared information, and maybe they even have reports in front of them that show that. But, perhaps, one member of the team actually has done some work in emerging markets. They've spent time in India and China, Brazil and Argentina. Maybe they know how consumers are quite different in those markets, and they know very specifically what the differences are and why that product will have to be adapted if they take it to the global market. That might be private or unshared information that they know based on their experience in those emerging markets that the rest of the Americans in the group do not know. So, in many teams and organizational settings we have this situation. We have knowledge—some of it shared, some of it private, only held by particular individuals.

What did Stasser find in his work? He found that group members tend to discuss private information far less than common information. Even when the privately held information does come to the surface, often it's not discussed as much as the common body of knowledge. The lack of adequate information sharing is one of the most perplexing challenges that teams face, and it hinders their decision-making effectiveness. Why do members of small groups fail to share information, even when their interests are aligned, even when everyone really is working toward the same goal? Psychologists do not know for certain, but Stasser has argued that perhaps: "The bearer of unique information, like the bearer of bad news, incurs some social costs. ... These social costs may include the necessity of establishing the credibility and the relevance of the unique information." Stasser also points out that status dynamics may exacerbate the problem. In the study by James Larson and colleagues, medical residents, interns, and third-year medical school students examine information relating to a patient's symptoms. They found that residents were substantially more likely to repeat unique information than interns or students would do. They also asked more questions about unique information that came to light. This finding suggests that lower-status members of a group may feel a particularly heavy burden associated with the social costs of surfacing private information. Let me give you an example of how this might work out in this situation. So suppose, for example, that everyone in the group—the residents, the interns, and the medical students—all knew the vital signs of the patient. But perhaps the resident has noticed something in a CAT scan, or an MRI, or in an X-ray of the person's lungs. The others haven't noticed that. That's private information that could be brought to the table, and what they found here is that the residents were more likely to actually repeat that kind of information. Why is repeating it important? It's because by repeating it, they're saying to the group: "Let's focus on this a little more. Let's make sure we're not dismissing the private information. Let's make sure we're not only discussing what we all already know in common." So, that's a very important thing, that ability to get everybody to focus, and it's the higher-status individuals who tend to do that.

How can we improve it? How can we improve information sharing? One might think that a consensus-oriented, participative leadership style will encourage more communication and information sharing within your team, while a very directive or authoritative approach would hinder information flow. That's certainly the conventional wisdom, but here, research evidence provides an interesting twist on this conventional wisdom. Again, we go to the research of James Larson and his colleagues. They contrasted participative and directive leaders. They defined the form of participative leaders as people who shared power with their subordinates, and who withheld their views until others had been given an opportunity to voice their opinions. These scholars defined directive leaders as those who took charge and stated their views at the outset, while often playing the devil's advocate as other opinions and views surfaced. What did Larson and his colleagues find? Surprisingly, they discovered that participative leaders, while they do tend to surface more privately held information, it's the more directive leaders that tend to repeat the unshared information more often—even when that data did not support the directive leader's initial viewpoint. Therefore, a directive leadership approach may actually encourage a group to analyze the unshared data more closely and actually encourage the group to incorporate it into the team's dialogue and their decision-making process—very, very interesting finding, indeed.

Directive leaders, though, have to be careful, because a forceful statement of their views might quash dissenting opinions and hinder candid dialogue. Deference to the boss can be very problematic if leaders become overly directive. Amy Edmondson, Michael Watkins, and I have done research on the subject, and we have argued that leaders can avoid that problem by adopting a directive approach to facilitating the group process, while not trying to dictate the content of the decision. David Nadler has also made a similar argument in his work. So, what's going on there? How can you be directive about the process without telling people what to do? What we're saying is that the leader can intervene and help manage the dialogue—really actively drawing out the quiet people, making sure that private information gets attended to and discussed—without trying to tell the group: This is the decision that needs to be made. So, what can leaders do? They can "manage airtime," ensuring that a few people don't dominate the discussion. They can reiterate or paraphrase ideas and statements that have emerged. They can show people where inadequate attention is being paid. They can ask clarifying questions as people bring forward new information. They can encourage people to express alternative viewpoints. They could actually induce debates so as to surface more data and assumptions. Perhaps most importantly, leaders need to take time near the end of a decision-making process to highlight the areas of remaining uncertainty that would ideally be resolved before making the decision. They could actually really go to the team and say: Here's what's still uncertain. Here's what we still don't know? Does anyone have any additional knowledge to bring to bear on that subject, to offer? Can you bring it forward and sort of invite that additional information to come to the table? That's what we mean by being directive about the process without telling people what to do, and we think it's important for combating this information process loss.

One final process loss that we need to talk about in this lecture, one final reason I'd like to point out that teams don't always achieve their potential—information filtering. It occurs in many groups. It's a situation where people sometimes funnel data as it moves up the hierarchy; where they don't let the leader know what they know. They prevent a leader (or a team) from having access to key data that may help them make a decision. Why do people filter information and not share it with their superiors? Why don't they give it to their team leader? It's not always for bad reasons, and that's important to remember. The intent may be very positive in many instances, but the outcome may be problematic. So, for example, many people sort of prevent or stop information from flowing up the hierarchy because they say, look, we're just overwhelming the leader, they're busy, they have a busy schedule, they have lots of meetings, and this is detail they don't need to know; we need to summarize it for them. In that attempt to improve the efficiency of the leader's work and in an attempt to sort of streamline that information, they filter out stuff that turns out to be very important.

There's some other more negative reasons why filtering happens. Sometimes it's pressures for conformity. It's information that gets filtered out that happens to show a dissenting view from that that people believe the leader already holds. There's confirmation bias, the notion we talked about in some past lectures, where we're actually looking to and emphasizing the information that confirms an existing hypothesis or an existing view of the world, and we sort of filter out information that, perhaps, disconfirms existing views. Finally, of course, some people filter out information because they're advocates for a particular position, and that information happens to show risks or negatives associated with that position, and so they filter it out. Very, very important this notion of information filtering, and I want to give you an example, a sad example, of how this happened—again in the federal government, again with respect to foreign policy.

The example is the Son Tay incident. This was an operation designed to free prisoners of war in North Vietnam during the Nixon administration. During the summer of 1970, intelligence indicated the location of a prison camp located in North Vietnam with a number of prisoners of war, American soldiers who had been captured. We had photographic evidence that these prisoners were there. The U.S. prepared a special rescue operation, and President Nixon approved it. We had an amazing amount of preparation for these Special Forces. We actually designed some camp in Florida at a military base that resembled the prison camp that we thought existed in North Vietnam, and we trained the soldiers as to how they would go in at night, in secret, and spring these prisoners of war and bring them home. During the fall, though, information arose at lower levels of the hierarchy that suggested that, perhaps, the prisoners were no longer at the camp; perhaps the North Vietnamese had moved them to another location; and the Central Intelligence Agency had some information also suggesting that, perhaps, these people were no longer at the camp. But key officials chose to withhold that information from the president. They didn't tell him. He didn't know that the intelligence had changed, and the operation kept moving forward. Some have argued that Nixon's behavior caused his advisers to think that his mind was already made up, and that he didn't want to hear the new information, and that might be one reason why people didn't bring it to his attention. Others believed that it was simply a matter of people not believing enough in the credibility of the new information, and they didn't want to go forward with it because they didn't know for certain that the intelligence showed that the prisoners had moved. Of course, they'd also gone very public, in front of the president, and argued of the importance of this operation, that they had evidence that the prisoners were there, and to now contradict that, that was a very difficult thing to do.

So, filtering took place; the group never looked at the new information with the president—they withheld it from him. The mission went ahead. The soldiers performed brilliantly. They got to the camp. They, in fact, actually found some Russian or Chinese soldiers or advisers that were there as well, and they got into some combat. They did very well, and there were very few injuries, and it was overall remarkable in the way they were able to execute it, but there were no prisoners at the camp. It was a major blunder. They had all moved. We had put these brave men and women, these soldiers, these Special Forces, at great risk, at great peril, and it turns out there was not a single American prisoner of war in that camp. It had, indeed, been abandoned. Oh, when the press found out, this was a major debacle for the Nixon administration, an embarrassment, and, of course, later we find out that people knew, or at least they thought they knew. They had some pretty strong intelligence that the prisoners had moved, but that information had been filtered out as it moved up the hierarchy. Information filtering happens in all teams and all organizations—again, sometimes for good reason. It's the final process loss I want to emphasize in this lecture. It's an important one.

What do you do to solve the filtering problem? There are all sorts of things you can do, including making sure that as a leader, you seek different voices, and you connect with people on the periphery of your organization, and that you go out and listen with your own ears to people on the ground who are perhaps several levels down the hierarchy. You talk to people who don't normally interact with your team, people who aren't normally customers of your organization or suppliers of your organization. You get their perspective. All of those kinds of things make sure that you don't remain sheltered as a leader, so that you do get access, and that you're not simply watching the information that others have packaged for you.

I want to point out the importance here of team design. How do you solve these process losses? You have to take time really thinking about how you put your team together; who they are; what the goals are; what the roles, and responsibilities, and shared norms of the team are—all that is important. As Richard Hackman said, effective leaders "set the organizational stage for great team performances." They create a set of conditions that enable groups to perform well, and that's something we're going to talk about in the lectures ahead. But first, in our next lecture, we're going to talk about, perhaps, the most important process loss of them all: groupthink. Once we've done that, we'll then embark on a series of lectures that help us understand how to fix these problems, how to improve our decision-making and create vigorous, and candid, and open dialogue within our teams.

Lecture Nine
Groupthink—Thinking or Conforming?

Scope:

Building on the concept of process losses, we will examine a key reason why groups tend to make flawed decisions—namely, that they experience groupthink. Drawing on the famous Bay of Pigs case study, we will explore Irving Janis' theory of groupthink: the phenomenon in which a cohesive group finds itself prematurely converging on a solution to a problem due to powerful pressures for conformity. Through an in-depth analysis of President John F. Kennedy and his advisers, we will describe the factors that cause groupthink, as well as the symptoms and results of groupthink. We will show why dissenting views often do not surface in teams and how the lack of dissent can inhibit decision-making effectiveness.

Outline

I. Groupthink is one of the most famous examples how and why a group can make very flawed decisions even if the group is cohesive and its members have great intellect, in-depth knowledge, and good intentions.

    A. What is groupthink? According to social psychologist Irving Janis, groupthink is when a cohesive team experiences tremendous pressures for conformity, such that people strive for unanimity at the expense of critical thinking.

    B. Put another way, groupthink is when we see team members "going along to get along."

    C. Janis has argued that groupthink is more likely to arise when groups are highly cohesive and when they face a great deal of stress or pressure.

II. Janis developed his theory of groupthink based on an analysis of a number of decision fiascoes involving American presidents. The central case that he studied was the Bay of Pigs decision by President Kennedy.

    A. With the approval of President Eisenhower, the CIA trained a force of Cuban exiles in Central America to prepare them for a possible invasion to overthrow communist dictator Fidel Castro.

B. Within a few days of Kennedy taking office in 1961, the CIA presented its plan for using these exiles to invade Cuba.

    1. Kennedy asked the Joint Chiefs of Staff to take a look at the plan. They concluded it could work, but only with certain caveats—either they had to add U.S. soldiers to the plan or they had to be able to count on a substantial internal uprising within Cuba to help the exiles.

    2. After a few weeks, the CIA argued that the time was now to invade. They cited several factors arguing for immediate action.

    3. The CIA acted as both the advocates for the plan as well as its principal evaluators or analysts. It had a vested interest in going forward with the plan.

    4. The entire decision-making process took part under the veil of secrecy. Key experts from within the administration did not join the cabinet meetings for their deliberations.

C. Candid dialogue and debate did not take place at these meetings.

    1. A number of people held back their concerns about the plan.

    2. Many assumptions were made during these meetings, but they were not well vetted.

    3. One key subordinate's concerns were not shared by his boss with the president and the rest of the cabinet.

    4. The CIA dominated the meetings, and the one group with lots of status and experience that could have challenged the CIA—namely, the Joint Chiefs of Staff—tended to remain quite silent.

D. The group spent most of its time trying to tweak the proposal rather than examining other options.

    1. The group failed to consider any alternatives. It focused on a go/no-go decision.

    2. It ended up paring down the original proposal, but the proposal still retained its core weaknesses.

    3. Over time, the plan gathered tremendous momentum.

    4. There is evidence of the sunk-cost effect, causing the CIA to feel as though it had to go forward based on its past investments in this effort.

E. Ultimately, the president went ahead with the plan, despite his own concerns.

    1. The effort was a complete fiasco.

    2. Most of the rebels were either captured or killed.

    3. Castro retained power, and his internal prestige grew.

    4. The invasion harmed the United States' reputation in the world, and specifically, it harmed U.S.-Soviet relations at the height of the cold war.

    5. The invasion may have led the Soviets to put nuclear missiles in Cuba in the following year.

III. What are the symptoms of groupthink, which are clearly evident in the Bay of Pigs case?

    A. The group feels that it is invulnerable—that it cannot fail.

    B. The group rationalizes away disconfirming data and discounts warnings.

    C. People have a belief that they are inherently better than their rivals.

    D. The group maintains stereotyped views of the enemy.

    E. The majority pressures group members who express a dissenting view.

    F. The group comes to a belief that it unanimously supports a particular proposal, without necessarily knowing what each individual believes.

    G. People self-censor their views, afraid to challenge the majority. They do not want to be marginalized or ostracized.

    H. Certain individuals filter out information that might challenge the conventional wisdom within the group.

IV. What are the results of groupthink, which are clearly evident in the Bay of Pigs case?

    A. Groups discuss few (or no) alternatives.

    B. People do not surface many of the risks associated with a plan that appears to have the support of the majority.

    C. Once an option is dismissed, it rarely is reconsidered later to see if could be bolstered and made more plausible.

    D. The group does not seek outside experts who do not have a vested interest in the matter.

E. The group exhibits the confirmation bias with regard to how it gathers and analyzes information.

F. The group does not discuss contingency plans.

V. What are some of the signals that your group is not having a sufficiently candid dialogue? Consider this a list of warning signs.

   A. Do management meetings seem more like hushed, polite games of golf or fast-paced, physical games of ice hockey?

   B. Do subordinates wait to take their verbal and visual cues from you before commenting on controversial issues?

   C. Are planning and strategy sessions largely about the preparation of hefty binders and fancy presentations, or are they primarily about a lively, open dialogue?

   D. Do the same people tend to dominate management team meetings?

   E. Is it rare for you to hear concerns or feedback directly from those several levels below you in the organization?

   F. Have senior management meetings become "rubber stamp" sessions in which executives simply ratify decisions that have already been made through other channels?

   G. Are people highly concerned about following rules of protocol when communicating with people across horizontal levels or vertical units of the organization?

   H. Do you rarely hear from someone who is concerned about the level of criticism and opposition that they encountered when offering a proposal during a management team meeting?

VI. What are some of the major barriers to candid dialogue in teams and organizations?

   A. Structural complexity in and around the team can hinder open dialogue.

   B. When people's roles are ambiguous, that can be problematic.

   C. Teams that have a very homogenous composition can have a harder time engaging in a high level of vigorous debate.

   D. Large status differences among team members can squelch the level of candid dialogue.

E. Leaders who present themselves as infallible, who fail to admit mistakes, can squelch candid dialogue.

Suggested Reading:

Janis, *Victims of Groupthink.*

Schlesinger, *A Thousand Days.*

Questions to Consider:

1. What are the primary drivers of groupthink?
2. When is groupthink most likely to arise?
3. What can be done to break down the barriers to candid dialogue in groups?

Lecture Nine—Transcript
Groupthink—Thinking or Conforming?

In this lecture, we will discuss the powerful pressures that emerge within groups to suppress dissenting opinions and get in the way of candid dialogue. We'll be talking about a theory called groupthink. Barry Rand, the CEO of Avis, once said: "If you have a yes-man working for you, one of you is redundant." It's such an interesting and funny quote, but many people talk about sycophants running around organizations, yes-men and yes-women who say only what the boss wants to hear. But in most of my research over the past decade or two looking at this, I didn't find a series of people in organizations who lacked the backbone and the courage to stand up, and speak their opinion, and air their views in front of senior leaders. Instead, I found a series of problems and flaws in the organizational cultures of companies in the way senior leaders conducted themselves that made it difficult, in fact that hindered candid dialogue, that suppressed the vigorous debate and dissent that are necessary to make good decisions. So, I want to talk in this lecture about what are those barriers to candid dialogue, and we'll start by talking about groupthink.

Groupthink is a theory first exposed by Irving Janis. Irving Janis was a social psychologist at Yale University for many decades, and he taught and conducted research on group dynamics. He conducted a series of very interesting studies back in the 1950s and '60s, culminating with a book he published in 1972 called *Victims of Groupthink*. Janis studied foreign policy decisions, such as the Bay of Pigs decision, the decision by President Kennedy to support a rebel invasion to try to overthrow Fidel Castro. He studied why the U.S. did not foresee the Pearl Harbor attacks. He studied a series of other decisions conducted in the 20th century by American presidents. Along with those studies, he also conducted experiments to try to understand specific facets of group dynamics, to understand how stress affected people, and why cohesive groups sometimes actually don't have enough vigorous debate.

Groupthink—what is it? He would say it's smoothing or avoiding behavior (i.e., it's smoothing over our differences). It's a lack of confronting conflict and debate, confronting when differences of opinion occur. Here's his specific definition that he wrote about in his book. He said:

> "Groupthink" … refer(s) to a mode of thinking that people engage in when they are deeply involved in a cohesive in-group, when the members' striving for unanimity overrides their motivation to realistically appraise alternative courses of action. … Groupthink refers to a deterioration of mental efficiency, reality testing, and moral judgment that results from in-group pressures.

Another way of putting this, a very simple way of putting this is, this is when we go along to get along. We're in a group and sort of there's a natural human tendency to want to feel a sense of belonging with others in a group, and that can be dangerous at times. Really, groupthink represents one of the most famous examples of how and why groups can make very flawed decisions, even if the group is cohesive—even if the members have great intellect, in-depth knowledge, good experience, and good intentions. This, in a sense, is smart people who have good intentions; who share a goal; who, though, want to have a great sense of belonging to one another. That sense of belonging, that desire to "go along to get along," can be dangerous.

Janis argued, in fact, that groupthink is most likely to arise when groups are highly cohesive (or have a strong desire to be more cohesive) and when they face a great deal of stress or pressure. To help us understand this theory in more detail, what are its symptoms, what are the results or consequences of groupthink, I'd like to go into one of Janis's cases in great detail. I'd like to talk about the Bay of Pigs invasion of 1961.

I will tell this story drawing on a variety of historical works, but, in particular, I'm going to draw on the work of Arthur Schlesinger. Arthur Schlesinger—a long-time presidential historian—was also involved in the Bay of Pigs decision. He was a presidential adviser who left the university and went to Washington to work for John Kennedy, and so he was there in the meetings involved in the decision to support these rebels who had been exiled, who left Cuba when Castro came to power, and now were going to go back to try to overthrow Castro, having been trained by the United States. So, Schlesinger, being there, having been part of the Kennedy administration, wrote a very famous book called *A Thousand Days*, representing the 1,000 days that John Kennedy was president of the United States, until his assassination in 1963. So, what we have is a firsthand account, but I'm not only relying on Schlesinger, though I will quote him at times during my account. I'll also tell you from a perspective of what we know based on the fact that many of these meetings were taped at the time. This was before Nixon got caught taping, and so now we don't have these kinds of interesting White House tapes. But back then we did, and so historians have been able to look back and corroborate Schlesinger's account with listening to real discussions on tape that are there. We also know that many others who were involved—Ted Sorensen, for example, another presidential adviser—also wrote accounts of what happened based on being there. So, we have some powerful records to draw upon to tell the story—not from a geopolitical sense, not simply from a historical or political science sense, but to look very closely at the group dynamics, which is what I'm interested in.

So, how does this story start? It starts, actually, with the Eisenhower administration. Dwight Eisenhower was the President of the United States prior to John Kennedy. He served two terms and left the White House in January of 1961, turning it over to John Kennedy. During Eisenhower's administration, the CIA trained a force of Cuban exiles and developed a plan to employ these rebels in an invasion of Cuba. The CIA plan called for no direct U.S. military involvement in the invasion. You'll recall that Castro had come to power as a communist dictator in the 1950s, and this caused great concern in the United States—and, of course, we were very worried about the influence of Soviet communism just off of our shores. Eight days after John Kennedy becomes president, after his inauguration, the Central Intelligence Agency, the CIA, presented this plan to the new president and his staff. Kennedy was wary and cautious. He was a new president. He was very young and inexperienced in foreign policy, and he asked the Defense Department to take a look at the plan.

The Joint Chiefs of Staff, the leaders of each branch of the United States military, concluded that the plan could work; however, they offered some caveats. They weren't necessarily completely persuaded that the plan could work in its current form. They argued that it could only work if it was coupled with an internal uprising, if Cuban citizens—normal citizens—rose up who, perhaps, belonged to resistance organizations; who formally had been in the military; if they could come to the beaches and join the rebels when they arrived on the shores of Cuba and assist them, so as to be able to overthrow

Castro's regime. Or, they said, if not for an internal uprising, we had to actually add U.S. military troops in one form or another. We might have troops join the rebels in the landing on the beaches, or perhaps we should offer air cover (i.e., the U.S. Air Force would actually help from the air, control the skies, and help the rebels land safely on the beaches and make progress against Castro's military).

So, the Joint Chiefs offered an endorsement, but a cautious endorsement, and an endorsement only if some other changes were made to the plan that the CIA had put forth. In early March, President Kennedy was confronted with a "now or never" choice by the CIA. They were saying: "Mr. President, we've talked about this awhile. We've been training them for quite some time, but really now is the time to strike," and they offered three reasons why there was time pressure here. These rebels were being trained in Guatemala at the time, and the Guatemalan government was becoming very concerned. After all, they were worried that this secret operation would be revealed, and that their citizens would become quite disturbed by the fact that they were working with the CIA to train Cuban exiles in their country. So, the Guatemalans wanted the Cuban exiles to stop training there and to leave. Meanwhile, Castro was expected to receive a major shipment of Soviet fighter jets in June of that year. Moreover, the rainy season was about to start, complicating any invasion effort. This would make it very difficult not only to land on the beaches safely, but to move across the beaches and the rough terrain in Cuba. On March 11, the president convened a meeting of his Cabinet. Allen Dulles and Richard Bissell, Jr.—highly respected and experienced CIA officials—argued for the invasion. I should note that neither of these men was appointed by John Kennedy. They were long-time members of the CIA—carry-overs from prior administrations. They presented to a Cabinet that consisted of all men, and all men who were newly arrived in Washington. They did not have the experience in the federal government that Dulles and Bissell had. They presented, quote from Schlesinger, they presented:

> a proposal on which they had personally worked for a long time and in which their organization had a heavy vested interest. This cast them in the role less of analysts than of advocates, and it led them to accept progressive modifications so long as the expedition in some form remained.

In other words, they were willing to let this thing be amended, but they very much were interested in keeping the momentum going and keeping the pressure on the Cabinet to go forward with this plan that they had invested a great deal of time in, their own personal reputation in—so, they really were biased, of course. They were not actually unbiased experts looking at this with an objective view. They were pushing to try to get their plan finally to be implemented after years of working to build the plan and to train the rebels.

Schlesinger said: "The determination to keep the scheme alive sprang in part … from the embarrassments of calling it off." In other words, he's saying, look, at this point they had put so much into it that they very much weren't willing to walk away. They, in fact, were worried about seriously feeling embarrassed in front of their colleagues at the CIA, and more broadly in the federal government, if they had to back away from this. He said: "having created the Brigade as an option, the CIA now presented its use against Cuba as a necessity." Kennedy still wasn't sold, though, at this point. He began to ask his advisers to consider a revised plan that would enable the invasion to occur at lower political risk. During these meetings, many participants presumed that uprisings within Cuba would be essential to the plan's success, consistent with what the military chiefs had said to Kennedy at the outset of this process. Dulles, from the CIA, argued that thousands of people belonged to underground resistance organizations, and they would actively support the invasion by the rebels.

All of this was done in secret, mind you—very few people were involved in the deliberation. The Deputy Director of Intelligence "was not informed at any point about any aspect of the operation." Even Tom Mann—who was over at the Cuban desk at the State Department, an expert on the Cuban domestic situation—was not consulted much during this decision process. Schlesinger said: "The same men, in short, both planned the operation and judged its chances of success." So, very secret, not a broad group of people involved—in fact, one noted group is not involved here: the rebels themselves. They're not brought to the White House to be involved heavily in these discussions. They're the ones who know the terrain of Cuba, who understand the domestic situation, and will actually have to implement the plan. They've been training on the details of how they'll engage in this invasion effort, but they weren't involved either. Again, secrecy was paramount.

The Cabinet now began in late March to meet every three or four days, and Kennedy was skeptical still as problems and issues arose in the plan. Dulles and Bissell from the CIA redoubled their efforts. They argued that even if the plan failed, the cost was minimal. Schlesinger said: "Somehow the idea took hold around the Cabinet table that this would not matter much so long as U.S. soldiers did not take part." There was this interesting erosion of accountability. People didn't feel like they had that much at stake here. Dulles argued that the rebels could "melt away into the mountains" if the invasion failed. Amazingly, those mountains to which he referred were 80 miles from the landing site at the Bay of Pigs on the shores of Cuba. Amazing that this assumption was made that these rebels could simply melt away given those conditions. At this point, said Schlesinger, "our meetings were taking place in a curious atmosphere of assumed consensus." The CIA was dominating the meetings. They were running it, they controlled the agenda, and they controlled the dialogue, and they were the military chiefs. Schlesinger said they "seemed to be going contentedly along." They weren't challenging the plan. They weren't going back to the caveats they had offered. They were simply sort of going along, perhaps going along to get along.

At one point Secretary of State Dean Rusk was absent from these meetings. He was working on other diplomatic matters and traveling at times, and so Chester Bowles, his deputy, sat in on one meeting, and he was horrified at this plan that he had not heard of to that point, but he didn't speak up during the meeting. He didn't express his opposition. Instead, he went back to his office, and he wrote a memo to his boss, Dean Rusk, outlining his opposition to the Bay of Pigs invasion. This memo was never given by Rusk to President Kennedy. Arthur Schlesinger writes that, like Bowles, he, too, had grave concerns about the plan, but he didn't express them in these meetings. Schlesinger wrote:

> In the months after the Bay of Pigs, I bitterly reproach myself for having kept so silent. ... [He said though] it is one thing for a Special Assistant to talk frankly to a President at his request and another for a college professor, fresh to the government, to interpose his unassisted judgment in open meeting against that of such august figures as the Secretaries of State and Defense and the Joint Chiefs of Staff.

So, Bowles and Schlesinger, both with grave concerns, both keeping silent during these discussions. In fact, I've interviewed Robert McNamara, who was Secretary of Defense at the time, and he, too, says he was not a huge fan of the plan, but he was new to the government, new to Washington and the Defense Department—and he, too, sort of held back. He said: "I didn't oppose the plan. I didn't speak on the issue. I sat back really to a large degree, because I really wasn't an expert on these sorts of matters at that point."

What happened? In early April, Kennedy finally made up his mind. At that point Schlesinger says "He felt that ... he had successfully pared it down from a grandiose amphibious assault"—to a much smaller, more controllable, more low-risk plan. In fact, he says he felt that he had reduced failure, the risk of failure, "to a tolerable level." Remember that Kennedy was only in office a mere couple of months when he made this decision to support the invasion of Bay of Pigs. He and his team were fresh to Washington, and Schlesinger says that's part of the reason, perhaps, why they made such a flawed decision. He said:

> The decision resulted from the fact he had been in office only 77 days. ... [T]he authority of his senior officials in realm of foreign policy and defense was unanimous for going ahead. ... [T]hey all spoke with the prerogative of men vested with the unique understanding of arcane matters. ... Had one adviser opposed [it], I believe Kennedy would have cancelled it. Not one spoke against it [he said].

So, what's happening here? If you notice, the group spent most of its time trying to tweak the proposal. They never considered multiple alternatives, one of the key flaws of any decision process. In fact, all we have here is a go/no go decision, and go/no go is not multiple options. It's very hard to evaluate a proposal if you have nothing to compare it against, and so the failure to consider alternatives is a fundamental flaw here. We also see this continual paring down of the original proposal, because it did contain some weaknesses, rather than looking at options. So, we took a big bad plan and turned it into a smaller bad plan. We have tremendous momentum going on here, and we have secrecy. In fact, the people who have to implement the decision are not involved in the decision process, a key flaw that many organizations encounter when they're trying to make choices. Not involving those who have to execute it, who will understand where the pitfalls, and obstacles, and hurdles will be—and they're not brought in for reasons of secrecy, or for other reasons, perhaps. We have evidence of the sunk cost effect as well. Remember, the CIA has been working on this for some time. We talked about the sunk cost effect, you recall, in the Everest story. We said it's one of the key cognitive biases that trip up decision-makers, and here we have it as well—though the cost is not financial so much as it is psychological. It's the time, it's the personal reputation, it's the psychological commitment that the CIA has put into this plan. They want to go forward based on those past investments. They don't want to waste all that investment that they put forth to that point. We have a failure to test assumptions: melt away into the mountains; that thousands would join up in resistance—a failure to really validate those, to explore those in detail. In part, they couldn't explore them because they didn't bring in experts because they wanted to keep it so closely held, so secret within the Cabinet room of the White House.

So, there are many flaws here in this decision process. Janis would say it's one of the classic sort of flawed decision processes. Ultimately, the president, of course, did go ahead, despite his concerns, and the effort was a complete fiasco. Most of the rebels were either captured or killed. Fidel Castro retained power, and his internal prestige grew. The invasion harmed the United States's reputation in the world—and specifically, of course, it harmed U.S.-Soviet relations at a time where really we were at the height of the Cold War. The invasion, in fact, may have contributed to the fact that Soviets put nuclear missiles in Cuba in the following year, a case study that we will discuss in the following lecture. In fact, we'll be looking at how Kennedy, perhaps, improved and changed his decision process as he addressed that crisis in 1962.

So, this, of course, is this just a matter of politics? Does this happen to political leaders? Does it not happen in other circumstances? Do business people and others who run organizations—who have intellect, and good intentions, and a strong base of experience—do they have these kinds of problems with groupthink, where we have no candid dialogue? The Bay of Pigs, we had people who disagreed, who were unwilling to speak up. We had only one alternative considered. I mean, does this happen in other instances? I would submit to you that it does. I think, for example, we know from the evidence that many mergers and acquisitions in the field of business fail. They fail to produce shareholder value—and yet, we look at the decision process, and what do we see? In many mergers and acquisitions we see secrecy. We see implementers not involved in the decision process. We see a huge sunk cost effect—momentum and deal fever (much like the summit fever on Everest). We see a failure to consider multiple alternatives; instead, we see people focused on that one firm they're interested in buying. We see lots of assumptions that go into the financial analysis, the return on investment analysis, that's done prior to a merger, but we see a failure to really test those assumptions. In fact, in many mergers, we see wildly optimistic assumptions about the kind of synergies that will result after the two organizations come together.

Lastly, of course, in many of those mergers and acquisitions, it's the people advocating for the plan, who are completely biased in favor of the plan, who are providing the analysis. Everyone from the internal folks within the firm who would like to do the deal, to the investment banks who will only collect a large fee if the merger actually takes place—and yet, they're the ones providing financial analysis in support of the deal. It's no wonder so many acquisitions fail. They look eerily like the decision process in the Bay of Pigs.

So, groupthink, what is it? It's this tendency to really converge on one idea, to not engage in candid dialogue, and there are a number of symptoms of it that Irving Janis identified by studying the Bay of Pigs and other decision processes like it. So, let's take a look at what some of those symptoms are. He said: "Groups might be experiencing illusions of invulnerability, where they feel like they just can't go wrong." He pointed out Kennedy felt he had the Midas touch. He had been so successful in the years prior—rising up as a young senator from Massachusetts and becoming President of the United States. Groups collectively rationalize and discount warnings; that's another symptom of groupthink. That occurred in the Bay of Pigs. It occurred also, for example, in the Pearl Harbor attacks, said Janis. Unquestioned belief in the group's inherent morality or feeling that they're right and that they're best. Stereotyped views of the enemy, or in business of a rival or competitor—not a realistic appraisal of what the rival looks like, but a stereotype view sort of based on some conventional wisdom that's out there. There's also direct pressure on any group member who argues against the group's stereotypes, illusions, or proposals. Worse than that in groupthink, worse than that, here's what Janis found. He said when groupthink takes place what you are seeing is not just pressure in the dialogue against people who dissent; you see self-censorship, people holding back their own views, never even putting them forward, because they feel there's an apparent consensus in the group. There's this shared illusion of unanimity and, therefore, people censor themselves. Finally, the last symptom he identified is what he called "self-appointed mindguards" who protect the group from adverse information that might shatter their complacency, who filter out disconfirming data. Rusk, of course, doesn't pass along that memo from Bowles that outlines the weaknesses in the Bay of Pigs plan—that's an example of the kind of mindguards and mindguarding process that he's talking about when he talks about the symptoms of groupthink.

What are the results of groupthink? I mean, what are the consequences, and what do we see in the Bay of Pigs when we look at the process? We see discussions are limited to only a few alternative courses of action. The alternative that's initially preferred by a majority is really not examined critically for non-obvious risks. We see alternatives that maybe were initially discarded because they were viewed as unsatisfactory. They were never really brought back to the table and reexamined as the process unfolds. They're sort of discarded quickly, because there is this premature convergence on one proposal that's on the table. We're not bringing outside experts in who are unbiased, who can provide an objective view, who are not advocating for the proposal. We see lots of selective processing of information; the confirmation bias is a fundamental element of groupthink. We see people favoring facts and opinions that support their initial preferences, and finally, little discussion of contingency plans of risk, of what might the difficulties and setbacks be—and those are, in fact, even if they arise, easily dismissed when groupthink takes place.

So, here it is, we have a group that wants to go along to get along. We don't have candid dialogue; we have an inability to actually get multiple alternatives on the table, and it could happen to the best of groups. It could happen to a group as intellectually capable as the Kennedy team. It was a tremendous group—remember? They weren't experienced, that is true, but Janis finds that this happens to experienced groups as well. Though, I would note that the fact that they were new certainly did play a role. In looking at candid dialogue within groups, I would say there are two points in a group's life when they're especially vulnerable to groupthink. I think they are vulnerable to it in those early days when people don't know one another, when they don't have trust in one another. My colleague Amy Edmondson would say that in those early stages, often groups lack what she calls "psychological safety." She defines psychological safety as "a shared belief within a team that it's a safe environment for interpersonal risk-taking." What does she mean by "interpersonal risk-taking"? She means people being willing to express a dissenting view, or ask a question, or challenge the conventional wisdom, or admit their own errors, or point out the errors or mistakes that the team more broadly might be making. She says psychological safety is a key element in good group dynamics, but it's often low, particularly when a group is new and they don't know one another and trust one another—when they're not able to identify one another's strengths and weaknesses effectively. So, in those early stages, I think we're particularly vulnerable to groupthink, but we're also vulnerable in the late stages when a group has been together for a long time, because the danger there is that it grows likeminded over time, and that can be a very, very risky situation. So, groupthink doesn't only happen to new teams, though it may be a particularly vulnerable point in time in a team's life.

More broadly, I'd like to put forth some questions for you to think about, to say: Are the teams you're working in or volunteering in— or that you, in fact, have interacted in, in the past—have they had this kind of a problem? Are there warning signs that you have insufficient candor within your team? Let me offer you some questions to consider. Do the management meetings seem more like hushed, polite games of golf—or are they like fast-paced, physical games of ice hockey (the notion being that ice hockey is a contact sport)? Are the meetings of your team a contact sport? Do subordinates wait to take their verbal and visual cues from you, the leader, before commenting on controversial issues? Are planning and strategy sessions largely about the preparation of hefty binders and fancy presentations—or are they primarily about a lively, open dialogue? Do the same people tend to dominate management team meetings? Is it rare for you to hear concerns or feedback directly from those several levels below you in the organization? That's the kind of question I ask of an executive, of a senior leader, to see if they understand if there's a warning sign there of insufficient candor. Have senior management meetings become "rubber stamp" sessions in which executives simply ratify decisions that have already been made through other channels? Are people highly concerned about following rules of protocol when communicating with others across horizontal or vertical levels of the organization? Do you rarely hear from someone who is concerned about the level of criticism and opposition that they encountered when offering a proposal during a team meeting? All these questions—which I think you need to ask yourself and ask other members of your team, and particularly you need to ask if you're the leader of the team—will help you understand if you might be in danger of groupthink, if you might have a lack of psychological safety, if there's insufficient candor in your organization.

I want to close by talking about some of the barriers to candid dialogue in organizations, and next time we'll talk about how you can prevent groupthink, how you can spur more candid dialogue in your organization. But there are a few key barriers that many organizations face, and the first is structural complexity—crazy organization charts with all kinds of dots and arrows, all kinds of complexity, that make it look like this dense forest where people aren't clear on who they report to, on where authority and responsibility lie. Jack Welch, the long-time CEO and chairman of General Electric, says that organizational complexity is like "wearing a heavy sweater on a cold day"; it insulates you from the weather around you, where you're not really feeling what's going on, and that's what complexity in an organization is like. Senior leaders don't really feel what's going on around them; they're not hearing what's happening out there. If people's roles are ambiguous, that can be problematic as well—if people aren't clear on who they report to and who has the authority and accountability for things. We said in the Bay of Pigs there was this erosion of accountability that occurred.

Homogenous groups—you have groups that all look the same, that sound the same, that have the same backgrounds, that all come from the same colleges and industries. Homogeneity can deter the ability to achieve candid dialogue. We're better off with diverse groups. Large status differences among members of a team can squelch the level of candid dialogue. Think of, as my colleague Amy Edmondson has studied, medical surgery teams, where the cardiac surgeon has so much higher status than the nurse, and that status difference can be a huge barrier to having candid dialogue in the operating room. Finally, there are leaders who present themselves as infallible, who fail to admit their own mistakes. The leaders who actually are willing to be open about the errors they've made, they tend to encourage more candid dialogue, an aura of infallibility—that tends to be a key barrier to candid dialogue. So, from here next time, we'll talk not about these barriers, but how to break these barriers down—how to prevent groupthink in the teams in which you interact, and we'll talk about some very specific techniques to help us achieve this.

Lecture Ten
Deciding How to Decide

Scope:

Drawing on a case study of President Kennedy's decision making in the Cuban missile crisis, we will examine how teams can prevent groupthink and improve their decision making. As it turns out, Kennedy and his advisers reflected on their failure after the Bay of Pigs, and they devised a series of process improvements that were aimed at preventing groupthink and encouraging dissenting views. In this session, we will introduce the concept of "deciding how to decide"—that is, how leaders can shape a decision-making process so that it will tend to yield more constructive dialogue and debate among team members rather than strong pressures for conformity.

Outline

I. Let's take a look at how President Kennedy behaved in another momentous decision that took place a year after the Bay of Pigs invasion. The Cuban missile crisis took place in October 1962, and that decision process illustrates how to prevent groupthink.

    A. In October 1962, the CIA showed President Kennedy and his advisers photographs of missile bases being constructed in Cuba.

    B. Kennedy formed a group—called ExComm—that met over the next 12 days to discuss how to deal with the situation.

    C. Most people initially believed that the U.S. military should attack by air to destroy the missiles.

    D. ExComm met repeatedly in conference rooms over at the State Department, not in the cabinet room at the White House.

    E. President Kennedy did not attend all the ExComm meetings. He did not want to inhibit the dialogue, and he did not want the press to find out what was going on.

    F. Robert McNamara proposed an alternative to an air strike. He suggested a naval blockade of the island of Cuba.

    G. The CIA showed ExComm more photographs of missiles. They estimated that the missiles could kill 80 million Americans.

H. The group seemed to shift to favoring a blockade, but the president did not find their assessment and analysis completely persuasive. He asked them to continue deliberating.

I. ExComm split into 2 subgroups at that point. They developed white papers in support of 2 options: naval blockade versus military air strike.

J. The groups exchanged papers, and they critiqued each other's proposals.

K. The group leveled the playing field during these meetings, with no chairman, rank, or rules of protocol.

L. Robert Kennedy and Ted Sorensen served as devil's advocates during the decision-making process.

M. Finally, the 2 subgroups met with President Kennedy. They debated the issues in front of him. He listened, asked many probing questions, and ultimately decided in favor of a blockade.

II. The Cuban missile crisis decision-making process had many positive attributes.

    A. Clearly, they developed multiple options.

    B. They engaged in vigorous debate and probed key assumptions.

    C. The subgroups developed detailed plans for each option, and they wrote down those plans. Putting them in writing had many positive attributes.

    D. Everyone clearly felt accountable; no one lacked "skin in the game."

    E. The devil's advocates questioned all the ideas and probed for key risks. Using 2 devil's advocates, rather than one, had many positives.

    F. Everyone "spoke as equals" —people did not simply defer to the experts or to those with more status or power.

    G. The subgroups were trying to help each other bolster their options; it was a collaborative effort to present the president with the 2 strongest alternatives from which to choose. They didn't view it simply as a win-lose proposition in which they were competing with the other subgroup.

III. As it turns out, President Kennedy tried to learn from his failure in the Bay of Pigs situation.

    A. He met with Dwight Eisenhower after the Bay of Pigs.

        1. He sought advice and input from Eisenhower.

        2. Eisenhower asked him about how he had gathered advice from his advisers.

        3. It was interesting to see Eisenhower ask about the decision process rather than focus only on the military tactics.

        4. In a way, it is not surprising, given Eisenhower's history. It's important to recall that he was chosen as supreme allied commander in late 1943 in large part due to his leadership skills, not his brilliance as a military strategist.

    B. Kennedy worked with his advisers in 1961 to come up with a set of principles and techniques that would improve their decision-making process. These tactics were to be used in critical, high-stakes situations in the future.

        1. Kennedy would absent himself from the group to foster a more frank discussion at times.

        2. People would be asked to serve as skeptical generalists, not simply as specialists representing their agency. People were asked to speak even on issues not pertaining to their area of expertise.

        3. They would suspend the rules of protocol.

        4. They would split into subgroups to generate and debate alternatives.

        5. They would assign devil's advocates to question and critique all proposals on the table.

        6. Kennedy would directly communicate with lower-level officials with relevant knowledge and expertise.

        7. The group would welcome outside, unbiased experts to join the deliberations.

IV. Kennedy's behavior illustrates an important approach for preventing groupthink, which I call "deciding how to decide."

    A. Kennedy's best decision, in a way, was not the naval blockade. It was his decision to reform his decision process. It was the roadmap and the principles and techniques that he established regarding how he would approach critical decisions in the future.

B. What are the key dimensions of deciding how to decide?

    1. Composition: Who should be involved in the decision-making process?

    2. Context: In what type of environment does the decision take place?

    3. Communication: What are the "means of dialogue" among the participants?

    4. Control: How will the leader control the process and the content of the decision?

C. In deciding how to decide, Kennedy recognized that leaders have to think about how directive they would like to be, both in terms of the content of the decision as well as the process of decision making.

    1. In terms of content, they have to think about how much they want to control the outcome of the decision.

    2. In terms of process, they have to think about how they want to shape the way that the deliberations take place.

    3. In the Bay of Pigs, Kennedy was highly directive in terms of content but lost control of the decision process.

    4. In the Cuban missile crisis, Kennedy had a more balanced approach in terms of his control of both content and process.

D. Finally, Kennedy was effective at learning from his failure. He engaged in both content-centric and process-oriented learning.

    1. He reflected on what they could have done differently in terms of the tactics of how to deal with an invasion, a dictatorial regime, and so on. This is content-centric learning.

    2. He also reflected on what they could have done differently in terms of their decision-making process. This is process-centric learning.

    3. Leaders need to take time to reflect on their decision processes and to identify what attributes they want to change moving forward.

    4. Leaders should consider conducting systematic after-action reviews following all major high-stakes decisions, whether successes or failures.

Suggested Reading:

Johnson, *Managing the White House*.

Kennedy, *Thirteen Days*.

Questions to Consider:

1. What lessons can we apply from the process Kennedy employed during the Cuban missile crisis?

2. Why don't leaders "decide how to decide" in many situations?

3. What are the positives and negatives of employing a devil's advocate in a decision-making process?

Lecture Ten—Transcript
Deciding How to Decide

In the last lecture, we talked about the phenomenon of groupthink, of why some teams smoothed over their differences, why they avoid conflict, why the suppression of dissent occurs, and why some people self-censor—why they're not willing to come forward and offer their views if they challenge the conventional wisdom or the majority view in a group. We talked about the barriers to candid dialogue in groups, and now, today, in this lecture, what I'd like to do is talk about how we prevent groupthink, how do we actually stimulate constructive conflict, get the debate going within a group, get our differences on the table. I'd like to do that by talking about another one of the case studies that Irving Janis studied when he wrote his book *Victims of Groupthink*. In that book, he talked about a number of flawed decisions, such as the Bay of Pigs, but he also selected one decision, also made by President Kennedy, where a group seemed to do a wonderful job of actually preventing groupthink, of coming up with techniques that put their differences on the table, and that allowed vigorous dissent and debate. So, I want to look at that case study, tell you the story, and then from it, tease out some of the key lessons, some of the key techniques, that we can use in teams to actually spur more candid dialogue—more frankness, more honesty, more of an open exchange of views.

So, let's talk about the case study of the Cuban Missile Crisis. I'm going to tell this story from the perspective of Robert Kennedy. Robert Kennedy, as you all know, was the brother of the president, but he was also Attorney General of the United States in President John Kennedy's administration. He was involved, like Schlesinger was in the Bay of Pigs, in all of these meetings, and he wrote a book after the Cuban Missile Crisis called *Thirteen Days*—13 days, of course, representing the 13 days of the Cuban Missile Crisis in October of 1962. I will quote from that book as I go through this account, but, again, I've gone through the history, gone through various firsthand accounts, as well as historians' accounts of what happened here, so as to corroborate Robert Kennedy's view of events. I hope we'll be able to present a story that's relatively unbiased, that provides an objective view of how the process unfolded. Again, we're not interested in geopolitics or foreign policy—that, of course, is the domain in which this took place—but we're interested in the group dynamics. What happened within the team? Why didn't groupthink take place here, though it had happened on the Bay of Pigs? Why do we have a starkly different process of team decision-making in this—a decision that took place just a year and a half after that highly flawed decision about the Bay of Pigs invasion.

This choice took place, or this process began, in the early morning of October 16, 1962. At that point, John Kennedy was told that evidence from spy plane missions indicated that the Soviet Union had begun to place nuclear missiles in Cuba. Later that morning, the CIA, the Central Intelligence Agency, showed Kennedy and his staff photographs of the construction of a missile base in Cuba. The group that met on October 16 to look at those photos met almost continuously for the next 12 days. This was an unbelievably high-stakes situation, a crisis of enormous proportions, and this group was called to delve into this in great detail and give advice to the president. The group came to be called "ExComm"—the Executive Committee of the National Security Council. They did not meet, interestingly, in the White House Cabinet Room, but instead were sent off to meet in secret in conference rooms at the State Department of the United States.

Most of the advisers to the president, including the president himself, actually believed, initially, that some action had to be taken, and they felt that a military air strike against those bases in Cuba was really the only appropriate course of action. Bobby Kennedy says, interestingly, that: "To keep the discussions from being inhibited and because the president didn't want to arouse attention from the press and the general public, he decided not to attend all the meetings of our committee," a very important choice by Kennedy that we'll come back to later in this lecture. An alternative to a military air strike emerged during the discussions of October 16. Defense Secretary Robert McNamara argued for a naval blockade. The military chiefs, the Joint Chiefs of Staff, unanimously argued for an immediate air strike. I'll point out, by the way, that as part of this understanding of the crisis, as part of the study of this case that I've done, I've been able to talk personally with Robert McNamara about what happened—both in the Bay of Pigs and, more importantly, here in the Cuban Missile Crisis. McNamara came and visited with me and my students several years ago, talking about these incidents openly with the students, talking about his experience and how Kennedy changed what he did after the Bay of Pigs, and how he implemented this particular process of decision-making in the Cuban Missile Crisis. I'll come back later to some of McNamara's observations.

On October 17, after McNamara had proposed the blockade the prior day and the Joint Chiefs had unanimously argued for an immediate air strike, more photos were brought to the table the next day on October 17, photos showing several other installations in Cuba, with 16 to 32 missiles. It was estimated that these missiles could kill 80 million Americans, and the pressure rose, and the group felt it. In observing Kennedy's frustration at one point, General David Shoup told him: "You are in a pretty bad fix, Mr. President." And Kennedy shot back quickly: "You're in it with me, General"—You're in it with me.

By October 18, a majority of the group seemed to favor the naval blockade of the island of Cuba, but Bobby Kennedy wrote: "However, as people talked and the President raised probing questions, minds and opinions began to change again, and not only on small points." And Kennedy sent the group back to deliberate further. At this point, the group is really struggling. They're feeling the pressure, and they're not really sure if this blockade makes sense. Part of them thinks that the military air strike is a far superior option, and their minds are changing. Robert Kennedy says:

> Finally, we agreed on a procedure by which we felt we could give intelligent recommendations to the President. ... We split into two subgroups to write up our respective recommendations, beginning with an outline of [Kennedy's] speech to the nation and the whole course of action thereafter. In the early afternoon, we exchanged papers, each group dissected and criticized the other, and the papers were returned to the original group to develop further answers.

During all these meetings, they really did try to treat each other as equals. They suspended the rules of protocol. Subordinates could talk openly with their bosses. They could exchange views. There was no waiting or deference to the experts in the room. There was no chairman of these two subgroups that were meeting. "There was no rank in the room," said Robert Kennedy. These deliberations, he said, in these deliberations "we all spoke as equals." This is very different, mind you, than the Bay of Pigs. Keep that in mind as I go through this case, all the differences that you're hearing, that you're observing, between these two decision processes.

Two people played a key role in this process quite different than the others in the room. These two people, and Irving Janis noticed this as he went through this, he noticed very clearly, and then, of course, this was corroborated by people in the Kennedy administration who said this was rather purposeful, that two people had a special role. They were assigned a special role. In fact, these two were Robert Kennedy and Theodore Sorensen, another close adviser of the president. Their role was as intellectual watchdogs, told to essentially scrutinize each proposal, to poke holes in it, to offer criticism, to try to find the risks in each option on the table. Janis says they were trying to prevent errors arising from too superficial an analysis of the issues.

Janis went on to say that Bobby Kennedy accepted his role rather avidly. He said: "At the expense of becoming unpopular with some of his associates, [he] barked out sharp and sometimes rude questions. He deliberately became the devil's advocate." So, we have these two interesting roles in the process played by Bobby Kennedy and Ted Sorensen, pushing each of these two subgroups, who are developing multiple options. This process is looking a lot different than the Bay of Pigs.

Finally, ExComm meets with the president. McNamara presents the arguments for a naval blockade, and the Joint Chiefs present the arguments for a military air strike. Kennedy listens to the debate, asks many tough questions, and decides in favor of a naval blockade. The naval blockade, coupled with diplomatic negotiations, ultimately resolves the crisis: The missiles are removed from Cuba, and the world—which was at the brink, perhaps, of nuclear war—comes back to a peaceful resolution. It's an amazing decision process that we see. We've seen the attributes in this decision process of a very high-quality dialogue, a very high-quality team dynamic.

What kinds of things do we see? The kinds of things we didn't see in the Bay of Pigs. First of all, we see multiple alternatives: We have a naval blockade; we have a military air strike; in fact, we had a third alternative that was dismissed fairly early on, which was to purely go the diplomatic route. So, we have multiple options on the table, and the president was really pushing for multiple options. He told his brother, Robert, to push for multiple options in the dialogue. We see testing of assumptions, real probing of what is it we're assuming, and what do we know, and what do we not know. What is fact, and what is assumption? We see vigorous debate. We see constructive conflict, two groups offering different options, exchanging papers and debating one another. We see people taking a broad perspective, actually trying to write the speech that the president will give to the nation. In doing so, they're not looking at this thing simply from the perspective of their silo, of their agency within the federal government; they're taking the view of the person with the broadest perspective—that's the president. There's no strict deference to experts here. Unlike the Bay of Pigs, where the CIA was dominating the discussion, here we have everyone contributing—even if foreign policy is not their primary domain of expertise, even if they work in other parts of the government. And we have this suspension of rules of protocol, this view that the team is equal, this lessening of the salience of the hierarchy and the salience of the status differences among the team members here in ExComm.

So, we have a number of key differences. We have a number of things they did to sort of encourage more open dialogue. I just note a few things I think are kind of interesting, including the fact that they met over in the State Department. Why is that relevant? Why is that an interesting thing that they did primarily for reasons of secrecy, but that had this added benefit of creating an atmosphere of more psychological safety? Well, think about it. How do you sit in a Cabinet Room of the White House? What's it like? What's the atmosphere like there? I mean, first of all, you don't simply go take a chair, go take a seat wherever you like. The Secretary of State, one of the high-status members of the administration, of any administration—from George Washington to George Bush, the Secretary of State gets a seat close to the president. They get a prominent seat, and it's very clear that they have a lot of power and status. The Secretary of Agriculture, they're lucky if they make it onto the White House grounds. They're a very low-status member of a typical administration. So, we have key status differences that are highly salient in this room filled with history, and power, and status—in the State Department, a very different, more informal atmosphere, where it's easier to cultivate a culture of equals, where status and hierarchy don't mean as much. So they did a number of things that were very interesting that helped to create a better atmosphere. It's got the attributes of a much higher-quality decision process. Most importantly, we see conflict here. Where we saw avoidance of conflict in the Bay of Pigs, here we see an effort to truly stimulate debate, to bring the differences openly to the table, and to argue it out, to argue it out, very important. Andy Grove, the former chairman and CEO of Intel, says that conflict is so important, and he wrote a book called *Only the Paranoid Survive*. In that book he talks about how important it is to always be aware of the threats to your organization, and he talks about some of the mistakes that he made at Intel over the years. He says at key points, when you have to change your strategy, it's really important to have that open debate so that you get it right. He calls these "strategic inflection points," when there's a discontinuous change in your external environment, when there's a crisis like the Cuban Missile Crisis, and those are the moments, those high-stakes moments, where conflict is most important and where the leader needs to inject differences, inject frank dialogue and debate into his team, into his organization—has to induce conflict, if you will.

Grove said in his book: "Debates are like the process through which a photographer sharpens the contrast when developing a print. The clearer images that result permit management to make a more informed—and more likely correct—call." Very, very important—that conflict actually enhances the quality of the choices we make. That's Grove's argument, and there's lots of research to back that up. I'll point out, though, that conflict and debate are not just about getting to better decisions. I think, too, they help us make more ethical and more responsible choices. I think they help people. If you can inject conflict, if you can encourage psychological safety, they help those people who have some qualms, perhaps, with the ethical choices being made—who are wondering about the appropriateness of certain actions; it helps make sure those views come to the table. After the corporate scandals of the early part of the 21st century in 2001 and 2002, *Business Week* talked about a crisis in corporate governance, and they wrote a special report, a special issue, on the crisis in corporate governance. They talked about the role of conflict with regard to the ethical mistakes that were made in many companies. Here's what *Business Week* wrote, they said:

> The best insurance against crossing the ethical divide is a roomful of skeptics. CEOs must actively encourage dissent among senior managers by creating decision-making processes, reporting relationships, and incentives that

encourage opposing viewpoints. ... By advocating dissent, top executives can create a climate where wrongdoing will not go unchallenged. [Very, very important]

So, conflict matters; they stimulated it here. How did they do it (is the question)? Why is this process so different than the process in the Bay of Pigs? You couldn't have two decision processes that look more distinct, more different.

As it turns out, after the Bay of Pigs, Kennedy, who was very frustrated by his failure, tried explicitly to learn from his failure. One of the things he did to help spur that learning is he called his predecessor, the General and President Dwight Eisenhower, to come to Washington to discuss the Bay of Pigs, and he sought Eisenhower's advise and input. Interestingly, he asked President Eisenhower, former General Eisenhower, who had been Supreme Allied Commander of the effort to liberate western Europe during World War II, he asked him about various tactical military choices they had made. Should they have landed on a different beach? Should they have armed the troops or trained them differently? Should they have added U.S. military soldiers or air cover to help in the invasion of the Bay of Pigs? Eisenhower turned and asked, according to historian Steven Ambrose, he asked Kennedy: "Tell me about how you brought your advisers together. Tell me about the decision process you used." He wanted to know more about the dialogue than about the tactical choices they had made. That's a very interesting set of questions, and I looked back at Eisenhower (who I'll talk about in a subsequent lecture as well) and looked at his history. Today, we look and say, he must have been an obvious choice to Winston Churchill and Franklin Roosevelt to pick Dwight Eisenhower to be Supreme Allied Commander in late 1943, to be the person in charge of the D-Day invasions on the beaches of France. But, in fact, it wasn't so obvious a choice. Dwight Eisenhower didn't graduate at the top of his class from the Academy. He didn't have necessarily the same background in the field leading armies that people like Montgomery from Great Britain or Patten from the United States had. He wasn't necessarily viewed as a brilliant military strategist. Why was he chosen?

He had to bring together an incredibly diverse team of clashing personalities and interests—people as diverse and as tough to deal with as De Gaulle, and Churchill, and Roosevelt, and Marshall, and

Montgomery, and Brooke. I mean, think about the people he had to deal with. His skill lay in bringing them together. In fact, Montgomery, the British Field Marshal who was jealous that Eisenhower had gotten the job as Supreme Allied Commander, said he wasn't a great military strategist, his usual way of disparaging Eisenhower, but he did admit in his dairies that Eisenhower was a great choice to lead this team. So it's no surprise to me, given that history, that Eisenhower is asking Kennedy: "Think about the team, think about the dynamic of how you're making decisions. Don't only think about the tactics, the content of the choices you make."

We don't know if this is what spurred Kennedy to do what he did next, because, of course, Kennedy died and didn't have a chance to write about this process, but soon after those meetings with Eisenhower, Kennedy goes to his team and says tell me how we can improve our decision process. Tell me what we can do differently, not about the tactics of how we might conduct another invasion, or how we might confront communism in the future; tell me instead about how generically should we approach any high-stakes foreign policy decision. What kinds of techniques can we use so that we can get more candid dialogue, more frank discussion, more debate and dissent, so we don't end up with groupthink? He didn't know what groupthink was—Janis had not yet written about groupthink, of course—but he's saying how can we avoid that kind of phenomenon, where afterward people told me that you disagreed with what we did, yet you never spoke up about it.

So, there were a number of process improvements that were made after the Bay of Pigs that were discussed during this dialogue between Kennedy and his advisers. They decided that you had to get the president out of the room: "Mr. President, you can't be in all of our discussions because when you're there, people will be reticent to speak candidly. They might say what they think you want to hear. You, by getting out of the room, will encourage more frank discussion." They decided they had to suspend the rules of protocol—invite subordinates who had key expertise and knowledge to come to meetings and tell them it's okay to speak without waiting for their boss to speak first, and they could actually openly even debate superiors in the administration. They said we want everyone to be skeptical generalists, not simply spokespeople for their own departments. In other words, if you happen to be an expert on treasury matters, on financial matters, but if you've been invited to come to a foreign policy discussion, you are free to speak as a generalist as openly as any expert on foreign policy. We don't want deference to the people who are considered the technical experts. We want people to be speaking openly based on a general perspective.

We're going to split into subgroups at times to generate and debate alternatives. Oh, that's a fundamental choice they made and that they used in the Cuban Missile Crisis, where they went off, took the naval blockade, took the military air strike, developed those proposals, and then used the subgroup mechanism to exchange white papers to generate and debate those options—and to openly, then, bring them to the president. They're going to employ devil's advocates, they decided. We're going to have people whose sole responsibility is to challenge, to poke holes, to criticize the proposals, the options on the table. In the Cuban Missile Crisis, those devil's advocates were Bobby Kennedy and Ted Sorensen. We're going to ensure that the president has direct contact with lower-level officials so that if information is being filtered as it makes its way up the hierarchy, he can find out if key bad news is not getting to his office. So, he's going to reach down with the knowledge of his direct reports, reach down to lower-level officials and find out what they're thinking. Lastly, we're going to bring outside, unbiased experts to the table. We're going to get the view of people who are a little more objective and who may have direct knowledge of the kind of technical issues that are involved in our discussion.

This is a phenomenal list. This is an amazing list—getting JFK out of the room, the notion of splitting into subgroups, the use of devil's advocates. These are not things that Kennedy's team simply decided to do in the midst of crisis in October of 1962; these are a set of choices they made about improving their decision process that were made way back in 1961 after the Bay of Pigs. I would argue the most important decision John Kennedy made in the Cuban Missile Crisis is not the naval blockade—it's these process choices he made based in 1961 in his learning about his failure in the Bay of Pigs. This is what I call "deciding how to decide"—the notion that Kennedy developed a roadmap of how he wanted to lead and conduct a decision process, a set of techniques that would set up a strong foundation for candid dialogue. He decided how he wanted to decide in the future, and I would argue deciding how to decide is a critical leadership skill that improves the way teams make decisions. It improves the way the dialogue takes place; it helps prevent groupthink.

In any decision, we're looking for certain outcomes. We're hoping we get a quality decision that we can implement effectively in a timely manner, but in the moment we don't know whether we'll be able to achieve those things. We hope we can, but what can we do to enhance our odds of getting there, of getting to those good outcomes? Well, we can certainly stop in the middle of a dialogue, in the middle of a decision process, and sort of audit the process. We can say: Do we have multiple options on the table, or have we prematurely converged on one idea? What are our assumptions? How are they different from the facts? Can we distinguish the two? Can we probe, and test, and validate those assumptions? Have we got all the debate on the table that we need? Are there dissenting views that haven't arisen yet? Are we managing the conflict appropriately, or are we sort of discarding people who might have a minority viewpoint? Are we making sure the conflict stays constructive? We can do all sorts of things to sort of audit the process in real time, but better than that, we can decide how to decide. We can pull some levers up front to set up the process and dialogue so that we raise the odds that we get a productive discussion—so that we sort of stimulate a great debate.

What are the kinds of levers we can choose? Well, we can think about four things—what I call the four C's of decision-making. The composition of the group—who should be invited to come to the room? Kennedy thought about that. Who should be there? Who should be a member of ExComm? Very critical. The context—the second C. What is the atmosphere going to be like (both the physical atmosphere, going to the State Department, but also the psychological atmosphere)? What are the shared norms and ground rules that we want when we bring people together? This is suspending the rules of protocol and asking people to be skeptical generalists, not just spokespeople for their departments. Then there's a set of decisions about the third C—communication. How will we discuss, and talk about, and exchange views about the options? Here we see the use of subgroups, the use of devil's advocates, devices to enhance communication—again, designed in advance. And finally, the fourth C: How will I, as the leader, control the process? Will I always be in the room, or not? Kennedy absented himself. How will I ultimately make the final choice? Am I asking them to come to me with a package solution, or do I want them to come to me with options that they debate in front of me?

So, composition, context, communication, and control— these are the four levers, the four dimensions of deciding how to decide. They help shape a better process, which ultimately raises the odds of a better outcome. But there's one last piece to the puzzle here, to this model of how to prevent groupthink, and that's the notion that after the outcome happens, after you either succeed or fail in the decision, you need to learn, you need to reflect on your experience, the experience of your team, and then revise the four C's. Think about how you should change composition, context, communication, and control in the future, and that's what Kennedy did. With the help of Eisenhower, he was able to go back and revise his approach and really think explicitly about the kinds of process choices he wanted to make to enhance the level of discussion.

So, a very important difference between the way he acted in the Bay of Pigs and Cuban Missile Crisis, and I'd point out that we have this view of leadership often that there's sort of two styles of leadership that sit on the ends of a spectrum. One style is very authoritative or very directive, and the other side is very empowering or participative. But I think that's a false dichotomy, because if you think about the way that Kennedy behaved in the Cuban Missile Crisis—was he directive authoritative? Was he? Well, in terms of the content of the process (what should we do?), he wasn't that directive. He left the meetings. He let his group discuss the issues without him. He backed off a bit to give his team room to have candid dialogue and to speak frankly. But, he was very directive with regard to the process of decision-making. I mean this is absolutely critical. He laid out the kinds of choices he had made about devil's advocacy, and subgroups, and absenting himself from the room, and the kinds of shared norms he wanted the group to use as they went through their dialogue. He was very clear about the kind of process he wanted. So, was he directive or not? The answer is both. He was both directive in some ways and not in others. He backed off on the content, but he was very clear on how the process should take place. So, any leader, as they approach a decision process, if they want to prevent groupthink, has to ask themselves, on any choice, not just what should we do, but also how should we decide? (A very fundamental question that every leader must ask.)

I'll note that Kennedy learned—we talked about how important that was that Kennedy learned, and the key here I think is that he didn't just think about "content-centric learning," what I call content-centric learning, which is: What have I learned about making decisions regarding this particular content domain? He also thought about: What have I learned about the way we make decisions in this organization? What have I learned about process? That's process-centric learning. You have to do both as a leader—not just think about the substance of the decisions you make, but also the approach that you've taken with your team—and that's what deciding how to decide is all about. I'll note, I'll close, with two quotes and a short story from Robert McNamara.

Louis Pasteur once said: "Chance favors the prepared mind." John Kennedy was not a prepared mind in the Bay of Pigs—not because he was inexperienced, although he was, but because he didn't have a roadmap for how he wanted to make decisions with his team. He hadn't decided how to decide. In the Cuban Missile Crisis he had a roadmap—he was a prepared mind. Ben Franklin once said: "By failing to prepare, you are preparing to fail." If you want to make better decisions with your team, if you want to prevent groupthink, you've got to prepare; you've got to think about context, and communication, and control, and composition. Those are key choices you make upfront to build a good foundation for good decision-making.

I'll close with what Robert McNamara told me about what happened after the Bay of Pigs, I think a lesson in learning and taking responsibility that we should all keep in mind. He said that John Kennedy decides to go on TV after the Bay of Pigs and to take responsibility for the failure. He said: "Successes have many fathers, failures have none, but I am the father of this failure." Robert McNamara said: "Mr. President, let me go on TV and let me tell the American people, after you've gone and addressed them, that, in fact, your advisers gave you bad advice, that we were all there in the room and no one expressed a dissenting view." McNamara told me that John Kennedy said to him: "No, no, Bob. No, you're not going to go on TV and say that. This is my failure. I am its father, and I need to take responsibility for it." McNamara said to me: "That's so important that Kennedy learned from the Bay of Pigs: First, that you need to induce conflict and stimulate it within your team, but also that you need to take responsibility for your failures." As McNamara said: "Failures should not be without fathers."

Lecture Eleven
Stimulating Conflict and Debate

Scope:

In this lecture, we will examine the techniques that leaders and their teams can use to foster constructive conflict so as to enhance their decision making. Drawing on case studies about Emerson Electric, Sun Life Financial, and Polycom, we will describe and analyze 4 ways in which leaders can stimulate the clash of ideas within teams. First, teams can employ role-playing to stimulate debate. Second, they can employ mental simulation techniques. Third, they can use techniques for creating a point-counterpoint dynamic in the conversation. Finally, teams can apply diverse conceptual models and frameworks to ensure that people analyze an issue from multiple perspectives.

Outline

I. If an organization has become saddled with a culture of polite talk, superficial congeniality, and low psychological safety, how can a leader spark a heightened level of candor? What specific tools can leaders employ to ignite a lively yet constructive scuffle?

   A. Let's consider the story of Steve Caufield, the leader of an aerospace/defense firm that had to make an important strategic alliance decision.
   1. He invited a select set of executives and outside experts to a series of off-site meetings.
   2. He tried to create a highly diverse group, both in terms of expertise and personality.
   3. He divided them into 2 teams.
   4. He assigned 2 facilitators, one for each team. The facilitators were to lay out clear ground rules for how the discussion should take place.
   5. He chose not to attend the early meetings.
   6. He worked with the facilitators to establish 6 criteria for evaluating the alternatives. He also worked with them and others in the organization to identify 9 plausible alternatives.

7. Each group analyzed the 9 alternatives. One group rated all 9 on 3 criteria, while the other team evaluated all 9 options based on 3 different criteria.

8. Then Caufield joined the entire team to hear their evaluations and recommendations. He played the devil's advocate.

B. Caufield certainly "decided how to decide" quite effectively.

1. In terms of composition, he chose the participants, invited outside experts, and chose the subgroup assignments.

2. In terms of context, he chose to move it off-site, set the tone with his initial instructions to the group, and established clear ground rules for the deliberations.

3. In terms of communication, he outlined the options and decision criteria and developed a system for the subgroups to evaluate the options based on 6 criteria.

4. In terms of control, he did not attend the early meetings, but he provided a clear process roadmap for the group. He played the devil's advocate himself, and he designated others to serve as facilitators.

II. Let's now consider some specific techniques in the leader's tool kit that one can use to stimulate conflict and debate in an organization. These techniques can be employed as one "decides how to decide."

A. You can ask your management team to role-play the competition.

1. Professional football teams do this all the time, with their so-called scout teams.

2. In one famous example, Patriots' coach Bill Belichick credited a player who didn't even take the field for much of the Patriots' defense's success against the Colts in the American Football Conference championship game in 2004. He credited the back-up quarterback, who had role-played Colts' star quarterback Peyton Manning all week in practice.

3. Companies can do this as well. In my research, one company conducted extensive role-plays of their competitors.

4. For another role-play approach, sometimes companies can role-play what it would be like if another set of senior executives were leading the firm.

5. An example of this is when Intel leaders Andy Grove and Gordon Moore imagined in the early 1980s what it would be like if new leaders came to Intel. They used that simple role-play to help them make a very tough decision to exit the memory chip business.

B. You can employ mental simulation methods to stimulate conflict and debate.
1. By that, we mean mechanisms and techniques for envisioning and mapping out multiple future scenarios.
2. Royal Dutch Shell has pioneered scenario-planning techniques.
3. Gary Klein has introduced the notion of premortem analysis as a way of envisioning future scenarios, particularly ones where current ideas and proposals do not work out well.

C. You can introduce a simple set of models or frameworks that may be applied to a particular business problem and then designate people to use these different lenses during the decision-making process.
1. Kevin Dougherty did this when he was leading Sun Life Financial's Canadian group insurance business unit.
2. Back in 2000, he held an off-site where he wanted his team to consider how the Web was disrupting their business and how they could employ the Internet to build new business models.
3. He had an outside expert describe 4 models for how other companies, in a wide array of industries, were building businesses using the Web.
4. Then he divided his top leaders into 4 teams and had each team take one model. They had to create a new business proposal for Sun Life that was based on that model.

D. Finally, you can use various point-counterpoint methods to stimulate debate.
1. Formally, scholars now describe the 2 point-counterpoint methods we discussed as dialectical inquiry and devil's advocacy.
2. Polycom uses a version of this when they form red teams and blue teams to examine the pros and cons of making an acquisition.

3. Electronic Arts builds this type of point-counterpoint dynamic right into their organizational structure. Two people lead each development team, each with a different role. It is purposefully stimulating creative tension.

4. President Franklin D. Roosevelt purposefully used to create overlapping roles in his administration so as to create some point-counterpoint dynamics.

III. Sometimes, despite the best intentions, these methods do not work effectively. There are dangerous side effects that emerge, or approaches that render these methods ineffective.

A. Sometimes groups employ devil's advocacy, but they actually domesticate the dissenters. They engage "token" devil's advocates more to make everyone feel good about their approach, rather than to truly hear dissenting views.

B. Sometimes leaders create a system of communication whereby their subordinates are simply trying to persuade the person at the top, as opposed to actually debating one another.

C. Crowded agendas can diminish a debate's effectiveness. People do not have time to listen, digest what they have heard, and offer thoughtful critiques and responses.

D. We can allow people to become too entrenched in subgroups, such that they become quite polarized. They cannot come back together to synthesize what they have been doing separately.

E. Groups can strive for false precision. They become overly focused on minute details, as opposed to debating the big themes, ideas, and concepts.

IV. To close, we should point out that practice makes perfect when it comes to stimulating conflict in organizations.

A. Research shows that groups in experimental settings become more adept at debate, at methods such as dialectical inquiry and devil's advocacy, as they gain more experience with the processes.

B. In the real world, we see how some very effective leaders make conflict and debate a normal event—part of the usual routine of decision making, not a unique thing that happens only once per year at some off-site meeting.

C. As an example, consider Chuck Knight, long-time chairman and CEO of Emerson Electric. Knight designed that firm's strategic planning process as "confrontational by design." Everyone at the firm came to expect vigorous debate each and every day. It was a way of life at Emerson.

D. At Emerson, Knight enjoyed remarkable success. In Knight's 27-year tenure as CEO, Emerson's profits rose every single year.

E. General Electric had a similar approach when Jack Welch was CEO. Constructive conflict was even built in as one of the core values of the firm.

F. It reminds us of the wisdom of a famous quote by Aristotle: "We are what we repeatedly do. Excellence, then, is not an act, but a habit."

Suggested Reading:

Knight, *Performance without Compromise.*

Welch and Byrne, *Jack.*

Questions to Consider:

1. What techniques have you used that have helped stimulate a constructive debate within a team?

2. Why do some mechanisms for generating debate not function as expected?

3. Why does repeated practice help teams get better at managing conflict?

Lecture Eleven—Transcript
Stimulating Conflict and Debate

How can we stimulate conflict, dissent, and debate in our teams and groups? If an organization has become saddled with a culture of polite talk and low psychological safety, of what Jack Welch calls "superficial congeniality," how can a leader spark a heightened level of candor within that group? What specific tools can leaders use to ignite a lively, yet constructive scuffle? That's the topic of today's lecture. How can we stimulate the clash of ideas? And the clash of ideas is so important. David Hume once said: "Truth springs from argument amongst friends," and that's what we're looking for is how can we create an argument amongst friends in the teams that we lead, in the teams that we work with, on key decisions.

I'd like to tell the story of the case of an aerospace firm that made an important strategic alliance decision. It's a case that I studied doing my research about a decade ago in the industry. Since it's aerospace, I can't reveal the actual name of the firm or the name of the leader involved. I'm going to call him Steve Caufield, the disguised name that I use when I discuss this case. This strategic alliance decision was very important for this firm. They were involved in bidding for some major shipbuilding projects, and they knew they needed a partner in order to compete effectively on this contract bid. So, Caufield invited a select set of executives and outside experts to a series of off-site meetings for his firm, for his firm's management team. He tried to create a highly diverse group, both in terms of expertise and personality, and he divided them into two teams. He assigned two facilitators, one for each team. The facilitators were to lay out clear ground rules for how the discussions should take place. Interestingly, Caufield chose not to attend the early meetings of these teams. He worked with the facilitators to establish six criteria, though, for evaluating the alternatives. He also worked with them and others in the organization to identify nine of the most plausible alternatives. He asked each group then to analyze these nine options. One group was asked to rate all nine alternatives on three specific criteria, while the other team evaluated those same nine options, but on three different criteria. Then, after they had gone through their analysis, Caufield joined the entire team, bringing both subgroups together. He listened to their evaluations and their recommendations, and he himself then chose to play the devil's advocate during these deliberations.

What we see here is that Caufield really exemplifies what Kennedy did in the Cuban Missile Crisis; he's deciding how to decide. He's doing this very explicitly and effectively. In terms of composition, he's choosing the participants, he's inviting outside experts, and he's selecting the subgroup assignments. In terms of context, he chose to move it off-site. He set the tone with his initial instructions to the group. He established clear ground rules, shared norms, for how the deliberations should take place, trying to make sure that not only would they have conflict and debate, but that people would talk constructively, and openly, and politely—not so politely as to squelch dissent, but politely enough so that this could remain sort of a constructive and vigorous dialogue. In terms of communication, he outlined the options and decision criteria and then developed a system for the subgroups to evaluate the options based on these six criteria. Finally, in terms of control, he didn't attend the early meetings, but he provided a clear process roadmap for the group, and then he played the devil's advocate himself. He designated others to serve as the facilitators to make sure the discussion was moving in the right direction, that it didn't get bogged down in stalemate or impasse.

So, Caufield's story really does help us understand, gives us a great example of how we might stimulate conflict, and it offers us a roadmap—a roadmap of how deciding how to decide can take place. But it's not the only way, and I want to talk in this lecture about some specific techniques that we can use to stimulate the clash of ideas. I want to talk about four types of techniques in this lecture. I think it's important that we have sort of a toolbox, a wide array of methods that we can draw upon in a particular situation—not that we should simply emulate Kennedy or Caufield, but that we should have sort of a cafeteria that we can look to and select what we want to use for this particular situation, for this particular team, to stimulate the clash of ideas. These techniques are part of deciding how to decide. They are what you draw on as you "decide how to decide," as you build your process roadmap. The key point here is that conflict and debate often don't just come naturally to teams. We can't just sit back and say we know we've got a great group of people—they have intellect, they have expertise, they have experience, and naturally, they'll have a vigorous discussion. No, instead, we have to sort of induce them to actually come to some disagreement. We have to sort of ignite a bit of a scuffle, but a constructive one.

McNamara, the Secretary of Defense for John Kennedy, told me this in our discussions. He said, you know, you simply have to force them to debate sometimes in front of you. You want, as a leader of a team, to hear that give and take. You don't want them to resolve it all and then simply come to you with a packaged solution. You want them to come to you with their differences. You want to hear those differences and then provoke, and prod, and ask questions, and so, let's go through some techniques for doing so.

The first technique I'd like to talk about is role-playing the competition. Role-playing the competition can be a powerful way to ignite more divergent thinking within a team. I'll note that professional football teams do this all the time with their so-called scout teams. What's a scout team? A scout team is usually the second- or third-string players, and they are told during the week of practice to sort of study up what the opposing team will do this week. They are told to go to practice and to emulate the behavior, the strategies, the techniques, that the opposing team will use during that game. This gives the first-stringers, the players who will start the game, a chance to practice against something that looks like the competition, that works like the competition, that plays like it, that strategizes like the competition. Scout teams are so important in the game of professional football. In one famous example, the New England Patriots' Coach Bill Belichick credited a player who didn't even take the field for much of the Patriots' defensive success against the Indianapolis Colts in the American Football Conference championship game in 2004. He credited the backup quarterback, who had role-played Colts' star quarterback, Payton Manning, all week in practice. This backup never played in the actual championship game, yet throughout practice that week, he had mastered Payton Manning's techniques—right down to his mannerisms, the way he barked out the calls at the line of scrimmage. That ability to mimic the way Manning would behave in the game, well, Belichick said that was unbelievably important to help him prepare his defense for how they should play during that championship against the Colts.

Companies can do this as well. In my research, one company conducted extensive role-plays of their competition. They did this, importantly, both to spark new debate, to shed light on their venture's weaknesses, their efforts' weaknesses, and also to generate insights about the rival's behavior. One manager even made the analogy to the scout team in professional football when he explained this decision process to me. He said:

> We actually had someone role-play the other alliance that was forming, and they did a competitive assessment of us, just like a football team. You know, you scrimmage using the other guy's plays. The results portrayed the other alliance's view of us, and it was very revealing.

So, there's this important dimension of divergent thinking that's introduced when we get some people within our teams to actually behave as our opponent, as the people we're competing against.

For another role-play approach, sometimes companies can role-play what it would be like if another set of eyes, if another set of senior executives, were actually leading this particular team or this particular firm. There's an example of this, a wonderful example, from Intel and its leaders Andy Grove and Gordon Moore. Back in the early 1980s, the firm was at a critical point in its history. It had grown up and succeeded in the 1970s as a memory chip company, a D-RAM company, and been wildly successful at first, but then that market commoditized, and the Japanese entered the market and became the clear low-cost competitors. Intel couldn't differentiate their product, and they had higher cost, and they lost market share precipitously. Their market share dwindled down to the low single digits, yet they continued to pour research and development dollars into that memory chip business. They desperately wanted to save it. Perhaps we see a bit of the sunk-cost effect going on there, and they used a simple role-play exercise to help them eventually make a very tough decision to exit the memory chip business.

This is very interesting, this decision, because they resisted and resisted. Market share is dwindling, they're still pouring R&D in, but lower-level managers actually had begun to shift production capacity in Intel's manufacturing plants to the microprocessor market, a burgeoning market that was just emerging as the personal computer revolution was taking off. "Thank goodness," Andy Grove has said, "that middle managers didn't listen to the top, didn't listen to their bosses, and actually shifted away from memory chips and toward this new market of microprocessors." But anyway, Grove said it's important this little role-play that they did. What is it that they did? It's interesting—they apparently were in the office, Gordon Moore and Andy Grove, and they were discussing this topic, and they looked out, and they saw a Ferris wheel in the distance at a carnival that was going on in California, near the corporate offices of Intel. The Ferris wheel was turning, and they said: "Gee, you know, what happens if this office rotated like that Ferris wheel did, and a new set of executives came in, and they weren't so bound up—both in their personal identity and in the organization's identity as a memory chip company? Would they exit this business in the face of such intense Japanese competition, in the case of a clear low-cost advantage for the Japanese rivals?" And Grove and Moore said: "Well, of course, two managers who weren't embedded in our culture, who hadn't actually grown, and developed, and built the memory chip business—they would get out, they would exit. There's no question about it."

Grove then said, and now he quotes in his book, he said:

> New managers come unencumbered by such emotional involvement. ... They see things much more objectively than their predecessors did. If existing management want to keep their jobs when the basics of the business are undergoing profound change, they must adopt an outsider's intellectual objectivity. ... That's what Gordon and I had to do when we figuratively went out the door, stomped out our cigarettes, and returned to do the job.

So, role-playing the competition—such a powerful way to introduce divergent thinking, to create a different set of ideas that come to the table to be discussed, and to engage in some debate about them. So, role-plays—the first of these methods for stimulating the clash of ideas, but not the only technique. I'd like to talk about some others.

Another one is what we might call "mental simulation," and by that I mean mechanisms and techniques for envisioning and mapping out multiple future scenarios. Royal Dutch Shell is a company that's pioneered scenario planning techniques. What they do each year as part of their strategic planning process is actually map out complete scenarios for how the industry—in their case, the energy industry—might evolve in the future. They paint detailed, complete pictures of what the industry might look like 10 or 15 years out, and they create four or five of these alternative scenarios. They use those to really shake people out of their conventional view, out of the conventional wisdom of what the industry will be like. Painting those diverse views creates, then, a platform for vigorous debate within the senior management team at Royal Dutch Shell.

Gary Klein, the psychologist we've talked about when we talked about intuition, he's also studied this notion of how can we use mental simulation techniques to paint different pictures before us to spur divergent thinking. He's introduced the notion of a pre-mortem analysis as a way of envisioning future scenarios, particularly ones where current ideas and proposals do not work out well. Pre-mortems? What is Klein talking about? Well, we've all heard of a post-mortem, of course. A post-mortem—something many of us have engaged in as we're involved in a project, we're involved in a team, and we have a failure, and then we go through what the U.S. Army would call an After-Action Review, or what companies sometimes call lessons learned exercises. We go back and review our past actions—we look for what were the causes of this failure, what went wrong, how do we fix it—and that's a very powerful thing to do, post-mortem analysis. I would argue it's something that's critical, and it's so essential to an organization's future success—their ability to learn from their failures. We saw it with John Kennedy after the Bay of Pigs. He conducted a post-mortem, and it led to later success. But Klein says if we really want to spur divergent thinking and prevent failure (create more vigorous debate before we make a decision), let's conduct a pre-mortem, let's envision the failure before we even set out and make the decision. By painting a picture of how this thing might play out two or three years down the road as a failure, we can then sort of reverse engineer the situation and perhaps alter the decision we're about to make. We can refine the decision-making process.

How does this work? How does a pre-mortem unfold? It's really a 10-step process, and I want to walk you through those 10 steps. First step, and most important: Identify who you want participating in this exercise, and establish norms and ground rules for the discussion. Any decision process ought to have that step, and so should any pre-mortem.

Step 2: Make certain that all participants have a strong shared understanding of the decision under consideration. Step 3 then, importantly—now we're beginning to spur the divergent thinking:

We say to the group, imagine a complete failure that transpires as a result of this decision. Then, Step 4: Brainstorm the different paths or scenarios that may lead to that failure. Step 5: Identify the probability and the severity of each of those scenarios. There's no need for detailed quantitative analysis here—we're simply trying to understand which scenarios are most likely, and which ones are likely to lead to the worst outcomes. Step 6: Determine the scenarios that you believe warrant the most attention, those that are both most likely and potentially most severe. Step 7: Should we make a different decision, or can we enhance our approach to implementation as a means of avoiding failure? That's the key question you want to ask in Step 7. And then in Step 8 you say, if you choose to proceed with this decision, then work on an implementation plan to prevent the bad scenario from unfolding—or devise a plan to deal with the bad scenario if and when it transpires so as to minimize the damage. Step 9: Summarize your learnings from the exercise and communicate them to everyone involved in the decision-making process. Finally, Step 10: When the decision is finally implemented, then you conduct a post-mortem, and go back to the process to revisit the conclusions from the pre-mortem. Identify ways that the pre-mortem process could have been improved to actually have helped prevent the failure from occurring.

So, pre-mortem is an initiative technique developed by Gary Klein that could potentially help create much more divergent thinking and much more vigorous debate during the decision-making process.

Let's turn now to the third potential technique we can use to stimulate the clash of ideas. This is introducing a new conceptual model or framework to your team and having them use that to work through the decision in a way different than they might normally do. Kevin Dougherty did this when he was leading Sun Life Financial's Canadian group insurance business, and I wrote a case about Kevin and his team back in the early part around 2000, 2001. In 2000, he held an off-site, where he wanted his team to consider how the web was disrupting their insurance business, and how they could employ the Internet to build new business models. He brought an outside expert in, and he asked that expert to describe four models of how other companies, in a wide variety of industries, were building businesses using the web. Then, Dougherty divided his top leaders into four teams—16 people, 4 per team. He had each team take one of these conceptual models, and their mission over several days was to create a new business proposal for Sun Life that was based on that particular model.

This is a very interesting way to create four totally different paths for how they might use the web to transform the group insurance business. By giving the teams these starkly different models and asking them to sort of focus completely on how that model might apply to their business, he created, he forced upon the team, essentially a structure that enabled them to create four diverse alternatives. Then, he let the discussion flow. Once he'd set up that framework, then he backed off and allowed them the freedom to offer their ideas, and to be creative, and to wonderfully debate these ideas and alternatives—to synthesize and not just to pick one over the other, but to see how they might fit together, how one might complement the other, to create whole new alternatives from those original four.

Lastly, I want to talk about point-counterpoint methods. We actually saw these, both in the Kennedy case and in the Caufield story that I used to start out this lecture. What do I mean by point-counterpoint? Well, they're very simply two ways of doing this that we've seen. One is to use subgroups to stimulate dialogue, and the other is to use devil's advocates. We have actual terms that we use to describe the subgroup methodology. Academics would call it "Dialectical Inquiry." Essentially, what you're doing when you create two subgroups and bring them together to debate, you're essentially creating a dialectic where you're pushing two opposing ideas together and allowing the clash between those ideas to create new knowledge to help push the dialogue further.

Academics have outlined how Dialectical Inquiry should take place. It really mirrors, in many ways, the way that Kennedy behaved during the Cuban Missile Crisis. You're basically asking two subgroups to generate different alternatives, to really develop them in depth, to identify all of their assumptions as part of their proposal, and then to exchange papers and to dissect and criticize one another's ideas. It's important to write it down to help the team really understand—both what they want to do and to help the other group really understand the rationale behind that decision. Then, by writing it down and exchanging papers, the idea of Dialectical Inquiry is not to create a win-loss situation, where one group is trying to beat the other in the debate; instead, they're taking each other's papers, and they're giving them questions and ideas so that they can strengthen their proposal before ultimately they debate it with the leader. So, the idea here, like in the Kennedy cases, is the two teams aren't so much competing to win to get their idea essentially put in place by the leader—they're actually competing in debate, but also collaborating to try to strengthen each other's proposal through the give and take.

We see this in companies. Polycom, a leading provider of video conferencing and audio conferencing equipment, is a company that I've written cases about. They've made a number of acquisitions over the years, and they explicitly form what they call red teams and blue teams to examine the pros and cons of making any deal. The red team is assigned to put forth all the arguments for why the deal should take place. The blue team is there to present all the arguments for why the acquisition should not take place. The CEO always wants to hear the red team and blue team debate it out before he puts the final seal of approval on any acquisition.

Sometimes, we can build point-counterpoint into the structure of the organization. President Franklin Roosevelt, for example, purposefully used to create overlapping roles in his administration so as to create some point-counterpoint dynamics. This was frustrating to many of the people who worked in Roosevelt's Cabinet, I mean, imagine having rather ambiguous lines of authority or scope with which to work within. I mean, this was frustrating at times—yet for Roosevelt, it made sure that he wasn't vesting too much power in any particular individual. It allowed him to make sure that he had multiple people with expertise in particular areas, and that he could see how their differences of opinion might inform his ultimate choice. Point-counterpoint in the organization structure—it can happen in business, too, not just in Roosevelt's administration. Consider, for example, how Electronic Arts, the market share leader in the video game industry, manages the product development process. Most of its rivals appoint one person with total responsibility for overseeing the design of a new game. Electronic Arts has done it quite differently. They've created two separate leadership roles. Each person maintains distinct areas of accountability. The producer focuses on product quality, building a creative game that consumers will love to play. The development director tries to come in under budget and on schedule. They're focused not on the creativity, but on the fiscal discipline required to be a profitable game producer. Paul Lee, who was Chief Operating

Officer of Worldwide Studios at the firm when I interviewed him, describes the purpose of this unique organizational structure. He said to me:

> We have created a system of checks and balances or creative conflict. The producer focuses on ensuring that the game design is the best. ... The development director focuses on project management, budget, schedule, on-time delivery. And they clash. We force that conflict and that discussion so that the team will push the envelope.

They're building conflict into the structure. It's the last way I want to point out that we can stimulate the clash of ideas by really embedding point-counterpoint into the way the organization works all the time.

I am not suggesting that this is not without risk or danger. Sometimes, despite the best intentions, these methods don't work effectively. There are dangerous side effects that emerge, or approaches that render these methods quite ineffective. I call these the "watch-out situations" that any team should be aware of before they go forward and try to induce conflict and debate among them. Sometimes, for example, groups employ devil's advocates, but they actually domesticate the dissenters. What do I mean by that? They engage "token" devil's advocates more to make everyone feel good about their approach, rather than to truly hear dissenting views. They say: "You know, John, please play the devil's advocate for us," and it sort of just becomes routine. "Yeah, yeah, we know we need to do that. It makes us feel good, makes us feel like we're being rationale, and thoughtful, and rigorous in our decision process, but, really, we've sort of marginalized that person. We know we're really not going to take their views seriously," and that happens in many groups. Some have said that happened to Lyndon Johnson with regard to George Ball and others who were devil's advocates, if you will, during the Vietnam War discussions in the 1960s in the Johnson administration. Sometimes, leaders create a system of communication whereby their subordinates are simply trying to persuade the person at the top, as opposed to actually debating one another. I make this distinction between point-to-point communication and hub-and-spoke communication.

A hub-and-spoke communication system within a team is where the leader is the hub, and everybody is at the end of a spoke, and they're all talking to the leader, at the leader, trying to persuade the leader why their idea is best. That's not a true debate. That's not constructive conflict. A true debate is when we have point-to-point communication among members of the team—where the leader is sitting there able to listen to the give and take between and among members of his team. That's a much more productive type of communication. So, a watch-out situation is when the leader becomes the hub, and all the debate is not really a debate, so much as it is a persuasion mechanism—everybody pointing at the leader, trying to convince the leader of the merits of their ideas. Watch-out situations also include crowded agendas. People don't have the time to listen, digest what they've heard, and offer thoughtful critiques and responses when we're moving from one item to the next on an agenda that's got 10 or 15 items in a two-hour meeting—that is very destructive.

We also can allow people to become too entrenched in subgroups, such that they become quite polarized. They can't come back together to synthesize what they've been doing separately. So, when we use subgroups like Kennedy did or Caufield did in his case in the aerospace firm, don't let people stay in those subgroups for a long period of time because they will get entrenched and polarized, and you won't have a productive debate. Finally, the last watch-out situation: Be careful of false precision. We can become overly focused on minute details, as opposed to debating big themes, ideas, and concepts. We need to keep our eye on the big picture and not get mired in the weeds.

I'd like to close this lecture, though, by pointing out that this is tough. I'm not suggesting that it's easy to stimulate the clash of ideas. How do we do it in a way that we don't fall down, that we don't end up in destructive conflict? It's the topic of the next lecture. But before we get there, I'd like to point out that practice does make perfect—this is very important to remember. Research shows that groups in experimental settings become much more adept at debate, at methods such as Dialectical Inquiry or Devil's Advocacy, as they gain more experience with these types of processes. They get better at not being as defensive, at critiquing things in a constructive way and not using offensive language. In the real world, we see how very effective leaders make conflict and debate a normal event, part of the usual routine of decision-making. It's not a unique thing that happens only once per year at some off-site meeting—it's an everyday occurrence. There are two firms I'd like to point out that offer real exemplars to us of making conflict part of the "everyday" of the firm.

Consider Chuck Knight, longtime chairman and CEO of Emerson Electric. Knight designed that firm's strategic planning process to be as he says "confrontational by design." Everyone at the firm came to expect vigorous debate each and every day. It was a way of life at Emerson. It wasn't just something that happened at an off-site meeting—once every couple of years, when they were supposed to be thinking big thoughts. It was an everyday occurrence. At Emerson, Knight enjoyed remarkable success. In his 27-year tenure as CEO, Emerson's profits rose every single year. The other organization I point to in terms of practice makes perfect with regard to conflict is General Electric. General Electric had a similar approach to the approach taken by Knight when Jack Welch was Chief Executive Officer. Constructive conflict was even built in as one of the core values of the firm. Welch used to talk about a values card that people carried at GE, and one of the values that he emphasized when he got there was constructive conflict. This reminds us, this notion of practice makes perfect, reminds me of the wisdom of a famous quote by Aristotle. He said: "We are what we repeatedly do. Excellence, then, is not an act, but a habit." You need to make conflict a habit in your organization, in your team, if you expect to do it well—if you expect to become effective at debating one another and having a clash of ideas.

Lecture Twelve
Keeping Conflict Constructive

Scope:

While stimulating debate is essential to good group decision making, unfortunately, not all conflict remains productive. Here, we will describe how leaders must manage the 2 forms of conflict—task-oriented and interpersonal—within their teams. Drawing on a case study about Sid Caesar's famous comedic writing team, as well as cases about firms in healthcare and the nonprofit sector, we will look at how a leader can diagnose a debate to look for the warning signs of dysfunctional conflict. We will explore a number of techniques for leaders to curb interpersonal conflict in teams without compromising the level of task-oriented debate. In particular, we will examine what leaders can do before, during, and after a team decision-making process to manage conflict more productively.

Outline

I. In the 1950s, comedian Sid Caesar starred in one of the most popular shows on television, *Your Show of Shows*.

    A. The show had a famous writers' room, filled with what would later become known as some of the greatest comedic writers of a generation. The writers included Mel Brooks, Larry Gelbart, Neil Simon, Woody Allen, and Carl Reiner.

    B. They fought and argued. The ideas flowed freely.

    C. The arguments got very loud. It was contentious.

    D. However, the arguments were passionate yet productive. People channeled their emotions in such a way that enabled people to debate without tearing apart personal relationships.

    E. How can leaders create this kind of atmosphere of productive creative tension?

II. How can you diagnose whether a debate is becoming unproductive and dysfunctional?

    A. You can ask the following questions.

        1. Have people stopped asking questions intended to gain a better understanding of others' views?

        2. Has the group stopped searching for new information?

3. Have individuals stopped revising their proposals based on the feedback and critiques offered by others?
4. Has no one asked for help with the interpretation of ambiguous data?
5. Have people begun to repeat the same arguments, only more stridently and loudly over time?
6. Has no one admitted concerns about their own proposals recently?
7. Have less outspoken individuals begun to withdraw from the discussions?

B. It's important to understand that there are 2 forms of conflict.
1. Cognitive conflict is task oriented. It's debate about issues and ideas.
2. Affective conflict is emotional and personal in nature. It's about personality clashes, anger, and personal friction.
3. The key is to stimulate the cognitive conflict while minimizing the affective conflict.
4. Note that effective leaders channel the emotions; they do not try to eliminate them. It's nearly impossible to eliminate emotions from a lively debate. In fact, emotions, at times, can be helpful.

III. What can leaders do before the decision-making process to help stimulate constructive conflict?

A. Establish ground rules for how people should interact during the deliberations. Paul Levy did this when turned around the decision-making culture at the Beth Israel Deaconess Medical Center in 2002.

B. Clarify the role that each individual will play in the discussions.
1. Kevin Dougherty at Sun Life assigned people to play roles that they usually did not play to get them to understand how their colleagues thought about problems.
2. At the nonprofit New Leaders for New Schools, one of the firm's leaders asked people in 2 subgroups to write up the arguments for why to go forward with the other side's proposal.

C. Build mutual respect, particularly with regard to differences in the cognitive styles of each team member.

  1. It's important for people to understand one another's cognitive styles.

  2. Teams can and should spend some time discussing each member's cognitive style, as the people at New Leaders for New Schools did.

IV. What can leaders do during the decision-making process to help stimulate constructive conflict?

A. Redirect people's attention and recast the situation in a different light.

  1. My colleague Amy Edmondson points out that NASA would have benefited from reframing the debate during the critical meeting on the eve of the launch of the *Challenger* space shuttle.

  2. Reframing requires asking curious, nonthreatening questions.

  3. The language people use in those questions matters a great deal.

B. Present ideas and data in novel ways so as to enhance understanding and spark new branches of discussion. Howard Gardner has argued that redescribing ideas by presenting data in a different manner can unlock impasses and get people to rethink their views.

C. Revisit basic facts and assumptions when the group appears to reach an impasse.

  1. One executive I interviewed discussed how he always brought people back to certain core facts and assumptions when the debate seemed to simply be at an impasse among a set of proposals.

  2. The idea is to find some points of common ground in those heated moments.

V. What can leaders do after the decision-making process to help stimulate constructive conflict?

A. Evaluate the process and develop lessons learned for application in the future. Conducting good after-action reviews can help improve a group's ability to manage conflict constructively.

B. Attend to damaged relationships and hurt feelings that may not have been apparent to all during the process. Emerson Electric's Chuck Knight always tried to repair any hurt feelings on the same day that a heated debate took place at a strategic planning meeting; he did not wait.

C. Ensure that people remember, and even celebrate, the effective ways in which they handled difficult disputes. Paul Levy did this at Beth Israel, building on the satisfaction of his people when they began to learn how to resolve conflicts more constructively. He celebrated good conflict management and shared that best practice with the entire organization.

Suggested Reading:

Boynton and Fischer, *Virtuoso Teams*.

Ury, *Getting Past No*.

Questions to Consider:

1. Why is it so difficult to mitigate affective conflict during a decision-making process?

2. What techniques for managing conflict have worked for you either personally or professionally?

3. What are some of the key ways that a team can work through an impasse?

Lecture Twelve—Transcript
Keeping Conflict Constructive

Last time, we talked about how to stimulate more dissent and debate in our teams so that we can generate more options, evaluate them more critically, test our assumptions, identify hidden risks—in sum make better quality choices. However, to implement those choices effectively, we have to be able to keep conflict constructive—that's the subject of this lecture. I'd like to tell you a story about Sid Caesar, the famous comedian. In the 1950s, Caesar starred in one of the most popular shows on television, the title—*Your Show of Shows*; it was number one in the ratings at a time when television was spreading like wildfire into American households around the country. The show had a famous Writer's Room filled with what would later become known as some of the greatest comedic writers of a generation. The writers for the show included Mel Brooks and Larry Gelbart, who later wrote for *MASH*; Neil Simon; Woody Allen; and Carl Reiner. These writers fought, and they argued, and the ideas flowed freely. The producer of the show was named Max Liebman, and he used to like to say: "From a polite conference comes a polite movie." The Writer's Room for *Your Show of Shows* was far from a polite atmosphere.

The arguments got very loud. It was contentious. It was written that: "Chunks of plaster were knocked out of walls; the draperies were ripped to shreds; Mel Brooks frequently was hanged in effigy by the others." But nevertheless, the writers produced legendary skits week after week, worked effectively together for years—and remained friends, and confidantes, and collaborators for decades afterward. Somehow, the heated arguments represented what writer Mel Tolkin described as "good creative anger." The arguments were passionate, yet productive. People channeled their emotions in such a way that enabled people to debate without tearing apart personal relationships. Imagine, though, if a stranger walked into the Writer's Room one day, not knowing anything about the team's history, and here she witnessed the madness that Caesar and others have described. Naturally, one might have had a hard time believing that this team could produce such a spectacular show, or that the members would actually enjoy working together for years. Tomorrow, if you tried to emulate this pattern of behavior within your team, you might very well have a disaster on your hands. However, in the Writer's Room, the heated nature of the conflict did not become a liability. With astute leadership over a long period of time, Sid Caesar had created an atmosphere, as well as a creative decision process, in which the writers could argue in a passionate, yet productive way. He'd created a context in which hanging a team member in effigy did not represent aberrant or dysfunctional behavior, but a healthy, funny, "normal" way of coping with task-oriented conflict and debate, with letting the differences of opinion flow freely without becoming defensive.

In this lecture, we'll examine how leaders can act before, during, and after a decision-making process to ensure that conflict within their teams remains vigorous—yet constructive. We will not advocate direct emulation of the antics of Sid Caesar and friends, but we will try to develop a set of principles that applies in settings ranging from the Writer's Room to the corporate boardroom.

How can you diagnose if a debate is becoming unproductive and dysfunctional within your team? Again, like I've done in other lectures, I'd like to provide a set of diagnostic questions that you might ask yourself, or that team members might ask of one another when they're thinking about whether debate has become unproductive or dysfunctional. First you might ask: Have people stopped asking questions intended to gain a better understanding of others' views? Has a group stopped searching for new information? Have individuals stopped revising their proposals based on the feedback and critiques of others? Has no one asked for help with the interpretation of ambiguous data? Have people begun to repeat the same arguments, only more stridently and loudly over time? Has no one admitted concerns about their own proposals recently? Have less outspoken individuals begun to withdraw from the discussions, sitting quietly at the fringes of the dialogue?

Those questions, thinking about them carefully, even discussing them openly with other team members, will help you understand if you are at risk within your team of an unproductive dialogue—or if you've already gotten to the point where impasse and stalemate have set in, and interpersonal conflict is beginning to bubble up. Remember, there are two forms of conflict. In academic terms we call them "cognitive conflict" and "affective conflict." Cognitive conflict is task-oriented. It's debate about the issues and ideas. Affective conflict is emotional and personal in nature. It's about personality clashes, anger, and personal friction. The key for any team is to figure out a way to stimulate the cognitive conflict, while minimizing the affective. That's hard to do, creating what I call the "cognitive affective gap," but we're going to help you find some techniques in this lecture whereby you can achieve that, but that gap is key because we know that the teams that can create a gap between cognitive and affective, that can keep the task-oriented debate high and minimize the personal friction—those teams perform better. They not only make better decisions, but they can work together in harmony to implement those decisions more efficiently and more effectively.

It's important to note that leaders, effective leaders, do channel emotions, but they don't eliminate them. It's nearly impossible to eliminate emotions from a lively debate. In fact, emotions, at times, can be helpful. I mean, we want our people to be passionate about their ideas. I mean, every entrepreneur, for example, often has great passion for the business that they founded, and he or she wants to build a team that's just as passionate about bringing that value to customers, about introducing that new product or service to the marketplace, about satisfying the people that are purchasing their goods and services. Passion is important in business, and we don't want to eliminate that, but there are two different forms of conflict. Cognitive conflict, task-oriented—it's really focused on judgmental differences about how to best achieve common objectives. Important to note common objectives—the presence of a strong, shared goal really helps to keep that conflict cognitive in nature. Affective conflict is not just emotional, but it begins to focus on personal incompatibilities, on personal disputes, and it really is about anger and defensiveness introducing itself, injecting itself, into what should have been a productive, issue-oriented debate.

Any general manager, any leader, any person who is trying to bring a group together is thinking about the choices they make. Remember, they're going to hopefully decide how to decide when they make those choices about what kind of a roadmap, what kind of a process, they want to use. When they're trying to stimulate cognitive conflict, they're doing so because they want to make sure they generate lots of alternatives, test their assumptions, and critically evaluate every idea—and all that leads to better decisions. But if all you have is conflict, both cognitive and affective in nature—see, if you can't control the affective—then there is harm to be done. High affective conflict will diminish two important things that are critical preconditions for the ability to implement effectively. High affective conflict diminishes shared commitment. It means people are less likely to want to buy into the decision and cooperate in its implementation. High affective conflict also tends to diminish shared understanding. It gets in the way of making sure there's a common comprehension of what a decision is all about, of its rationale, and of the roles various people will have to play to execute the decision. So, when you make choices, you want to stimulate that cognitive conflict, but you want to beware that too high on the affective scale and you will diminish shared commitment and shared understanding, and you won't be able to implement even the best of decisions. That's what conflict management, then, is all about.

Remember, we can't eliminate emotion. Sometimes, people believe that regulating affective conflict entails a dispassionate, unbiased approach to decision-making, like Spock from *Star Trek*. Yet, eliminating passionate emotion from the decision-making process may not only be nearly impossible, I think it can be counterproductive. In the Writer's Room, Caesar's team achieved success in part because everyone came to the table with great zeal and excitement for their ideas. The same can be said for the process of creating new video games at Electronic Arts, a company I've touched on now in several lectures. Bruce McMillan, who was a senior executive at the firm for many years, talked to me about passion and decision-making at Electronic Arts, and he explained that passion and emotion play a critical role in business decisions. He wants proponents of an idea to display ardor and enthusiasm because he knows that those feelings will fuel a powerful drive to execute that project successfully. One cannot—and should not—simply ask people to put their passion aside. McMillan likens the situation to a disagreement with your spouse. In his case, he talks about, imagine a disagreement with your wife, and he says: "Imagine that you said to your wife: 'Honey, let's take the emotion out of this issue for a moment.' What do you think her reaction would be?" Effective leaders channel others emotions—they don't eliminate them.

So, how then can we channel emotions productively? How can we keep conflict constructive? I think there are (sort of) three elements to any decision process—sort of what happens before the process begins, what happens during the deliberations, and what happens after the decision has been made. We can think carefully about techniques in each of those three broad phases that we can employ to keep conflict constructive. Let's start by talking about what you do upfront. This foundational work is critical to managing conflict effectively.

First, you need to establish ground rules for how people should interact during deliberations. One of the case studies that I've conducted is of Paul Levy, a CEO of the Beth Israel Deaconess Medical Center in Boston. Mr. Levy took over that hospital in 2002, and it's a case study we'll talk about in more detail in subsequent lectures. In 2002, when Levy took over, the hospital was on the verge of bankruptcy. As a nonprofit, it actually was vulnerable to takeover by the state of Massachusetts who were worried that by bleeding cash for so many years, the hospital executives were actually squandering the trust that had funded the hospital for many years, squandering this nonprofit's endowment. Levy took over in these difficult circumstances and did turn around the hospital successfully, and he did it first and foremost by changing the decision-making culture, as we will discuss in later lectures. He understood that they weren't very good at the hospital at having productive dialogues, and the first thing he did to help change that culture was to set out some new ground rules for how people should behave, to get them to think about how to be more productive in the way they had to give and take. He said: "We need to learn that we can disagree without being disagreeable," and key ground rules that he actually wrote down and shared with each member of the senior team were critical to changing that culture. He held them accountable to these new ground rules. He actually had an open discussion about what these ground rules were, why they were important, and how he was going to hold people responsible for staying true to those rules. So that's key.

The second is to clarify the role that each individual will play in the discussions that you have. Let's go back to Kevin Dougherty, that general manager at Sun Life Financial that I talked about in a prior lecture. Remember, I talked about an off-site meeting he had where he did a very good job of creating divergent thinking and stimulating the clash of ideas. During that meeting, he did something very interesting with his 16 members of his top team. He assigned them all to look at the issues that they were discussing from a different perspective. He actually asked them to play roles that they usually do not play—to get people to understand how their colleagues thought about problems. For example, he asked the Chief Financial Officer to imagine that they were the Chief Marketing Officer. He asked the Chief Operating Officer to imagine that they were the Executive Vice President of Sales. By asking people to step into the shoes of their colleagues, he was hoping they would really understand the way their colleagues thought, what perspective they would take, what goals and interests their colleagues had, and that that would fuel a more productive dialogue.

I also studied a nonprofit called New Leaders for New Schools, an interesting nonprofit whose intent was to train principals, principals who would have the leadership skills to improve America's public schools. The feeling was that many principals had great education skills, but had not gotten the kind of executive training required to lead 21st-century schools effectively. New Leaders for New Schools set about to do this, but there were some disagreements early on about what the strategy should be for this nonprofit. At one point they had reached sort of a bit of an impasse, and they were worried that the conflict was becoming dysfunctional, and one of the firm's top leaders did something very interesting. He realized that there were two factions before him: one in favor of strategy A, and the other in favor of strategy B. So, he took the group in favor of strategy A, and he asked them to go off and write a 10-page plan, a 10-page document, that argued why strategy B was, in fact, the right plan for the company. And he asked the group that actually believed in B to go write a proposal for why strategy A was the right plan to move forward. By asking people to actually make the argument of the other side, the leader's intent was to get them to really understand how the other side was thinking, the feeling being that this would help them have a much more productive dialogue and debate. It's very important to get people to step into others' shoes, to understand their perspective, so that you're not attributing bad intentions or motives to the other side, but instead understanding they have every right to think the way they do, and that they have good intentions— they share the overall goal to help the organization move forward, they just have a different view of how to get there.

So, before the decision process, we're setting norms, we're setting some expectations about people's roles, and remember we talked about role-playing in a previous lecture. We said role-playing can help stimulate divergent thinking. It turns out that role-playing can also be helpful as leaders try to minimize affective conflict and resolve intense disputes. By putting individuals in others' shoes, a leader can help them understand better the motivations and interests of people with different views on a contentious issue. We've clearly said that's important, and I think one of the reasons is it's very easy for us to get caught up in what our position is, rather than understanding what people's interests are and why their goals and objectives are different than ours. William Ury and Roger Fisher, our famous negotiation scholars, who really focus on the need to get away from what your position is, to really understanding one another's interests—they argue that helps make negotiations more productive. I would argue it helps make any dialogue more productive, a focus on interests instead of positions. They say:

> Positional bargaining becomes a contest of will. … Anger and resentment often result as one side sees itself bending to the rigid will of the other while its own legitimate concerns go unaddressed. Positional bargaining thus strains and sometimes shatters the relationship between parties. … Bitter feelings generated by one such encounter may last a lifetime.

So, clearly these issues are important about understanding the other side—putting yourself in one another's shoes. Lastly, I think we need to remember that we need to build mutual respect, particularly with regard to differences in the cognitive styles of each team member. Remember, we don't all think the same; we make decisions in different ways. Some of us are more intuitive, others more analytical, and some of us rely on our emotions more than others. We have different cognitive styles, and if we understand one another's cognitive styles before we set out to make a tough decision, I think it's helpful in making that dialogue more productive.

What could we do during the decision process? I think there are a number of techniques we can do when we're in impasse, when we've reached a stalemate, to kind of keep that from degenerating into dysfunctional conflict. One idea is to present concepts and data in novel ways so as to enhance understanding and spark new branches of discussion. Howard Gardner, the education scholar known most famously for his theory of multiple intelligences, has argued that redescribing ideas by presenting data in a different manner can unlock impasse and get people to rethink their views. So, redescription—a very important technique you could use when you reach impasse, or when you're about to reach impasse. You also can revisit basic facts and assumptions when you appear to have reached a stalemate. One executive I interviewed discussed how he always brought people back to certain core facts and assumptions when the debate simply seemed to be in a deadlock among a set of competing proposals. The idea is to use that reachback to facts and assumptions to find points of common ground in those heated moments.

We also, at times, need to redirect people's attention and recast situations in a different light when a stalemate appears to be emerging. William Ury, that negotiations scholar I cited earlier, has called this "changing the frame," and we talked about frames in an earlier lecture and how powerful they can be. He said stalemate is one of those times when reframing can be very productive. Here's what he said:

> Reframing means redirecting the other side's attention away from positions and towards the task of identifying interests, inventing creative options, and discussing fair standards for selecting an option. ... Instead of rejecting their hard-line position, you should treat it as an informative contribution to the discussion. Reframe it by saying, "That's interesting. Why do you want that? Help me understand the problem you are trying to solve." The moment they answer, the focus of the conversation shifts from positions to interests [to goals]. You have just changed the game.

Reframing requires asking curious, non-threatening questions. The language you use in asking those questions matters a great deal. Language is powerful. It can lead to very destructive dialogues if not used appropriately.

I want to talk for a moment about a particular case study of a dialogue that didn't go well at all, that became emotional and unproductive, and I want to talk about how it might have been reframed to lead to a much more productive outcome. The case I'd like to talk about is the Challenger Space Shuttle accident. This is the space shuttle accident that took place back in 1986. This has been studied by Amy Edmondson, one of my colleagues from Harvard Business School. The infamous teleconference is what I want to talk about. This is a teleconference that occurred on the eve of the ill-fated launch in 1986. It represents a powerful example of the lost opportunity to reframe a debate. Lots of anger and emotion emerged in that meeting; it was clearly not a productive conversation.

For those who aren't familiar with the Challenger Shuttle accident, again it's a topic we're going to cover in much more detail in a later lecture, but let me just summarize what happened there. The shuttle exploded during the launch that day because O-ring erosion occurred because of the cold temperatures in Florida on the day of the launch. The O-ring erosion allowed hot gases to leak out on the solid rocket boosters, and that leaking of gases led to the explosion that killed Christa McAuliffe (that schoolteacher on board that day) and all of the other astronauts on the Challenger. It's a tragic outcome. As it turns out, at the teleconference on the evening prior to the launch, there was concern expressed about the cold temperatures at the launch. Roger Boisjoly, an engineer at NASA, argued quite stridently and forcefully that: "We shouldn't launch, that temperatures are too cold. I believe cold temperatures are what cause O-ring erosion." O-ring erosion had been happening on prior launches of the Challenger, and he seemed to think there was some correlation between cold temperatures and that problem with the O-rings, and that day they were talking about a launch that would take place at 40 degrees Fahrenheit, or perhaps colder. There was ice overnight on the launch pad, and Boisjoly was very concerned—but, he couldn't get his point across. He couldn't convince management to delay the launch, and there were heated words exchanged during that teleconference.

My colleague, Amy Edmondson, has pointed out that the meeting participants could have avoided a dysfunctional debate—and perhaps even prevented the disaster—by reframing the discussion as a collective learning and problem-solving process, not as a win-lose proposition. She points out that the people did not ask inquisitive questions during the debate, but instead found themselves repeatedly defending their own positions. People didn't try to understand each other's thinking; they didn't put themselves in each other's shoes. The lack of inquiry meant that people didn't learn from one another, and they didn't leverage the collective expertise in the room. They simply became frustrated and emotional.

During the meeting, Roger Boisjoly presented data on the temperatures at launch for those past flights with O-ring erosion incidents. The evidence showed no apparent correlation between temperature and O-ring failure—thus, senior management was clearly unconvinced of the threat: "You haven't shown correlation, why should we delay the launch? This seems to be some belief you have not grounded in any data in reality." However, if the group had looked at all flights in the graph that they actually put together—all flights, not just those with O-ring incidents, but all flights—if they had plotted that graph, they would have recognized very quickly that a correlation did exist—that, in fact, the only time that they'd had O-ring problems was when it was relatively cold, and every flight without an O-ring incident was a very warm weather launch. No one during the discussions asked for more data of this kind, no one asked for more data, and this, of course, is the tragedy of that teleconference.

Amy Edmondson stresses the power of asking curious, non-threatening questions to help reframe a contentious debate and break a stalemate. For instance, she points out that someone could have asked senior management the following question: "What kind of data would you need to change your mind and postpone the launch?" Edmondson argues that the likely response to that question might have been: "I would need data that suggests a correlation between temperature and O-ring erosion on past shuttle launches," and this might have spurred a great deal of further investigation and learning within the group. Specifically, group members together may have uncovered the correlation data that would have convinced senior executives at NASA to delay the launch. So, how can we reframe the debate? What kinds of non-threatening, curious questions can we ask, and how can we use language productively?

Fisher and Ury, those negotiation scholars, have said there are five types of questions we ask in reframing a debate, and they've offered advice on how to ask those five questions. The first is the "Why?" question. You might ask somebody why they believe what they believe, but they think the right way to ask that is by saying: "Help me understand why you believe X, Y, or Z." By saying: "Help me," you're really making it a non-threatening question. Then there's the "Why not?" question. It's important to ask: "Why not pursue these other options?" Instead of just criticizing the proposals by some other subgroup or some other individual on your team, instead of focusing on their option, bring other options to the table that can help reframe the debate. Then there's the "What if?" question. "What if we found this assumption proved to be false?" Here again, we're getting away from focusing only on people's positions, and we're backtracking to look at underlying assumptions, another way of reframing the dialogue so it's not just is A right or B right, but wait, are the assumptions underlying A and B correct? Then there's the fourth type of question, the "What would you do?" question, and here they say the question you want to ask is: "What would you do if you were in my shoes?" Again, trying to get people to empathize, to put themselves in other shoes and understand their vantage point. Finally, "What makes that optimal?"—the fifth kind of question for reframing a debate. Here you might say: "You must have good reasons for thinking that's an optimal solution. I'd like to hear them." In other words, if someone is simply stating their position and then restating it over and over, you say to them: "No, no, explain to me your thinking; give me your rationale. Take me inside your mind." Ask for help in understanding what they're saying, another way of reframing the dialogue to get to more-productive discussion.

Finally, what can we do after the decision process has ended? Here we can evaluate the process and develop lessons learned for application in the future. We've talked about the importance of that After-Action Review, but there's more than just that that we can do. We need to attend to damaged relationships and hurt feelings that sometimes simply are going to happen no matter how well we manage the debate. Importantly, sometimes those damaged feelings don't become apparent to everyone during the process. Chuck Knight, longtime chairman and CEO at Emerson Electric, remember he designed his meetings to be confrontational by design when he planned strategy for that firm—but he told me that he always tried to repair any hurt feelings on the same day that a heated debate took place. "Don't wait," he said to me, "it's so important to act quickly." One thing he did at the end of a conference, at the end of a day of intense strategic planning, he would take his team out to dinner, and he would always be sure to sit next to the person who'd sort of been bruised the most during the dialogue, who'd really been on the sort of rough end of some debates. Sit next to them, make sure that you work with them, and keep an eye on that relationship, and repair any damage that might have been done.

Finally, ensure that people remember, and even celebrate, the effective ways in which disputes have been handled. When a tough dispute is worked through productively, hey, make that an exemplar; celebrate it with your team. Levy, the chief executive at the Beth

Israel, did this in an important way at one point when a contentious dispute emerged. He built on the satisfaction of his people when they learned to actually resolve that conflict more constructively, and he celebrated that instance with his team and with the broader organization. He got lucky in this regard, because there was a heated debate, and it got very dysfunctional at a particular meeting, and then they worked through it, and they figured out how to make it a more productive dialogue. Several weeks later they'd come to a good decision, and people felt good about it. Interestingly, the two combatants, as he called them, actually coined a song about it. They coined the song to the tune of "Down by the Levee," a play on the chief executive's name, and they sang the song at a senior management meeting. Levy laughed, and then he told the story of the song and of these two combatants who had resolved their differences effectively. He told that story over, and over, and over—celebrating how they'd learned to have a productive dialogue and giving that as an example to the rest of the organization, a very powerful thing to do to teach others the importance of key techniques for how to manage conflict effectively.

To close, let me say that leaders certainly can't resolve every dispute that arises during a complex decision-making process. They need help. They must develop the skills of their subordinates. Moreover, once a leader unleashes the power of divergent thinking, they inherently give up some control over the ideas and options that are discussed. Yet, leadership always entails a broad responsibility for establishing the context in which people behave, as well as the processes that groups employ to initiate and resolve conflict. Leaders can and should shape and guide how people disagree, as well as the atmosphere in which that debate takes place. Along these lines, Larry Gelbart once reflected back on Sid Caesar's leadership of the wildly creative process in the Writer's Room for *Your Show of Shows*. Gelbart remarked: "He had total control, but we had total freedom."

Glossary

affective conflict: Disagreement that is rooted in personality clashes and personal friction. It involves emotion and anger. It is not issue- or task-oriented in nature.

anchoring bias: Refers to the notion that we sometimes allow an initial reference point to distort our estimates.

cognitive bias: The decision-making traps that afflict all of us as we try to make choices. We fall into these traps because of cognitive limitations that are characteristic of all human beings. Cognitive biases include such judgment errors as the sunk-cost trap and the confirmation bias.

cognitive conflict: Task-oriented or issue-oriented debate within a group. It is disagreement based on the substance and content of a decision, rather than based on personalities and emotions.

confirmation bias: The tendency to gather and rely upon information that confirms our existing views, while avoiding or discounting information that might disconfirm our existing hypotheses and opinions.

consensus: Decision-making consensus is defined as the combination of commitment and shared understanding. It means that individuals are committed to cooperate in decision implementation and that they have a strong shared understanding of the rationale for the decision, their contribution to the final choice, and their responsibility in the execution process.

deferred judgment: A key principle of brainstorming. It means that individuals go through a phase of the brainstorming process in which they refrain from judging or criticizing others' ideas. Instead, they simply focus on generating as many new ideas as possible.

devil's advocacy: A structured group decision-making method whereby a team splits into 2 subgroups. One subgroup proposes a plan of action, while the other critiques the plan so as to expose flawed assumptions and hidden risks.

dialectical inquiry: A structured group decision-making method whereby a team splits into 2 subgroups that then discuss and debate competing alternatives.

groupthink: The term coined by social psychologist Irving Janis to describe the powerful social pressures for conformity that sometimes arise within groups, causing people to self-censor their views—particularly dissenting opinions.

high-reliability organizations: Those complex organizations in high-risk environments that have operated with very few accidents over many years.

intuition: Fundamentally a process of pattern recognition based on past experience. Through pattern matching, individuals are able to make intuitive judgments without going through an appraisal of multiple alternatives, as many "rational" models of choice would suggest.

normal accidents: Those catastrophic failures that are quite likely to eventually occur in high-risk organizations that are characterized by complex interactions and tight interconnections among components of the organizational system.

normalization of deviance: A phenomenon described by Diane Vaughan in her study of the *Challenger* space shuttle disaster. It is a situation in which organizations gradually come to accept higher levels of risk and to take those risks for granted over time.

practical drift: The term coined by Scott Snook to describe how accepted, taken-for-granted practice within organizations gradually can move away from standard operating procedure.

procedural justice: Refers to the perceptions among participants in a decision that the process is both fair and equitable.

procedural legitimacy: Refers to the perception that a group or organizational process meets certain acceptable and desirable behavioral norms, according to general societal standards and beliefs.

process losses: The failed attempts to capitalize on the synergistic potential of groups. A process loss occurs when a group of people do not manage to pool the talent and expertise of the individual members to create a better solution than any individual could come up with on his or her own.

prospect theory: Put forth by Amos Tversky and Daniel Kahneman, this theory argues that individuals will exhibit different risk-taking tendencies depending on how a decision is framed.

reasoning by analogy: This takes place when we try to determine what choice to make by drawing direct comparisons to a situation in the past that we deem to be quite analogous to the current circumstance.

recency effect: The tendency to overweight readily available information, specifically recent data, when judging the probability of certain events occurring in the future.

recovery window: The period of time between the identification of an ambiguous threat and the eventual catastrophic failure, during which some actions can be taken to prevent the failure from occurring.

sensemaking: The cognitive process whereby individuals and groups interpret and understand ambiguous situations.

small wins: Refers to a theory put forth by Karl Weick, whereby a large and complex problem is broken down into smaller components to enable a group to make progress toward finding an acceptable solution in a timely and effective manner.

sunk-cost effect (or sunk-cost trap): The tendency to escalate commitment to a failing course of action if one has invested a great deal of time, money, and other resources that are not recoverable.

Biographical Notes

Breashears, David (b. 1955): David Breashears is a highly accomplished mountaineer and award-winning filmmaker. He has reached the summit of Mount Everest numerous times. Breashears was filming the IMAX documentary *Everest* during the famous 1996 Everest tragedy, which was written about in books such as *Into Thin Air* by Jon Krakauer. Breashears observed those tragic events in May 1996. Having turned around before the other expedition teams kept climbing toward the summit and got caught in the terrible storm, Breashears later helped in the rescue efforts. He has earned 4 Emmy awards for his filmmaking, and he is the author of several books.

Churchill, Winston (1874–1965). Winston Churchill was the indefatigable British prime minister during World War II. He graduated from the Royal Military Academy at Sandhurst, and he participated in the British army's last full cavalry charge in the Sudan in 1898. Churchill won election to Parliament in 1900, and during World War I, he became First Lord of the Admiralty. He made great strides in building Britain's naval strength, but his disastrous advocacy for the Gallipoli landings on the Dardanelles cost him his job. Churchill was one of the earliest British politicians to sound alarms about Hitler's rise to power in the 1930s. He fervently opposed Prime Minister Neville Chamberlain's appeasement of Hitler. Churchill succeeded Chamberlain in 1940 and earned great acclaim for inspiring his countrymen to withstand Germany's relentless attacks until the United States entered the war. His close relationship with Franklin D. Roosevelt proved vital to the Allied cause. Despite Churchill's efforts to defeat Hitler, he lost a bid for reelection in 1945. Churchill later coined the phrase "iron curtain" to describe the alarming spread of communism and Soviet domination in Eastern Europe. Churchill again served as prime minister from 1951 to 1955. An accomplished biographer and author, Churchill won the Nobel Prize in Literature in 1953.

Dodge, Wagner (d. 1955): Wagner ("Wag") Dodge was the foreman of the smokejumper team involved in the Mann Gulch, Montana, fire of 1949, in which 12 United States Forest Service smokejumpers lost their lives. Dodge was one of the few survivors of the fire. When the fire escalated dramatically, most of the smokejumpers began running for the ridge, trying to elude the fire rushing toward them on the slope of Mann Gulch. Dodge estimated that the men could not outrun the rapidly approaching fire to the top of the ridge, which was roughly 200 yards away. Thus, he bent down and lit an "escape fire" in the grass with a match. Then Dodge placed a handkerchief over his mouth and lay down in the smoldering ashes. Dodge later testified to the review board that he had never heard of the concept of an escape fire prior to Mann Gulch. He simply felt that the idea seemed logical given the situation at the time. After the fire raced right around him, Dodge sat up from his burned patch. The escape fire had deprived the onrushing blaze of fuel, thus forcing it around him. Had the others followed him into his ingenious escape, they too would have lived.

Eisenhower, Dwight D. (1890–1969): Dwight Eisenhower grew up in Abilene, Kansas, and his family was quite poor. Eisenhower attended the United States Military Academy at West Point, and he began his military career in the infantry. He later served as a staff officer under several highly accomplished commanders—first General John J. Pershing and then General Douglas MacArthur. Eisenhower was appointed to the war planning division in 1942, working for General George Marshall, the U.S. Army chief of staff. Eisenhower went on to become the commander in chief of the Allied forces in North Africa, and he directed the Allied invasions of Sicily and Italy. Eisenhower became the supreme commander of the Allied Expeditionary Force in December 1943, and in that role, he directed the massive effort to liberate Europe in 1944–1945. After the war, Eisenhower retired from the military and became president of Columbia University. In 1951, he left that post to lead the military forces of the newly created NATO. In 1952, the American people elected Eisenhower as the 35th president of the United States. He easily won reelection in 1956.

Gerstner, Louis, Jr. (b. 1942): Louis Gerstner Jr. was chairman and chief executive officer of IBM Corporation from 1993 until 2002. He later served as chairman of the Carlyle Group, a private equity firm headquartered in Washington DC. Before becoming CEO of IBM, Gerstner served as CEO of RJR Nabisco and as a senior executive at American Express. He also had been a partner at McKinsey Consulting for many years prior to joining American Express. Gerstner has an undergraduate degree from Dartmouth and an MBA from Harvard Business School. In 2001, he was knighted by Queen Elizabeth II of England.

Grove, Andrew (b. 1936): Andrew Grove was born in Hungary, came to the United States and earned an undergraduate degree at City College of New York, and was awarded his Ph.D. from the University of California at Berkeley. In 1968, Grove became one of the founders of Intel Corporation, after having worked in research and development at Fairchild Semiconductor. He later served as chief executive officer of Intel from 1987 to 1998 and was chairman of the board at Intel from 1997 to 2005. He has served as a lecturer at the University of California at Berkeley and the Stanford University Graduate School of Business. Grove has also authored several books, including *Only the Paranoid Survive* (1996). He was named *Time* magazine's "Man of the Year" in 1997.

Kennedy, John F. (1917–1963): John F. Kennedy graduated from Harvard College and served courageously in World War II. After the war, he served in the U.S. House of Representatives and the U.S. Senate, representing the state of Massachusetts. In 1960, he ran against Vice President Richard Nixon for the presidency of the United States, and he won a tightly contested election. He was inaugurated as the 35th president of the country in January 1961. Kennedy's term was tragically cut short when he was assassinated by Lee Harvey Oswald on November 22, 1963, in Dallas, Texas. He was succeeded by his vice president, Lyndon B. Johnson. Two of the most famous foreign policy decisions of his presidency were the Bay of Pigs invasion and the Cuban missile crisis.

Kennedy, Robert F. (1925–1968): Robert F. Kennedy was born in Brookline, Massachusetts. He earned a bachelor's degree at Harvard College and graduated with a law degree from the University of Virginia. Kennedy served in the military during World War II, and he worked as a Senate lawyer in the 1950s. He became attorney general during his brother's administration and continued in that role during the early years of the Johnson presidency. However, he left the cabinet and won a seat in the U.S. Senate in 1965, representing the state of New York. While running for the Democratic nomination for president in 1968, Kennedy was assassinated in California.

Krakauer, Jon (b. 1954): Jon Krakauer has a degree from Hampshire College in Massachusetts. He is a highly acclaimed author as well as a mountaineer. He was writing an article about Mount Everest for *Outside* magazine when a number of climbers died in May 1996 during a horrible storm. He later wrote an article about that incident for *Outside* magazine. Based on the popularity of that article, he went on to author a bestselling book, *Into Thin Air*, about the tragedy. Krakauer has written a number of other books as well, including many others about outdoor adventures.

Kranz, Gene (b. 1933): Gene Kranz was born in Ohio and served in the Korean War as a member of the U.S. Air Force. He later became a flight director at NASA during the Gemini and Apollo programs. Kranz was the flight director during the famous *Apollo 13* mission, and he helped bring those astronauts safely home to Earth after an explosion damaged their vehicle in space. Kranz was featured in a movie about the incident, which was directed by Ron Howard. He retired from NASA in the early 1990s. Kranz's autobiography, *Failure Is Not an Option*, was published in 2000. He has earned the Presidential Medal of Freedom for his substantial contributions to America's space program.

Levy, Paul F. (b. 1950): Paul F. Levy was appointed chief executive officer of the Beth Israel Deaconess Medical Center in Boston in January 2002. During his time at the hospital, the institution bounced back from serious financial distress to become a very stable and healthy organization. It enhanced its reputation as a high-quality academic medical center. Prior to joining Beth Israel Deaconess, Levy served as Executive Dean for Administration at Harvard Medical School. Levy was responsible for the Boston Harbor Cleanup Project as executive director of the Massachusetts Water Resources Authority. He also has been chairman of the Massachusetts Department of Public Utilities and director of the Arkansas Department of Energy. Levy also has taught as an adjunct professor at MIT.

McNamara, Robert (b. 1916): Robert McNamara was born in San Francisco, California. He earned a bachelor's degree in Economics and Philosophy from the University of California at Berkeley in 1937 and an MBA from Harvard Business School 2 years later. He became a professor at Harvard Business School in the early 1940s and served in the armed forces during World War II. In 1946, he took a position in the finance organization at Ford Motor Company. He rose quickly to a series of senior management positions at Ford, ultimately becoming the first non–family member to serve as president of the firm. He gained fame at Ford for his highly analytical and quantitative approach to solving business problems.

When John F. Kennedy became president of the United States, he appointed McNamara as the secretary of defense despite the fact that he did not have a great deal of specific knowledge about military matters. McNamara instituted many sophisticated planning and budgeting techniques at the Department of Defense during his tenure. He served in his post until February 1968, at which time he became the president of the World Bank. He retired from that post in 1981.

Nixon, Richard M. (1913–1994): Richard Nixon served in the U.S. Navy during World War II and was elected to the U.S. House of Representatives after the war. Nixon became a U.S. Senator and then vice president of the United States during the Eisenhower administration. He failed to win election to the presidency during his first attempt at the office in 1960, when he was defeated by John F. Kennedy. Nixon finally won the presidency in 1968, defeating Vice President Hubert Humphrey and to become the 37th president of the United States. Nixon became president during the Vietnam War, and the war essentially ended on his watch, though only after years of additional conflict. He was responsible for the decision to try to rescue prisoners of war from the Son Tay camp in Vietnam. Nixon resigned in disgrace in 1974 because of the Watergate scandal.

Truman, Harry (1884–1972): Harry Truman served in World War I in the artillery. After the war, he became involved in politics and became a judge in Missouri. He was elected to the U.S. Senate in 1934. In 1944, he was elected as vice president of the United States, under Franklin D. Roosevelt. Shortly after taking office as vice president, Truman assumed the presidency because of the death of Roosevelt. Truman was responsible for the decision to drop the atom bomb on Japan, and he presided over the end of World War II and the rebuilding of Japan and Western Europe after the war. Truman was elected to the presidency in his own right in November 1948 in a stunning win over Thomas Dewey. He served as president while the cold war began, and he made the decision to defend South Korea when the communist North invaded in 1950. He left the presidency in January 1953, after choosing not to run for reelection.

Bibliography

Allison, G. T. *The Essence of Decision: Explaining the Cuban Missile Crisis.* Boston: Little, Brown, 1971. Allison takes a close look at the Cuban missile crisis through 3 very different conceptual lenses, helping us understand that the decisions of a complex organization are rarely simply the choices of a single rational actor who is at the top of the hierarchy.

Amason, A. C. "Distinguishing the Effects of Functional and Dysfunctional Conflict on Strategic Decision Making." *Academy of Management Journal* 39 (1996): 123–148.

Ambrose, S. *The Supreme Commander: The War Years of Dwight D. Eisenhower.* New York: Doubleday, 1970. Ambrose, one of Eisenhower's most prolific biographers, writes a detailed account of Ike's time leading the Allied effort to liberate Western Europe during World War II.

Bazerman, M. *Judgment in Managerial Decision Making.* New York: John Wiley & Sons, 1998. Bazerman's book is a thorough review of the academic literature on cognitive biases.

Benner, P. *From Novice to Expert: Excellence and Power in Clinical Nursing Practice.* Menlo Park, CA: Addison-Wesley, 1984. Benner takes a close look at the development of expertise in the nursing profession, with some key insights as to the role that intuition plays in expert decision making.

Bourgeois, L. J., and K. Eisenhardt. "Strategic Decision Processes in High Velocity Environments: Four Cases in the Microcomputer Industry." *Management Science* 34, no. 7 (1988): 816–835.

Bower, J. *Managing the Resource Allocation Process.* Boston: Harvard Business School Press, 1970. Bower examines how strategy is enacted in large organizations by delving into the process by which resources are allocated among sometimes competing projects and initiatives.

Boynton, A., and B. Fischer. *Virtuoso Teams: Lessons from Teams That Changed Their Worlds.* Upper Saddle River, NJ: Financial Times Press, 2005. Boynton and Fischer look at some amazing creative teams, including the remarkable comedy-writing team from *Your Show of Shows.*

Clark, M., with A. Joyner. *The Bear Necessities of Business: Building a Company with Heart*. Hoboken, NJ: John Wiley & Sons, 2006. This book, by the founder and CEO of Build-A-Bear, Maxine Clark, describes the key lessons that she has learned during her tenure leading this very creative and successful company.

Columbia Accident Investigation Board. *Columbia Accident Investigation Board Report*. Washington, DC: Government Printing Office, 2003. This remarkable volume is the official investigative report produced after the *Columbia* accident.

Dekker, S. *Just Culture: Balancing Safety and Accountability*. Aldershof, UK: Ashgate, 2007. Dekker examines how firms balance the issue of providing a safe environment for people to admit mistakes in with the need to maintain a culture of accountability and responsibility.

Drucker, P. F. *The Practice of Management*. New York: Harper, 1954. This is one of Drucker's most famous early books, in which he lays out many of his classic theories on effective management.

Edmondson, A. "Psychological Safety and Learning Behavior in Work Teams." *Administrative Science Quarterly* 44 (1999): 354.

Gavetti, G., D. Levinthal, and J. Rivkin. "Strategy-Making in Novel and Complex Worlds: The Power of Analogy." *Strategic Management Journal* 26 (2005): 691–712.

Gerstner, L., Jr. *Who Says Elephants Can't Dance? Inside IBM's Historic Turnaround*. New York: Harper Business, 2002. Gerstner writes a firsthand account of his time as CEO during the turnaround of IBM in the 1990s.

Hackman, J. R. *Groups That Work (and Those That Don't)*. San Francisco, CA: Jossey-Bass, 1990.

Harrison, F. *The Managerial Decision-Making Process*. 4th ed. Boston: Houghton Mifflin, 1996. Harrison's book provides an extensive overview of the field of organizational decision making, suitable for many college or MBA courses on the subject.

Heifetz, R. *Leadership without Easy Answers*. Cambridge, MA: Belknap, 1994. Heifetz describes how and why our usual view of leadership is ill-conceived, and how more effective approaches can be employed that involve empowering subordinates and marshaling their collective intellect for the good of the organization.

Janis, I. *Victims of Groupthink.* 2nd ed. Boston: Houghton Mifflin, 1982. Janis articulates his theory of groupthink in this classic book with fascinating case studies about the Bay of Pigs, Cuban missile crisis, Korean War, Vietnam War, and Pearl Harbor.

Johnson, R. T. *Managing the White House.* New York: Harper Row, 1974. This book emerged from Johnson's research as a White House Fellow and doctoral student in management during the early 1970s, and it provides a comparison of various decision-making styles used by American presidents in the 20th century.

Kahneman, D., and A. Tversky. *Choices, Values, and Frames.* Cambridge: Cambridge University Press, 2000. Kahneman and Tversky describe prospect theory, which argues that how one frames a problem affects the solution that will be chosen.

Kelley, T. *The Art of Innovation: Lessons in Creativity from IDEO, America's Leading Design Firm.* New York: Doubleday, 2001. One of the cofounders of IDEO provides an explanation for how IDEO engages in such remarkably creative product-design work.

Kennedy, R. F. *Thirteen Days.* New York: W. W. Norton, 1969. This book provides a riveting firsthand account of the Cuban missile crisis.

Kim, W. C., and R. Mauborgne. "Fair Process: Managing in the Knowledge Economy." *Harvard Business Review* 75, no. 4 (1997): 65–75.

Klein, G. *Sources of Power: How People Make Decisions.* Cambridge, MA: MIT Press, 1999. Klein describes his extensive research on intuition, based on interviews and observations of experts in fields such as the military, firefighting, and nursing.

Knight, C. *Performance without Compromise: How Emerson Consistently Achieves Winning Results.* Boston: HBS Press, 2005. Knight offers an explanation of how Emerson Electric achieved remarkably consistent financial results during his tenure as CEO, with a focus on the vaunted Emerson strategic planning process.

Krakauer, J. *Into Thin Air: A Personal Account of the Mount Everest Disaster.* New York: Anchor Books, 1997. Krakauer wrote a bestselling firsthand account of the 1996 Mount Everest tragedy based on his observations during the climb with one of the 2 expeditions that encountered serious trouble that year.

Lind, A., and T. Tyler. *The Social Psychology of Procedural Justice*. New York: Plenum Press, 1988. Lind and Tyler extend the work of Thibault and Walker in this book.

Nadler, D., J. Spencer, and associates, Delta Consulting Group. *Leading Executive Teams*. San Francisco, CA: Jossey-Bass, 1998. Nadler draws on his academic background and his extensive experience consulting with CEOs and their top management teams in this book on how to lead more effective senior teams.

National Commission on Terrorist Attacks Upon the United States. *The 9/11 Commission Report: Final Report of the National Commission on Terrorist Attacks Upon the United States*. New York: W. W. Norton & Company, 2004. This book is the official investigative report produced by the presidentially appointed 9/11 commission.

Neustadt, R., and E. May. *Thinking in Time: The Uses of History for Decision-Makers*. New York: Free Press, 1986. Neustadt and May examine how a variety of American presidents have drawn on analogies, either effectively or ineffectively, as they have made key policy decisions.

O'Toole, J. *Leading Change: Overcoming the Ideology of Comfort and the Tyranny of Custom*. San Francisco, CA: Jossey-Bass, 1995. O'Toole offers an interesting look at the power of taken-for-granted assumptions and mental models, with a particularly thought-provoking examination of the reasons for General Motors' decline.

Perrow, C. "Normal Accident at Three Mile Island." *Society* 18 (1981): 17–26.

———. *Normal Accidents*. New York: Basic Books, 1984. This book is Perrow's classic work in which he describes his theory of complex systems, using the famous case of the Three Mile Island nuclear power plant accident, among other cases.

Presidential Commission on the Space Shuttle Challenger Accident. *Report to the President by the Presidential Commission on the Space Shuttle Challenger Accident*. Washington, DC: Government Printing Office, 1986. The Rogers Commission produced this official report examining the causes of the *Challenger* accident and offering prescriptions for how NASA should change moving forward.

Reason, J. T. *Managing the Risks of Organizational Accidents.* Aldershof, UK: Ashgate, 1997. Reason examines how and why many small errors often compound one other to create a large-scale failure, and he examines how tactics such as the creation of redundancy might help prevent catastrophes.

Roberto, M. *Know What You Don't Know: How Great Leaders Prevent Problems before They Happen.* Upper Saddle River, NJ: Wharton School Publishing, 2009. My new book shifts the focus from problem solving to what I call the "problem-finding" capabilities of effective leaders. I examine how leaders can unearth the small problems that are likely to lead to large-scale failures in their organizations and how leaders need to shift from fighting fires to detecting smoke, so that they can detect and interrupt the chain of errors that often precedes a major failure. Then I identify 7 key problem-finding capabilities that all leaders must develop to become successful at averting crises in their organizations.

———. *Why Great Leaders Don't Take Yes For an Answer: Managing Conflict and Consensus.* Upper Saddle River, NJ: Wharton School Publishing, 2005. My first book focuses on how leaders can stimulate constructive debate in their teams and organizations.

Roberts, K. "Managing High Reliability Organizations." *California Management Review* 32, no. 4 (1990): 101–113.

Russo, E., and P. Schoemaker. *Winning Decisions: Getting It Right the First Time.* New York: Fireside, 2002. This book provides an extensive discussion of many of the cognitive biases that affect individuals and provides some simple prescriptions for overcoming these traps.

Salter, M. *Innovation Corrupted: The Origins and Legacy of Enron's Collapse.* Cambridge, MA: Harvard University Press, 2008. Salter provides a detailed academic examination of the reasons behind Enron's demise, including how reasoning by analogy played a role in the poor decisions made at the firm in the 1990s.

Schein, E. *DEC is Dead, Long Live DEC: The Lasting Legacy of Digital Equipment Corporation.* San Francisco, CA: Berrett-Koehler, 2003. MIT Professor Ed Schein draws on his time as a consultant to DEC founder and CEO Ken Olsen to write an account of the rise and fall of that company.

Schlesinger, A., Jr. *A Thousand Days*. Boston: Houghton Mifflin, 1965. Schlesinger provides a firsthand account of his time as a presidential adviser to John F. Kennedy in the early 1960s, with a particularly interesting description of the Bay of Pigs fiasco.

Schweiger, D. M., W. R. Sandberg, and J. W. Ragan. "Group Approaches for Improving Strategic Decision Making." *Academy of Management Journal* 29 (1986): 51–71.

Snook, S. A. *Friendly Fire: The Accidental Shootdown of U.S. Black Hawks over Northern Iraq*. Princeton, NJ: Princeton University Press, 2000. This book provides a riveting academic examination of a tragic friendly-fire accident that took place in the no-fly zone in northern Iraq in 1994.

Starbuck, W., and M. Farjoun, eds. *Organization at the Limit: Lessons from the* Columbia *Disaster*. London: Blackwell, 2005. These editors bring together scholars from many different fields to examine the causes of the *Columbia* space shuttle accident. The book includes a chapter written by me and my coauthors.

Stasser, G., and W. Titus. "Pooling of Unshared Information in Group Decision Making: Biased Information Sampling During Discussion." *Journal of Personality and Social Psychology* 48 (1985): 1467–1478.

Staw, B. M. "Knee Deep in the Big Muddy: A Study of Escalating Commitment to a Chosen Course of Action." *Organizational Behavior and Human Performance* 16 (1976): 27–44.

Staw, B. M., and H. Hoang. "Sunk Costs in the NBA: Why Draft Order Affects Playing Time and Survival in Professional Basketball." *Administrative Science Quarterly* 40 (1995): 474–494.

Staw, B. M., L. Sandelands, and J. Dutton. "Threat-Rigidity Effects on Organizational Behavior." *Administrative Science Quarterly* 26 (1981): 501–524.

Steiner, I. *Group Process and Productivity*. New York: Academic Press, 1972. Steiner explains the concept of process losses (i.e., why many teams do not achieve their potential for integrating the diverse expertise of various members).

Surowiecki, J. *The Wisdom of Crowds: Why the Many Are Smarter than the Few and How Collective Wisdom Shapes Business, Economies, Societies and Nations*. New York: Anchor Books, 2004. This book describes how and why we can get better answers to tough problems by pooling the judgments of a large group of independent people.

Tapscott, D., and A. Williams. *Wikinomics: How Mass Collaboration Changes Everything*. New York: Penguin, 2006. This book examines how the Internet and other technologies have enabled mass collaboration to take place by people around the world, many of whom may not know one another.

Thibault, J., and L. Walker. *Procedural Justice: A Psychological Analysis*. Hillsdale, NJ: L. Erlbaum Associates, 1975. This book is one of the seminal pieces in the academic literature on procedural justice.

Turner, B. *Man-Made Disasters*. London: Wykeham, 1978. Turner examines the causes of large-scale catastrophes and argues that there are often long incubation periods during which such catastrophes slowly unfold.

Ury, W. *Getting Past No: Negotiating Your Way from Confrontation to Cooperation*. New York: Bantam Books, 1993. Ury writes one of the classic books on conflict resolution and negotiation, with practical advice that we can all apply in our personal and professional lives.

Useem, M. *The Leadership Moment: Nine Stories of Triumph and Disaster and Their Lessons for Us All*. New York: Times Business, 1998. Useem provides engaging accounts of how 9 leaders behaved and performed in critical situations filled with risk and uncertainty.

Vaughan, D. *The Challenger Launch Decision: Risky Technology, Culture, and Deviance at NASA*. Chicago: University of Chicago Press, 1996. Sociologist Diane Vaughan wrote one of the definitive accounts of the *Challenger* space shuttle accident, in which she explains her groundbreaking theory of the normalization of deviance.

Weick, K. "The Collapse of Sensemaking in Organizations: The Mann Gulch Disaster." *Administrative Science Quarterly* 38 (1993): 628–652.

——. *Sensemaking in Organizations*. Thousand Oaks, CA: Sage, 1995. Weick explains how decision makers make sense of ambiguous situations, and how that process can go off track.

——. "Small Wins: Redefining the Scale of Social Problems." *American Psychologist* 39, no. 1 (1984): 40–49.

Wcick, K., and K. Sutcliffe. *Managing the Unexpected*. San Francisco, CA: Jossey-Bass, 2001. This book examines how some organizations in very high-risk environments manage to achieve remarkably good safety records.

Welch, J., and J. Byrne. *Jack: Straight from the Gut*. New York: Warner Business Books, 2001. Welch describes some of the key lessons he learned as CEO of General Electric from 1981 to 2001.

Wohlstetter, R. *Pearl Harbor: Warning and Decision*. Stanford, CA: Stanford University Press, 1962. Wohlstetter's book provides an in-depth look at the reasons why various military and political leaders discounted the possibility of a Japanese attack on Pearl Harbor in the early 1940s.

Notes